MEDIA, FEMINISM, CULTURAL STUDIES

The Sacred Cinema of Andrei Tarkovsky
by Jeremy Mark Robinson

Liv Tyler
by Thomas A. Christie

The Cinema of Hayao Miyazaki
Jeremy Mark Robinson

Stepping Forward: Essays, Lectures and Interviews
by Wolfgang Iser

Wild Zones: Pornography, Art and Feminism
by Kelly Ives

'Cosmo Woman': The World of Women's Magazines
by Oliver Whitehorne

The Cinema of Richard Linklater
by Thomas A. Christie

Andrea Dworkin
by Jeremy Mark Robinson

Cixous, Irigaray, Kristeva: The Jouissance of French Feminism
by Kelly Ives

The Erotic Object: Sexuality in Sculpture
From Prehistory to the Present Day
by Susan Quinnell

Women in Pop Music
by Helen Challis

Sex in Art: Pornography and Pleasure in Painting and Sculpture
by Cassidy Hughes

Erotic Art
by Cassidy Hughes

Jean-Luc Godard: The Passion of Cinema / Le Passion de Cinéma
by Jeremy Mark Robinson

Genius and Loving It! Mel Brooks
by Thomas Christie

The Comic Art of Mel Brooks
by Maurice Yacowar

Marvelous Names
by P. Adams Sitney

The Art of Katsuhiro Otomo
by Jeremy Mark Robinson

Akira: The Movie and the Manga
by Jeremy Mark Robinson

The Art of Masamune Shirow (3 vols)
by Jeremy Mark Robinson

Detonation Britain: Nuclear War in the UK
by Jeremy Mark Robinson

Julia Kristeva: Art, Love, Melancholy, Philosophy, Semiotics
by Kelly Ives

Luce Irigaray: Lips, Kissing, and the Politics of Sexual Difference
by Kelly Ives

Helene Cixous I Love You: The Jouissance of Writing
by Kelly Ives

FORTHCOMING BOOKS

Legend of the Overfiend
Death Note
Naruto
Bleach
Hellsing
Vampire Knight
Mushishi
One Piece
Nausicaä of the Valley of the Wind
The Twilight Saga
Harry Potter

Bibliography

Author Green, Daniel Chanan Matt. *Zohar, the Book of Enlightenment.* Paulist Press, 1983.

Bataille, Georges. *The Accursed Share.* Michigan: Zone Books, 2010.

Bhikku, Thanissaro. Translator "Alagaddupama Sutta: The Water-Snake Simile." 2004. *Accesstoinsight.org.* https://www.accesstoinsight.org/tipitaka/mn/mn.022.than.html.

Biernacki, Loriliai. *Renowned Goddess of Desire: Women, Sex, and Speech in Tantra.* Oxford University Press, 2007.

Brown, Peter. *15 Simple Ways to Awaken Your Kundalini Energy.* 2021. https://www.binauralbeatsmeditation.com/awaken-kundalini-energy/. 2023.

Campbell, Joseph. "Masks of Oriental Gods: Symbolism of Kundalini Yoga." Lambert, Neal E. *Literature of Belief: Sacred Scripture and Religious Experience.* Provo: Religious Studies Center Brigham Young University, 1981. 109-38.

—. *The Masks of God, Vol. III: Oriental Mythology.* Viking Press, 1963.

Joseph Campbell: Mythos Vol. 2. Dir. Robert Walter. Perf. Joseph Campbell. 2006.

Carabine, Deirdre. *The Unknown God: Negative Theology in the Platonic Tradition: Plato to Eriugena.* Oregon: Wipf and Stock Publishers, 1995.

Clothey, Fred W. *The Many Faces of Murukan?: The History and Meaning of a South Indian God.* Munshiram Manoharlal, 1978.

Coburn, Thomas B. *Devi Mahatmya: The Crystallization of the Goddess Tradition.* Delhi: Motilal Banarsiddas, 1984.

Cross, St. John of the. "Christian Classics Ethereal Library." *Dark Night of The Soul.* https://ccel.org/ccel/john_cross/dark_night/dark_night.vii.html?highlight=house&queryID=13788533&resu

ltID=137868#highlight.

Damyron, Ryan. Translator. "The King of Tantras, the Glorious Mahamaya." 2021. *84000 Reading Room.* https://read.84000.co/translation/toh425.html.

Dash, Mike. *Thug: the true story of India's murderous cult.* Grata Books, 2005.

Dass, Ram. https://www.youtube.com/watch?v=kjh1BAG5Pfs. 15 December 2014. 2023.

Davids, Thomas William Rhys. *Pali-English Dictionary.* Motilal Banarsiddas, 1993.

Deleuze, Gilles and Felix Guattari. *A Thousand Plateaus: Capitalism and Schizophrenia.* New York: Continuum, 1988.

Dongbin, Lu. *The Secret of the Golden Flower.* 2021. https://www.thesecretofthegoldenflower.com/contact.html.

Dyson, Michael Eric. *Holler If You Hear Me: Searching for Tupac Shakur.* Basic Books, 2006.

Emerson, Ralph Waldo. "Nature." *Nature and Other Essays.* Dover Publications, 2012. 3.

Emmanuel, Steven M. *A Companion to Buddhist Philosophy.* John Wiley & Sons, 2015.

Farrow, George W. Translator. *The Concealed Essence of the Hevajra Tantra.* Motilal Banarsidas Publishers, 1992. http://www.abhidharma.ru /A/Tantra/Content/Hevajra/0005.pdf.

Freud, Sigmund. "On Narcissism." *The Standard Edition of the Complete Psychological Works of Sigmund Freud, Volume XIV (1914-1916): On the History of the Psycho-Analytic Movement, Papers on Metapsychology and Other Works.* Random House UK, 2001. 67-102.

Gabrielle, Angelique Maria. "University of Victoria." December 2013. *Embodying asana in all new places: transformational ethics, yoga tourism and sensual awakenings.* http://dspace.library.uvic.ca/handle/1828/4453.

Gandi, Lakshmi. https://www.npr.org/sections/codeswitch/2013/11/18/245953619/ what-a-thugs-life-looked-like-in-nineteenth-century-india. 18 November 2013. 2023.

Gellert, Michael. "What Carl Jung Said About Race Relations in America." *Michaelgellert.com.* https://michaelgellert.com/pdfs/jung-said-about-race-relations-in-america.pdf.

Hanh, Thich Nhat. *You Are Here: Discovering the Magic of the Present Moment.* Boston: Shambhala, 2010.

Hegel, G.F.W. "The Phenomenology of Spirit." *The Phenomenology of Spirit.* Oxford University Press, 1977.

Jr., Henry Louis Gates. "The Signifying Monkey: A Theory of African

American Literary Criticism." *The Signifying Monkey: A Theory of African American Literary Criticism.* Oxford University Press, 1988.

Jung, C.G. *Man and His Symbols.* Doubleday, 1964.

—. "Psychic Energy." *The Collected Works of C.G. Jung: Complete Digital Edition.* Princeton University Press, 2014.

—. *The Red Book.* New York: W.W. Norton, 2009.

Khan, Sharful Islam. "Semen Contains Vitality and Heredity, Not Germs: Seminal Discourse in the AIDA Era." *Journal of Health, Popular Nutrition* (2006). https://www.ncbi.nlm.nih.gov/pmc/articles/PMC3001146/.

King, Sallie B. "The Buddha Nature: True Self As Action." *Religious Studies* Vol 20, No 2 (1984): 257.

Kitchens, Travis. "Unfortunate Son: The roots of Tupac Shakur's Rebellion." November 2016. *Baltimore Sun.* https://www.baltimoresun.com/citypaper/bcp-113016-music-tupac-shakur-and-baltimore-20161129story.html. 2023.

Lacan, Jacques. "The Signification of the Phallus." *Ecritus.* New York: W.W. Norton and Company, 1996. 579.

Lindhal, Kaplan, and Britton. "A Phenomenology of Meditation-induced Light Experiences: Traditional Buddhist and Neurobiological Perspectives." January 2013. *Frontiers in Psychology.* https://www.frontiersin.org/articles/10.3389/fpsyg.2013.00973/full.

Lochtefeld, James G. *The Illustrated Encyclopedia of Hinduism: N-Z.* Rosen Young Adult, n.d.

Matt, Daniel C. Translator. *The Zohar Vol. 1.* California: Stanford University Press, 2001.

McFarlane, Thomas. *Center for Sacred Sciences "Living Without A Why".* November 2009. http://www.centerforsacredsciences.org/index.php/Holos/holos-carabinc.html.

Nietzsche, Friedrich. "Literaturepage.com." December 2012. *Thus Spoke Zarathustra.* http://www.literaturepage.com/read/thusspakezarathustra 137.html.

—. *Thus Spoke Zarathustra.* Oxford University Press, 2009.

Pacheco, Chris. "If You Meet The Buddha On The Road, Kill Him?" November 2021. *Lion's Roar.* https://www.lionsroar.com/if-you-meet-the-buddha-on-the-road-kill-him/.

Patra, Sanjib Kumar. "Physiological Effect of Kriyas: Cleaning Techniques." January 2017. *International Journal of Yoga.* https://www.researchgate.net/publication/321799696_Physiological_effect_of_kriyas_Cleansing_techniques.

Plato. *Republic.* Open Road Media, 2014.

Powell, Kevin. "2paclegacy.net." May 2016. "*Ready To Live" Vibe Magazine*

1995. https://2paclegacy.net/tupac-interview-kevin-powell-for-vibe-magazine/. 2023.

Purana, Linga. *Hindu Online.* 2012. http://hinduonline.co/Scriptures/Puranas/LingaPurana.html. 2023.

Roelofs, Lyle D. "The Power of Sankofa: Know History." n.d. *Berea College.* https://www.berea.edu/cgwc/the-power-of-sankofa/.

Rowan, John. *Subpersonalities: The People Inside Us.* Taylor and Francis, 2013.

Shakur, Tupac. "1994 MTV Interview." n.d. *YouTube.* https://www.youtube.com/watch?v=aMXzLhbWtmk. 2023.

—. "2Pacalypse Now Promotional Interview." 1991. *Zettoplus.medium.com.* https://zettoplus.medium.com/the-1991-tupac-shakur-interview-that-all-americans-need-to-hear-in-2017-847978de0fd6.

—. "Genius." 1992. *Tupac Speech to Malcolm X Grassroots Movement.* https://genius.com/2pac-speech-to-malcolm-x-grassroots-movement-annotated. 2023.

—. *God Has Cursed Me To See What Life Should Be Like.* Ed Gordon. 1994.

—. *My Dream Came True.* Eva Sundqvist Olmos. 1996.

—. *Tupac Interview By Benjamin Svetkey.* Benjamin Swetkey. March 1994. https://2paclegacy.net/tupac-interview-by-benjamin-svetkey-march-1994-rare/ (.

Svatmarama, Swami. *Hatha Yoga Pradipika.* The Aquarian Press, 1992.

Svetkey, Benjamin. "2paclegacy." October 2016. *Tupac Interview 1994.* https://2paclegacy.net/tupac-interview-by-benjamin-svetkey-march-1994-rare/.

Trungpa, Chogyam. *The Lion's Roar: An Introduction to Tantra.* Shambhala, 2001.

Varma, Raja Ravi. *World History Encyclopedia "Kali".* 21 June 2013. https://www.worldhistory.org/image/1332/kali/. 2023.

Vivekananda, Swami. *Moola bandha: The Master Key.* Yoga Publications Trust, 2011.

Watts, Alan. *Awaken.* 12 November 2017. <http://www.awaken.com/2017/11/we-are-all-god-playing-hide-and-seek-alan-watts>.

—. "Tantric Buddhism." *YouTube.* https://www.youtube.com/watch?v=er-egjXmkUE.

Williams, Paul. *Buddhist Thought: A complete introduction to the Indian Tradition.* Taylor and Francis, 2012.

—. "Buddhist Thought: A Complete Introduction to the Indian Tradition."

—. *Buddhist Thought: A Complete Introduction to the Indian Tradition.* New York: Routledge Taylor and Francis Group, 2000. 237.

Wineberg, Yosef. *Chabad "Shaar Hayichud Vehaemunah.* 2021.

https://www.chabad.org/library/tanya/tanya_cdo/aid/7993/jewish/Chapter-7.htm. 2023.

CRESCENT MOON PUBLISHING

web: www.crmoon.com e-mail: cresmopub@yahoo.co.uk

ARTS, PAINTING, SCULPTURE

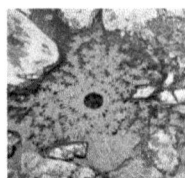

The Art of Andy Goldsworthy
Andy Goldsworthy: Touching Nature
Andy Goldsworthy in Close-Up
Andy Goldsworthy: Pocket Guide
Andy Goldsworthy In America
Land Art: A Complete Guide
The Art of Richard Long
Richard Long: Pocket Guide
Land Art In the UK
Land Art in Close-Up
Land Art In the U.S.A.
Land Art: Pocket Guide
Installation Art in Close-Up
Minimal Art and Artists In the 1960s and After
Colourfield Painting
Land Art DVD, TV documentary
Andy Goldsworthy DVD, TV documentary
The Erotic Object: Sexuality in Sculpture From Prehistory to the Present Day
Sex in Art: Pornography and Pleasure in Painting and Sculpture
Postwar Art
Sacred Gardens: The Garden in Myth, Religion and Art
Glorification: Religious Abstraction in Renaissance and 20th Century Art
Early Netherlandish Painting
Leonardo da Vinci
Piero della Francesca
Giovanni Bellini
Fra Angelico: Art and Religion in the Renaissance
Mark Rothko: The Art of Transcendence
Frank Stella: American Abstract Artist
Jasper Johns
Brice Marden
Alison Wilding: The Embrace of Sculpture
Vincent van Gogh: Visionary Landscapes
Eric Gill: Nuptials of God
Constantin Brancusi: Sculpting the Essence of Things
Max Beckmann
Caravaggio
Gustave Moreau
Egon Schiele: Sex and Death In Purple Stockings
Delizioso Fotografico Fervore: Works In Process 1
Sacro Cuore: Works In Process 2
The Light Eternal: J.M.W. Turner
The Madonna Glorified: Karen Arthurs

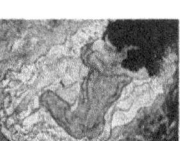

LITERATURE

J.R.R. Tolkien: The Books, The Films, The Whole Cultural Phenomenon
J.R.R. Tolkien: Pocket Guide
Tolkien's Heroic Quest
The *Earthsea* Books of Ursula Le Guin
Beauties, Beasts and Enchantment: Classic French Fairy Tales
German Popular Stories by the Brothers Grimm
Philip Pullman and *His Dark Materials*
Sexing Hardy: Thomas Hardy and Feminism
Thomas Hardy's *Tess of the d'Urbervilles*
Thomas Hardy's *Jude the Obscure*
Thomas Hardy: The Tragic Novels
Love and Tragedy: Thomas Hardy
The Poetry of Landscape in Hardy
Wessex Revisited: Thomas Hardy and John Cowper Powys
Wolfgang Iser: Essays and Interviews
Petrarch, Dante and the Troubadours
Maurice Sendak and the Art of Children's Book Illustration
Andrea Dworkin
Cixous, Irigaray, Kristeva: The *Jouissance* of French Feminism
Julia Kristeva: Art, Love, Melancholy, Philosophy, Semiotics and Psychoanalysis
Hélene Cixous I Love You: The *Jouissance* of Writing
Luce Irigaray: Lips, Kissing, and the Politics of Sexual Difference
Peter Redgrove: Here Comes the Flood
Peter Redgrove: Sex-Magic-Poetry-Cornwall
Lawrence Durrell: Between Love and Death, East and West
Love, Culture & Poetry: Lawrence Durrell
Cavafy: Anatomy of a Soul
German Romantic Poetry: Goethe, Novalis, Heine, Hölderlin
Feminism and Shakespeare
Shakespeare: Love, Poetry & Magic
The Passion of D.H. Lawrence
D.H. Lawrence: Symbolic Landscapes
D.H. Lawrence: Infinite Sensual Violence
Rimbaud: Arthur Rimbaud and the Magic of Poetry
The Ecstasies of John Cowper Powys
Sensualism and Mythology: The Wessex Novels of John Cowper Powys
Amorous Life: John Cowper Powys and the Manifestation of Affectivity (H.W. Fawkner)
Postmodern Powys: New Essays on John Cowper Powys (Joe Boulter)
Rethinking Powys: Critical Essays on John Cowper Powys
Paul Bowles & Bernardo Bertolucci
Rainer Maria Rilke
Joseph Conrad: *Heart of Darkness*
In the Dim Void: Samuel Beckett
Samuel Beckett Goes into the Silence
André Gide: Fiction and Fervour
Jackie Collins and the Blockbuster Novel
Blinded By Her Light: The Love-Poetry of Robert Graves
The Passion of Colours: Travels In Mediterranean Lands
Poetic Forms

POETRY

Ursula Le Guin: Walking In Cornwall
Peter Redgrove: Here Comes The Flood
Peter Redgrove: Sex-Magic-Poetry-Cornwall
Dante: Selections From the Vita Nuova
Petrarch, Dante and the Troubadours
William Shakespeare: Sonnets
William Shakespeare: Complete Poems
Blinded By Her Light: The Love-Poetry of Robert Graves
Emily Dickinson: Selected Poems
Emily Brontë: Poems
Thomas Hardy: Selected Poems
Percy Bysshe Shelley: Poems
John Keats: Selected Poems
Joh n Keats: Poems of 1820
D.H. Lawrence: Selected Poems
Edmund Spenser: Poems
Edmund Spenser: Amoretti
John Donne: Poems
Henry Vaughan: Poems
Sir Thomas Wyatt: Poems
Robert Herrick: Selected Poems
Rilke: Space, Essence and Angels in the Poetry of Rainer Maria Rilke
Rainer Maria Rilke: Selected Poems
Friedrich Hölderlin: Selected Poems
Arseny Tarkovsky: Selected Poems
Arthur Rimbaud: Selected Poems
Arthur Rimbaud: A Season in Hell
Arthur Rimbaud and the Magic of Poetry
Novalis: Hymns To the Night
German Romantic Poetry
Paul Verlaine: Selected Poems
Elizaethan Sonnet Cycles
D.J. Enright: By-Blows
Jeremy Reed: Brigitte's Blue Heart
Jeremy Reed: Claudia Schiffer's Red Shoes
Gorgeous Little Orpheus
Radiance: New Poems
Crescent Moon Book of Nature Poetry
Crescent Moon Book of Love Poetry
Crescent Moon Book of Mystical Poetry
Crescent Moon Book of Elizabethan Love Poetry
Crescent Moon Book of Metaphysical Poetry
Crescent Moon Book of Romantic Poetry
Pagan America: New American Poetry

THE SWORDSMAN

TONY CHING. TSUI HARK

A Critical Study

THE SWORDSMAN

TONY CHING. TSUI HARK

A Critical Study

Jeremy Mark Robinson

CRESCENT MOON

Crescent Moon Publishing
P.O. Box 1312
Maidstone, Kent
ME14 5XU, Great Britain
www.crmoon.com

First published 2024.
© Jeremy Mark Robinson 2024.

Set in Helvetica 9 on 12pt.
Designed by Radiance Graphics.

The right of Jeremy Mark Robinson to be identified as the author of this book has been asserted generally in accordance with sections 77 and 78 of the Copyright, Designs and Patents Act 1988.

All rights reserved. No part of this book may be reprinted or reproduced, stored in a retrieval system, or transmitted, in any form or by any means, electronic, mechanical, photocopying, recording or otherwise, without permission from the publisher.

British Library Cataloguing in Publication data available for this title.

I.S.B.N.-13 9781861718792

CONTENTS

Acknowledgements ❖ 9
Picture Credits ❖ 9
Abbreviations ❖ 9

PART ONE
TONY CHING SIU-TUNG
TSUI HARK
BIOGRAPHY

1   Tony Ching: Biography ❖ 14
2   Tony Ching: Aspects of His Cinema ❖ 32
3   Tsui Hark ❖ 61

PART TWO
THE SWORDSMAN

1   *The Swordsman* ❖ 81
2   *The Swordsman 2* ❖ 94
3   *The Swordsman 3: The East is Red* ❖ 111

Appendix: *Royal Tramp 1* and *2* ❖ 131
Filmography ❖ 140
Recommended Books and Websites ❖ 154
Bibliography ❖ 155

ACKNOWLEDGEMENTS

To the authors and publishers quoted.
To the copyright holders of the illustrations.

ABBREVIATIONS

LM *The Cinema of Tsui Hark* by Lisa Morton

PICTURE CREDITS

Golden Harvest. Shaw Brothers. Paragon. Cinema City. Film Workshop. China Entertainment. Paka Hill. Eastern Production. Win's Entertainment. Star East. Jing Productions. Media Asia. Beijing Polyabana Publishing. United Filmmakers Organization. China Film Co-Production. Big Pictures. China Juli Entertainment Media. Distribution Workshop. Different Digital Design. Huxia Film Distribution. New Classics Pictures.

NOTE

Parts of this book appeared in my full-length study of Tsui Hark: *Tsui Hark: Dragon Master of Chinese Cinema* (2023), published by Crescent Moon.

PART ONE
TONY CHING SIU-TUNG
TSUI HARK

1
TONY CHING SIU-TUNG: BIOGRAPHY

TONY CHING SIU-TUNG: INTRODUCTION

Tony Ching Siu-tung (b. 1953) started out as an actor and stuntman, working in movies in the late 1960s and 1970s; he moved into television as martial arts co-ordinator in the late 1970s and thru the 1980s (on several historical TV series); he moved up to directing movies with 1983's *Duel To the Death*.

Tony Ching Siu-tung's two signature works are probably *A Chinese Ghost Story* and *The Swordsman 2*. Critically, those two films (and their movie series, the *Chinese Ghost Story* series and the *Swordsman* series), have garnered the highest critical accolades (and they were big hits financially), and *The Swordsman 2* has been the subject of numerous analyses of gender-bending issues in cinema. The sight of Brigitte Lin in drag and later fooling around with Jet Li as a 'woman' who was a man seems to drive film critics goo-goo.

Tony Ching Siu-tung has won top awards for the action choreography for *The Witch From Nepal, Shaolin Soccer, New Dragon Gate Inn, Hero* and *The Swordsman*.

Like the other famous action directors in Hong Kong cinema (such as Yuen Woo-ping, Sammo Hung, Corey Yuen Kwai and Yuen Bun), Tony Ching Siu-tung has worked with every single star in Hong Kong, every producer, every cameraman, designer, stylist, costumier, etc, and probably every stuntman and stuntwoman.

Tony Ching Siu-tung has action director credits on: *Dangerous Encounter – 1st Kind, Twinkle Twinkle Little Star, Peking Opera Blues, A Better Tomorrow 2, The Killer, New Dragon Gate Inn, Moon Warriors, City Hunter, Butterfly and Sword*, the *Krrish* films, *Kung Fu Dunk* and *The Warlords*. He is an action director in high demand – for many TV shows as well as movies. Ching has worked many times with producer/ director/ dynamo Tsui Hark.

Tony Ching Siu-tung seems barely known outside of Chinese film circles, and in the West[1] his name is over-shadowed by directors such as Tsui Hark, John Woo, Wong Kar-wai, etc. Yuen Woo-ping has become known for the *Matrix* movies and others, and of course Jackie Chan remains a huge presence (tho' as a movie star, and not for his incredible directing skills. Few realize that Chan has directed several genuine masterpieces, including the *Project A* series and the *Police Story* series).

But consider the achievements of Tony Ching Siu-tung – they are very impressive: two of the finest and most celebrated of Hong Kong franchises – the *Swordsman* movies and the *Chinese Ghost Story* movies. Judged solely on the basis of those two film trilogies, Ching is a *kung fu* master and lion dancer among filmmakers. The first two *Chinese Ghost Story* films are masterpieces, as are the first two *Swordsman* films (some would include the third installment, too – it's very popular with critics and fans). Near-masterpieces would include Ching's first film as director, *Duel To the Death, The Sorcerer and the White Snake, Jade Dynasty* and *An Empress and the Warriors.* Add to those giant historical pictures his work as action director on masterpieces such *Hero, Peking Opera Blues, House of Flying Daggers, A Better Tomorrow 2* and *The Killer,* and a host of very enjoyable pictures, such as: *Butterfly and Sword, City Hunter, Moon Warriors,* the *Krrish* films, *Curse of the Golden Flower,* and *The Warlords.* (Some of those productions were enormous – *Krrish, The Warlords, Hero, Curse of the Golden Flower,* etc).

Technically, the movies directed by Tony Ching Siu-tung are breathtaking – in every department of film production, Ching's movies excel. Costumes are lavish, the sets are super-detailed, and the cinematography is stellar. Sometimes you really are looking at something very close to a classical, Chinese painting, where the billowing robes that the actors wear fit in perfectly, and are spot-on equivalents for the spiritual mood of Chinese art. The floating, ruffling clothes are also practical, on-set versions of the human figures in Chinese art, as if they have been animated from paintings on silk and given three-dimensional form.

Like Tsui Hark, Tony Ching is fascinated by visual effects, and his cinema contains every trick imaginable. Ching's cinema celebrates the magic of filmmaking, the artifice, the dream.

Talking about the issue of co-direction: Hong Kong cinema has a long-established tradition of sharing duties in many areras of production, direction included.[2] The high speed of production meant that if someone wasn't available, someone else would step in; it was simply a practical solution; the idea of waiting weeks until the main director became available again, because only the main director was capable or legally authorized to shoot the film, is just silly. Most of the celebrated film directors in Hong Kong have co-directed at some time or other. Tony Ching Siu-tung was happy to collaborate with Tsui Hark, as we know – and also to share

---
[1] By the early 2000s, many Hong Kong action directors were working in the West, including Tony Ching Siu-tung, Corey Yuen Kwai, Yuen Cheung-yan and, most famously, Yuen Woo-ping.
[2] A surprising number of actors and crew in the Hong Kong film industry have also directed. Actors, DPs, editors, writers and action choreographers often step into the director's chair.

direction with Wong Jing, Johnnie To, and others.

It's common in the Hong Kong industry for film directors to also be actors, for actors to direct, for writers to be actors, and for some of the really gifted people to have multiple roles (like Sammo Hung, Jackie Chan, Tsui Hark, Eric Tsang, Wu Ma, etc).

TONY CHING SIU-TUNG: FILM CREDITS

Tony Ching Siu-tung's films as director include:

Duel To the Death (1983)
The Witch From Nepal (1986)
A Chinese Ghost Story (1987)
The Terracotta Warrior (1989)
The Swordsman (1990 – co-directed)
A Chinese Ghost Story 2 (1990)
The Raid (1991 – co-directed)
A Chinese Ghost Story 3 (1991)
Swordsman 2 (1992)
Swordsman 3 (1993 – co-directed)
The Heroic Trio (1993, co-directed)
The Executioners (1993, co-directed)
Wonder Seven (1994)
Dr. Wai In "The Scripture With No Words" (1996)
The Longest Day (1997)
Conman In Tokyo (2000)
Naked Weapon (2002)
Belly of the Beast (2003)
An Empress and the Warriors (2008)
The Sorcerer and the White Snake (2011)
Jade Dynasty (2019)

Tony Ching Siu-tung's work as action director/ choreographer includes 84 films up to 2011 (this is in addition to most of the movies he also helmed, where he was the action director, and not forgetting the many TV series that Ching has action directed – see below).

The following is a partial list:

The Fourteen Amazons (1972)
The Rats (1972)
Love and Vengeance (1973)
Shaolin Boxer (1974)
The Tea House (1974)

Kidnap (1974)
Lady of the Law (1975)
Negotiation (1977)
He Who Never Dies (1979)
Monkey Kung Fu (1979)
The Bastard Swordsman (1979)
The Sentimental Swordsman (1979)
Dangerous Encounter - 1st Kind (1980)
The Spooky Bunch (1980)
The Sword (1980)
The Master Strikes (1980)
Gambler's Delight (1981)
Return of the Deadly Blade (1981)
Sword of Justice (1981)
The Story of Woo Viet (1981)
Rolls, Rolls, I Love You (1982)
Once Upon a Rainbow (1982)
Swordsman Adventure (1983)
Twinkle Twinkle Little Star (1983)
Cherie (1984)
Happy Ghost 3 (1986)
Peking Opera Blues (1986)
A Better Tomorrow 2 (1987)
The Eighth Happiness (1988)
I Love Maria (1988)
The Killer (1989)
All About Ah-Long (1989)
The Fun, the Luck and the Tycoon (1990)
Casino Raiders 2 (1991)
Son On the Run (1991)
New Dragon Gate Inn (1992 – co-directed)
Moon Warriors (1992)
Twin Dragons (1992)
Royal Tramp (1992)
Royal Tramp 2 (1992)
Gambling Soul (1992)
Justice, My Foot! (1992)
Lucky Encounter (1992)
Flying Dagger (1993)
Future Cops (1993)
Holy Weapon (1993)
The Mad Monk (1993)
Butterfly and Sword (1993)
City Hunter (1993)
Love On Delivery (1994)
A Chinese Odyssey 1: Pandora's Box (1995)
A Chinese Odyssey 2: Cinderella (1995)

The Stuntwoman (1996)
Warriors of Virtue (1997)
Hong Niang (1998)
The Blacksheep Affair (1998)
The Assassin Swordsman (2000)
The Duel (2000)
My School Mate, the Barbarian (2001)
Invincible (2001)
Shaolin Soccer (2001)
Hero (2002)
Spider-Man (2002 – uncredited)
House of Flying Daggers (2004)
The Curse of the Golden Flower (2006)
Krrish (2006)
In the Name of the King: A Dungeon Siege Tale (2007)
The Warlords (2007)
Dororo (2007)
Legend of Shaolin Kungfu I: Heroes in Troubled Times (2007)
Butterfly Lovers (2008)
Kung Fu Dunk (2008)
The Treasure Hunter (2009)
Future X-Cops (2010)
Just Call Me Nobody (2010)
Legend of Shaolin Kungfu 3: Heroes of the Great Desert (2011)
Krrish 3 (2013)

Tony Ching has been the action director on many television series, including:

The Spirit of the Sword (1978)
It Takes a Thief (1979)
The Roving Swordsman (1979)
Reincarnated (1979)
Reincarnated 2 (1979)
Dynasty (1980)
Dynasty 2 (1980)
Legend of the Condor Heroes (1983)
The Return of the Condor Heroes (1983)
The New Adventures of Chor Lau Heung (1984)
The Duke of Mount Deer (1984)
The Return of Luk Siu Fung (1986)
The New Heaven Sword and Dragon Sabre (1986)
The Storm Riders (a.k.a. *Wind and Cloud*, 2002)
The Storm Riders 2 (a.k.a. *Wind and Cloud 2*, 2004)
The Royal Swordsmen (2005)

It's worth noting a couple of things about the credits of Tony Ching

Siu-tung and other action directors:[3] (1) some sources have Ching as the director, confusing action director with director. (2) The action director does indeed oversee whole sequences of a movie. The director sometimes leaves action scenes (and more) up to them. Also, action direction often includes second unit work. So you could argue that some films are co-directed – especially action movies, where lengthy sections will have been overseen by the action director. (3) And some movies were officially co-directed by Ching, working as a director (often with Tsui Hark). As you can see from the credits and the dates of the movies, co-directing usually occurred in the ultra-busy time of the late 1980s and early-to-mid-1990s, when people were working on four movies simultaneously, and sleeping in their car.

In Tony Ching Siu-tung's case, we know that *New Dragon Gate Inn* ran into trouble, and Ching and Tsui Hark came in to oversee the direction in order to finish the movie (part of which was filmed on location in Mainland China). *The Swordsman* too had problems, with several directors contributing to it to get the whole thing done.

In the West, the division of labour includes stunt co-ordinator, who oversees the stunt team and the stunts, and second unit director, who takes up all of the material that the first or 'A' unit hasn't time to do. In Hong Kong, the action director tends to combine the role of the stunt co-ordinator with that of the second unit director (many of the big name action directors have their own stunt teams – Jackie Chan's guys being the most famous).

How could Tony Ching do so much work in action direction – often several movies in the same year? The answer is the action director or stunt co-ordinator will be hired for short periods, sometimes even a day, to deliver particular effects. Even if they oversee several action sequences, they won't be on board for the whole schedule (for the talky scenes, for instance). Some productions call for a lot more action, of course, which will take longer; but many films hire several action directors (plus assistants). Thus, the action scenes can be filmed simultaneously.

In addition, action teams are often collaborating with the same people on film after film, so they develop a shorthand way of working; they are used to working fast; they often work long hours (without film unions); and they sometimes work on other shows at the same time (having several action directors means that some can be working in the studio, while others are on location).

Tony Ching Siu-tung has provided action direction for Tsui Hark, Johnnie To, John Woo, Wong Jing, Ringo Lam, Zhang Yimou, Peter Chan, Andy Lau, Kevin Chu, and Stephen Chow, among others. That is, practically all of the major filmmakers in China. (Ching has worked many times with a group of directors that include Tsui, Jing, To, Chow, Zhang and Chu. Ching has worked with Jing more than anyone else, except perhaps Tsui). There's no doubt whatsoever that one of the reasons those directors are celebrated by critics and fans around the world is because

---

[3] The 'martial arts director' was a position partly created by director King Hu in the 1960s.

their action sequences were overseen by Ching and his contemporaties.

We might wish, selfishly, that Ching Siu-tung had directed more movies, as with Jackie Chan (13 or so), rather than providing action direction for other filmmakers. However, 22 features as director or co-director, between 1983 and 2019, is a solid career – some of those movies are masterpieces (22 films is more than celebrated directors such as Orson Welles, Andrei Tarkovsky and Luchino Visconti).

TONY CHING SIU-TUNG: BIOGRAPHY

Tony Ching Siu-tung – often known as Tony Ching or as Ching Siu-tung[4] – was born on October 30, 1953, in Anhui, Showhsien province.[5] Ching is a genius of action cinema.[6] No one in the West can touch him, and only his contemporaries among Chinese action choreographers, such as Yuen Woo-ping, Corey Yuen Kwai and Yuen Bun, offer serious competition. Ching is the director of two of the great recent fantasy franchises in Chinese cinema: the *Chinese Ghost Story* series and the *Swordsman* series – two trilogies of pure cinematic bliss.

If these two film trilogies were better-known, Tony Ching Siu-tung would be celebrated like the greats of cinema – Renoir, Rossellini, Mizoguchi, Hawks, and, yes, even Murnau and Griffith. Ching 'demands to be ranked with the most idiosyncratic visionaries in film history', Howard Hampton[7] asserted (*pace The Swordsman 3: The East Is Red*).

Tony Ching Siu-tung[8] has helmed 22 movies (*A Chinese Ghost Story* was only his third feature as director), and has been the action choreographer on some of the very finest action movies of recent times, including *Hero, House of Flying Daggers, The Curse of the Golden Flower, Shaolin Soccer, Moon Warriors, Peking Opera Blues, New Dragon Gate Inn, City Hunter, The Killer, A Better Tomorrow 2* and *Twinkle Twinkle Little Star* (Ching's first action director credits go back to 1972's *The Fourteen Amazons* (his first credit as action director, for a film directed by his father, Ching Gong), and he was an actor in classics such as *Come Drink With Me*, 1966).

Tony Ching won Golden Horse Awards for *New Dragon Gate Inn* and *Shaolin Soccer*, Hong Kong Film Awards for *The Witch From Nepal, The*

---

4 As usual in China, there are many variants on his name, including: Xiaodong Cheng, Cheng Sao Tung, Ching Ting Yee, Cheng Bao-shan, Cheng Hsiao-tung and Shao-Tung Cheng.
  The names in Chinese cinema are confusing: there are at least two and often more for each person: a Chinese name, and an Angelicized name. Further, names in Cantonese and Mandarin are different. There is also some confusion about first names and surnames or family names – names're often printed with the surname first. And a single vowel change can mean a different name: Chang or Cheng, for example. So it's easy to be confused by the many Wongs, Laus, Leungs, Cheungs and Yuens!
5 Other sources say it was Hong Kong.
6 'The world's greatest wire-rig wizard', said Lisa Morton (LM, 88).
7 Quoted in F. Dannen, 338.
8 Cheng Xiaodong in pinyin.

Swordsman and *Hero,* as well as awards for *A Chinese Ghost Story*.

Ching Siu-tung has returned to work in television from time to time. For ex, in 2002 and 2004, he was the action choreographer on the long-running series *The Storm Riders,* also known as *Cloud and Wind*. This Taiwanese production of 45 episodes was based on a comic (known in China as *manhua*) by Ma Wing-shing called *Fung Wan*.

Tony Ching Siu-tung's father is Ching Gong (b. April 7, 1924, also known as Cheng Kang), a writer and director at Shaw Brothers. Ching senior was directing Cantonese films occasionally from 1951 onwards, filmed 2nd unit for Shaws in the 1960s, became a full director in 1967, and his output (of some 30 titles) includes many swordplay movies. He was very active in the 1950s-1970s as a writer – he's known for films such as *The Magnificent Swordsman* (1968) and *The Fourteen Amazons* (1972). His last film as director was *Gambling Soul* (1992).

Ching junior worked at Shaws as a stuntman,[9] sometimes on his Dad's movies; he grew up on film sets. Later, Ching acted as action director on several of his father's films. (Unfortunately, as with so many Hong Kong movies, many of them are not widely available).

Ching Gong was a writer for many years before directing – he has an impressive list of credits. However, the desire to write didn't transfer to his son – Ching has very few writing credits.

Tony Ching trained for seven years in Peking Opera and in *kung fu* in the Northern Style, at the East Drama School, run by Tang Ti.

✳

Sidenote on the Shaws: the Shaw Brothers Studio at Clearwater Bay in Hong Kong was launched in 1957 by Sir Run Run Shaw (Shao Yifu). Dubbed 'Movie Town', the 49-acre complex included eleven sound stages, fifteen standing sets on the backlot (featuring old Chinese settings), post-production, dubbing and editing facilities, print laboratories, dormitories and apartments for the casts and crews, and its own film school. (Run Run Shaw was in Singapore before this, overseeing distribution and acquiring properties. He came to Canton to take over the business from his brother, Runde).

Shaw Brothers kept players and talent on contracts, as in the Hollywood system (some 1700 workers).[10] The pay was famously low. Altho' the Hong Kong operation was regarded as Shaw Brothers, each brother oversaw companies within the empire. Shaws wasn't just a production facility/ studio, it had a distribution network.

Run Run Shaw spent HK $800,000 (= US $103,000) per movie; they were filmed in colour and in widescreen (Shawscope). Shaw was a canny and energetic businessman. He made deals with overseas producers, such as Italian producers, and the British Hammer studio (a famous investment was $7.5 million for foreign rights in the Warner Brothers/ Tandem/ Ladd Company movie *Blade Runner*, 1982).

✳

---

9 As Ching was small, he sometimes doubled for women.
10 At its height, the Shaw Brothers operation had 1,500 actors and 2,000 staff, an 80,000 wardrobe dept, a drama school (of 120 students), and in-house magazines.

One of Tony Ching Siu-tung's specialities is wire-work (there is plenty in the *Chinese Ghost Story* series); another is swordplay. Ching can fly actors and stunties with a blissful disregard for anything as everyday as gravity. The speed, invention, spontaneity, timing, rhythm, and acrobatic dynamism of Ching's action scenes are truly marvellous. Also worth remarking upon is the visual style of Ching's films: they have a highly romantic, luxurious look, with particular attention to art direction, costumes and textures. His films exploit props and the physical environment to a striking degree (this is true of many Hong Kong action movies). But Ching seems to go further than anyone else in evoking mystery, beauty and romance. Ching is an all-round filmmaker, and his mark is everywhere in his movies. Even amongst many similar films in Hong Kong cinema, Ching's stand out. Ching has said that entertainment is the highest priority for him as a filmmaker – like Tsui Hark, he is a supreme example of the Filmmaker As Showman.

Tony Ching Siu-tung is also a master of visual effects – no doubt he learnt plenty from Tsui Hark and Film Workshop, but visual effects and practical effects are a key ingredient in the Chingian style of filmmaking. If there's a cinematic trick available, Ching will use it. 'I like being unconventional', he remarked.

The movies of Ching Siu-tung foreground the tricks and visual effects of cinema; Western filmmakers who also use this approach include: Orson Welles, Jean Cocteau, Walerian Borowczyk, Sergei Paradjanov, Tim Burton, Vincente Minnelli, Powell & Pressburger, Ken Russell and Francis Coppola. Films of Ching's such as *A Chinese Ghost Story* are filled with visual effects (the influence of producer Tsui Hark is clear in this production).

Only in Hong Kong has the kind of action choreography delivered by Tony Ching and his contemporaries been possible. Nowhere else on this planet has action direction this complicated, this fast, this imaginative and this entertaining, using wires, rigs, harnesses, pulleys, cranes and ropes, been seen in movies.

Ching Siu-tung was promoted to martial arts coordinator in movies in the '70s, and worked in television (at Commercial Television) as a martial arts coordinator (at the invitation of Anthony Leung). Ching was the chief martial arts adviser on the 1979 TV series *Meteor, Butterfly, Sword*. He worked for Rediffusion Television on TV series such as *The Spirit of the Sword* (1978), *It Takes a Thief* (1979), *The Roving Swordsman* (1979), *Reincarnated* (1979), *Reincarnated 2* (1979), *Dynasty* (1980) and *Dynasty 2* (1980).

Tony Ching continued to work in television throughout the 1980s, including Hong Kong Television Broadcast series such as: *Legend of the Condor Heroes* (1983), *The Return of the Condor Heroes* (1983), *The New Adventures of Chor Lau Heung* (1984), *The Duke of Mount Deer* (1984), *The Return of Luk Siu Fung* (1986) and *The New Heaven Sword and Dragon Sabre* (1986). This extensive work in television partly explains the gap of three years between the feature productions *Duel To the Death* and *The*

Witch From Nepal.

Tony Ching's first full-length, theatrical film as director was *Duel To the Death* (1983), which was, of course, a *wuxia pian*. Ching's first collaboration with Tsui Hark on a feature film was *Dangerous Encounter – 1st Kind* in 1980, tho' they had already worked together in television.

Tony Ching has moved into North American movies (with *Belly of the Beast* (2003), a Steven Seagal actioner), worked uncredited on *Spider-man* (2002), has choreographed the Indian superhero movie *Krrish* (2006), and the sequels, produced the pop video *L'Âme-Stram-Gram* (1999) for French pop star Mylène Farmer, and contributed to the 2008 Beijing Olympics (at the invitation of director Zhang Yimou).

Tony Ching has been an actor many times, taking lead roles in *Monkey Kung Fu* (1979) and *The Master Strikes* (1980). Ching launched his own production company in 1993, China Entertainment.

Tony Ching Siu-tung's directing credits (22 features up to 2019) include *Dr Wai, The Sorcerer and the White Snake, Jade Dynasty, Wonder Seven, An Empress and the Warriors, Belly of the Beast, The Terracotta Warrior, The Raid* (co-directed), *The Witch From Nepal* and *The Executioners*. Ching's credits as action director (84 films up to 2011!) include *Butterfly Lovers, The Warlords, Shaolin Soccer, Invincible, In the Name of the King, Holy Weapon, Spider-man, Moon Warriors*, the *Royal Tramp* films (sometimes credited with co-direction), *Peking Opera Blues, Krrish, Butterfly and Sword* (sometimes credited with co-direction), *Bloodmoon, Hero, House of Flying Daggers, The Curse of the Golden Flower, The Royal Swordsmen* (TV series), *The Duel, Chinese Odyssey, Kung Fu Dunk, City Hunter, Twin Dragons, Future Cops, The Killer, A Better Tomorrow 2, The Storm Riders* (a.k.a. *Cloud and Wind*, TV series, 2002/ 2004), and *Twinkle Twinkle Little Star*.

Altho' John Woo, Yuen Woo-ping and Tsui Hark receive many of the accolades from film critics (and fans) for their depiction of action on screen, I am struck with awe at the imagination and magnificence of Tony Ching Siu-tung's work. He is the equal of Tsui, Woo, Yuen *et al*, and in some respects he out-does them (he has also of course worked as an action choreographer for all of the big names in Hong Kong action cinema). For action with a high fantasy component, Ching can't be beat – look at his work in *Hero* or *The House of Flying Daggers* or *Moon Warriors*, for instance. (And let's remember that Ching worked as action director for many Hong Kong directors, including John Woo: one of the reasons that the *Better Tomorrow* movies or *The Killer* are so good is because it's Ching choreographing the action. And it's often the action that critics rave about in those Woo-helmed movies).

Producer Terence Chang said that Tsui Hark and Tony Ching Siu-tung complemented each other: while Tsui was enamoured of the historical pictures from the Shaw Brothers, Ching actually worked on them: 'they complemented each other and were tied together by their shared romantic vision', Chang remarked.

Indeed – of all of Tsui Hark's many, many creative collaborations, the ones with Tony Ching Siu-tung are among the most productive: they seem to have sparked each other to greater imaginative heights, as evinced by the *Chinese Ghost Story* series and the *Swordsman* series (both made in the busy late 1980s/ early 1990s period).

Jeff Yang noted that Tony Ching Siu-tung was about the only director able to work with Tsui Hark consistently, maybe because he got along with Tsui, or because he was happy to let Tsui take all of the glory (2003, 97). Also, directors in Hong Kong are happy to share director credits – most of the major directors have done it.

Maybe Tony Ching Siu-tung was able to accommodate Tsui Hark and his tendency to wade in heavy and strong to a film project and not get freaked out by it. Maybe Ching realized that the movies they were producing were extraordinary (so a bit of aggro didn't matter, and aggro doesn't last anyway). Maybe Ching was easy-going enough (where other filmmakers in this period found it just too difficult to work with Tsui, and some walked out).

Because Tony Ching Siu-tung clearly threw himself 100% into the three *Chinese Ghost Story* movies (and the *Swordsman* movies). These are film productions that literally *roar* with fire and energy and humour and action and sweetness and tenderness and mind-boggling eccentricity. There's *so much* energy on screen, these movies are like a conflagration.

As a director, Ching Siu-tung's career has been a tad uneven: low-points include *Naked Weapon* and *Belly of the Beast*, two mean-spirited films that Ching directed which were not worthy of his talents. However, in 2002 and 2003 Ching also action directed two sublime examples of action cinema: *Hero* and *House of Flying Daggers* (plus the great comedy *Shaolin Soccer*, and the TV series *The Storm Riders*). Soon after that, Ching provided the action direction for *Krrish* and *The Curse of the Golden Flower* (both 2006), and took up the directing reins in 2008 for his masterpiece *An Empress and the Warriors*.

PEKING OPERA.

Tony Ching trained in Peking Opera, a breeding ground for many future Hong Kong and Chinese stars. Peking Opera is known as *jingju* = theatre of the capital. The four performance skills in Peking Opera are *da* (acrobatics and martial skills), *chang* (singing), *nian* (reciting) and *zuo* (acting).

In Chinese Opera, as in many theatrical traditions, men play women's roles (so that only men're on stage). Yam Kin-fai and Pak Suet-sin, for instance, played across the gender divide in the Opera movies of the 1950s and 1960s. In Cantonese Opera, the fighting instructor was called *longhu* (= Dragon-Tiger Master).

The Peking Opera approach to entertainment was characterized thus by Bey Logan:

> extravagant costumes, bright full-face makeup, Olympic-class gymnastics, and both weapon and empty-handed combat, as well as a

rich tradition of character, music and drama. (9)

Beijing Opera is the most well-known form of Chinese Opera, but it's not the only one. There are 100s of Opera styles, including Cantonese Opera. Acrobatics, extravagant costumes, make-up, singing, music, and stylized gestures constitute the performance style. Most of the performers have traditionally been men. The heyday of Chinese Opera was the 1930s. Following its decline in the 1960s and 1970s, performers moved into the film industry.

Peking Opera's most famous academy was the one run by Sifu Yu Jim Yuen in Hong Kong, the stern taskmaster who oversaw the performance troupe that included Jackie Chan, Sammo Hung, Yuen Biao, Yuen Tak, Yuen Wah, Yuen Bun and Yuen Kwai (Corey Yuen). They were known as the Seven Fortunes (tho' there were fourteen of them). Their upbringing at the academy was immortalized in the 1988 movie *Painted Faces* (with Hung playing the *sifu*). As Hung, Chan, Biao and others have often remarked, the regime overseen by Yu was so harsh, no one would believe them! (Even though in the *Painted Faces* movie what the boys have to undergo is pretty tough).

HONG KONG CINEMA IN CRITICISM.

The critical response to Hong Kong cinema in recent years tends to celebrate the same movies, and the same filmmakers are enshrined by the critical academy: Tsui Hark, John Woo, Yuen Woo-ping, Wong kar-wai, Johnny To, Lau Kar-leung, Peter Chan, Stanley Kwan, Corey Yuen Kwai, Sammo Hung, Ronny Yu, Ann Mui, Ringo Lam, and of course Jackie Chan. Tony Ching Siu-tung is part of that list.

The same actors are exalted: Jackie Chan, Jet Li, Chow Yun-fat, Tony Leung, Andy Lau, Leslie Cheung, Sammo Hung, Yuen Biao, Donnie Yen, Stephen Chow, Leon Lai, Jacky Cheung, Simon Lam, Joey Wong, Zhao Wenzhou, Zhao Wei, Chingmy Yau, Anita Mui, Michelle Yeoh, Maggie Cheung, Brigitte Lin, Michelle Reiss, Carrie Ng, Cherie Chung, Rosamund Kwan, Sally Yeh and Zhang Ziyi.

The much-discussed Hong Kong movies include the *Once Upon a Time In China* series, the *Police Story* series, the *Project A* films, the *Armor of God* films, the *Better Tomorrow* series, the *Stormriders* series, the *Fong Sai-yuk/ Legend* series, the *Lucky Stars* series, the *Bride With White Hair* series, the *On Fire* series, *Rouge, Mr Vampire, Rumble In the Bronx, Zu: Warriors From the Magic Mountain, Peking Opera Blues, Painted Faces, Infernal Affairs, Dragons Forever, Drunken Master, Snake In Eagle's Shadow, Iron Monkey, Moon Warriors, The Spooky Bunch, Royal Tramp, Bullet In the Head, The Killer, Hard-Boiled, God of Gamblers, Chungking Express, Ashes of Time, Aces Go Places, Wicked City, City Hunter, Naked Killer, Sex and Zen*, etc. And of course every critic also cites the Bruce Lee movies, and the Shaw Brothers classics.

Tony Ching has several movies that're part of that list: the *Swordsman* series and the *Chinese Ghost Story* series; he has worked on many classics directed by others, too: *New Dragon Gate Inn, Moon Warriors, A Better Tomorrorw 2, Peking Opera Blues* and *The Killer*.

You try finding a study of Chinese cinema or Hong Kong cinema between 1980 and today that *doesn't* mention *any* of the above movies or directors or actors! So it's a narrow group of film classics, in short.

REMAKES AND UPDATES.

Much of Ching Siu-tung's cinema comprises updating and remaking previous movies and stories. Hong Kong filmmakers know their history, and how their industry is constantly recycling and updating earlier movies. As Ching notes, you have to be contemporary, you can't be out of date. As an action director, Ching has worked on many remakes and updates of earlier films: *A Better Tomorrow* was a remake of *Story of a Discharged Prisoner* (a.k.a. *True Colors of a Hero*, 1967), *New Dragon Gate Inn* updated the King Hu-helmed movie of 1967, and *The Warlords* was a remake of *The Blood Brothers* (1973).

In thriving film cultures, like France, Japan, Korea or the U.S.A., it is completely expected and normal to remake movies and stories all the time. *New actors in old stories* is one of the definitions of the Hollywood movie machine in the glory days of the 1930s thru 1960s, but the phrase still sums up a large proportion of the output of any flourishing filmmaking centre. Often, the remakes and updates are simply old stories dressed up in new clothes, with some new gimmicks to help sell them (such as 3-D, or visual effects, or a postmodern spin on an old chestnut).

CHING SIU-TUNG AND TELEVISION.

Television nurtured the New Wave filmmakers in Hong Kong – becoming something like a Shaolin Temple for cinéastes, as critic Law Kar put it. They worked at stations such as C.T.V. (Commercial Television), R.T.H.K. (Radio Television Hong Kong) and T.V.B.[11] (Hong Kong Television Broadcast, Ltd.). Selina Chow, a TV executive, was instrumental in hiring the 'New Wave' filmmakers in television.[12] They were also a film school generation: the New Wave directors studied at film schools abroad partly because they didn't really exist in Asia (the Chinese State film school, Beijing Film Academy, didn't re-open until 1978).

Ching Siu-tung worked a good deal in television, from the 1970s onwards. Before he helmed his first feature, *Duel To the Death* in 1983, Ching had already been an action director for TV shows such as *The Spirit of the Sword* (1978), *It Takes a Thief* (1979), *The Roving Swordsman* (1979), *Reincarnated* (1979), *Reincarnated 2* (1979), *Meteor, Butterfly, Sword* (1979), *Dynasty* (1980) and *Dynasty 2* (1980). Ching returned to television production periodically – in 2002 and 2004, for example, Ching action directed the *Storm Riiders* TV series (a.k.a. *Wind and Cloud*).

---

11 T.V.B. was the television arm of Shaws.
12 Lisa Morton, 221.

THE HONG KONG NEW WAVE.

Ching Siu-tung was not one of the New Wave of Hong Kong filmmakers who went to film school overseas – instead, Ching grew up in the film industry: his father Ching Gong was a film director at Shaws. However, Ching worked on many of the New Wave productions – three in 1980, for example: *The Sword, Dangerous Encounter* and *The Spooky Bunch*.

Many of the Chinese New Wave filmmakers were film school graduates: Ann Hui and Yim Ho studied in London; Tsui Hark in Austin, Texas; and Ringo Lam in Toronto (York University). They studied in the West, or in Western-style institutions in Hong Kong. They could speak English with critics, which no doubt helped, because they'd spent time in the West. And they were familiar with the art film traditions of Europe and the U.S.A.

Following film school, they went to work in television. (Hui, Ho and Tsui were part of the first wave of the New Wave, along with Allan Fong, Patrick Tam, Kirk Wong, and Tony Ching Siu-tung); the second wave included Stanley Kwan, Alex Law, Clara Law, Cheung Yuen-ting, Jacob Cheung, Wong Kar-wai, and Eddie Fong.

The Hong Kong New Wave did not have a style or an approach: it took on aspects of youth: 'school, sex, drugs and other travails of growing up in a materialistic society, misunderstood by parents and adults in authority', according to Stephen Teo (1997, 156).

It was no surprise that many of the first films of the Hong Kong New Wave were thrillers or crime stories – because they are a staple of Hong Kong cinema, and of cinemas the world over, because they tend to be cheap to make, because the genre was versatile, and because a huge proportion of source material was in the crime or thriller genre.

For Stephen Teo, the two strands of the Hong Kong New Wave cinema – realism and genre conventions – developed towards the latter: the New Wavers started out tackling realism but lent towards genre filmmaking (1997, 149). The forms and conventions of genres were updated for modern audiences in the 1980s. (The first official, Hong Kong New Wave film was *The Extras* (1978), but the unofficial film that launched it, according to Cheuk Pak-tong, was *Jumping Ash* (1976). In 1979, some of the first New Wave films included *The Secrets* (dir. Ann Hui), *The Butterfly Murders* (dir. Tsui Hark), *The System* (dir. Peter Yung) and *Cops and Robbers* (dir. Alex Cheung)). By contrast, Ching Siu-tung's first film as director was the high fantasy swordplay movie *Duel To the Death* in 1983.

At the height of the 1990s New Wave, actors and crew were commonly rushing from one movie set to another. Andy Lau Tak-wah slept in his car while filming a movie a month in 1991, and according to rumour making four movies in four locations at the same time. (Chinese filmmakers became geniuses at stretching footage of actors who could only give them a day or so, by using doubles, re-arranging scripts, focussing on reaction shots, etc).

You'll see the same actors and directors in the New Wave of Hong Kong and Chinese cinema, continuing up to the present day. The actors include: Jet Li, Jackie Chan, Brigitte Lin, Tony Leung, Leslie Cheung, Michelle Yeoh Chu-kheng, Zhao Wei, Donnie Yen, Maggie Cheung, Jacky Cheung, Zhang Ziyi, Yuen Biao, Chow Yun-fat, Josephine Siao, Stephen Chow, Gong Li, Rosamund Kwan, Zhao Wenzhou, Kent Cheng, and Xiong Xin-xin.

And directors such as Tsui Hark, Ronny Yu, Ringo Lam, King Hu, Sammo Hung, Zhang Yimou, Ann Hui, Wong Jing, Yuen Woo-ping, Wong Kar-wai, Stanley Tong and John Woo. Tony Ching Siu-tung is part of that group.

The second wave of Hong Kong filmmakers occurred in the mid-1980s, and included filmmakers such as Stanley Kwan (*Rouge, The Actress*), Wong Kar-wai (*Ashes of Time, Chungking Express*), Clara Law (*The Reincarnation of Golden Lotus*), Mabel Cheung (*An Autumn's Tale*), Lawrence Ah Mon (*Gangs, Queen of Temple Street*), Alex Law (*Painted Faces*), Eddie Fong, and Jacob Cheung.

*

Hong Kong is a city of seven million or so. The filmmaking community is small: everybody knows or has heard of everyone else. Over its history, the cast and crew of Hong Kong movies would've met many times at the Shaw Brothers' studios at Clearwater Bay, or the Golden Harvest studios in Diamond Hill, or the television studios at Hong Kong Television Broadcast, Ltd. They would visit the same bars and restaurants. Some American filmmakers prefer to shoot outside of L.A., because if you film in Tinseltown everybody knows what you're doing. No chance of avoiding that in Hong Kong!

You'll see the same downtown areas of Hong Kong, the same harbour fronts, the same strips of forest or beaches, and the same standing sets of 19th century China, in movie after movie. (And, with the problems of obtaining film permits, shooting on location on the streets often means guerilla-style filmmaking, which Hong Kong crews are experts at).

Ching Siu-tung on set.

Making Jade Dynasty (2019), this page and over.

小战战与河水结下了深刻的革命友谊

〔是他抢我的棍子〕

2

ASPECTS OF THE CINEMA OF TONY CHING SIU-TUNG

'MORE POWER!': SOME OF TONY CHING SIU-TUNG'S MOTIFS

Tony Ching Siu-tung's on-set mantra is, 'more power, more power!' Among the many motifs and techniques in Ching's style of action direction are:

• an emphasis on the beauty and flow of bodies in motion (Tony Ching Siu-tung is probably the most painterly of Hong Kong action directors);

• fluttering, flapping robes, banners and flags (fans are continually blowing on a Ching set);

• mass battles – chaotic movement everywhere; typically, someone will bounce on a hidden trampoline across the camera;

• extremely rapid swordplay accompanied by jumps and acrobatic spins, and often moving across the ground, covered in tracking shots;

• the lone swordsman entering the fray, weapon extended, like Superman;

• groups of figures lowered on wires – it might be the heroes arriving at a scene, or henchmen (*Krrish*), or some ghoulish characters (as in *A Chinese Ghost Story*);

• water explosions – multiple fountains of water from oil barrels, often erupting behind a magician (as in the *Chinese Ghost Story* series, *Moon Warriors*, the *Swordsman* films and *Royal Tramp 2*);

• long distance airborne travel – a palanquin complete with footmen hurtling thru the tree-tops at speed;

• ærial flight gags – ninjas[1] flying on kites;

• visual effects – these are everywhere in Tony Ching Siu-tung's cinema, combined with action;

• charas (often ninja) diving into frame from either side of a rapidly-tracking camera;

• exiting a scene by soaring upwards and crashing thru a roof;

---

[1] Bey Logan calls the ninjas that regularly pop up in the films of Tony Ching 'Chinjas'.

- hidden attacks from high above, sword pointing down;
- horror movie gags (giant tongues);
- gross-out gags – people or horses[2] split apart; people exploding in a flurry of blood and rags;
- massive gags and stunts – disintegrating wooden platforms, flying logs, collapsing buildings, crazy monsters, enormous explosions.

ELEMENTS OF CHING SIU-TUNG'S CINEMA

The 22 films directed (and co-directed) by Ching Siu-tung (up to 2019) feature the following elements:

- They all have Chinese casts (with one or two exceptions).
- They all use Hong Kong and Chinese crews.
- They are all set in Asia, and usually in China or Hong Kong, with one or two overseas locations.
- They are all Chinese stories (with one or two exceptions).
- They are all produced in China (with the odd overseas trip).
- They draw heavily on Chinese tradition and history.
- About half can be classed as swordplay movies (or *wuxia pian*). The rest are thrillers or action-adventures.
- Two-thirds are historical movies; one third are contemporary-set.
- Comedy is a significant element in at least half of the films.
- All of the films climax with a giant action scene.
- Ching Siu-tung has action director credits on all of them.

These elements speak for themselves: most of Ching Siu-tung's films have been about China, set in China, with Chinese stories featuring Chinese characters, using Chinese crews and casts, and two-thirds have been historical movies.

ASPECTS OF THE CINEMA OF TONY CHING SIU-TUNG

Tony Ching Siu-tung told the Hong Kong Film Directors' Guild:

> I like beautiful, romantic things, and have an almost extreme and idealized sense of perfectionism regarding the films I make, and strive to achieve the kind of poeticism found in traditional Chinese paintings.

---

[2] If you love horses and don't like to see them harmed – even if you know it's movie fakery – don't watch Hong Kong action movies! Horses are punched and wrestled to the ground (*An Empress and the Warriors*), decapitated (*Burning Paradise*), pushed down steep slopes (*Seven Swords*), and sliced in two (Tony Ching Siu-tung's films).

Keep those things in mind when considering Tony Ching Siu-tung's cinema: romance, idealization, perfection, painting and poetry. (And remember, too, that Ching trained in Peking Opera for 7 years).

Altho' Ching Siu-tung is known as an action director and a film director who showcases action, romance, comedy and a painterly vision are also key elements of his cinema. For instance, his first big hit movie was a romance (*A Chinese Ghost Story*), and romance was an important ingredient in the *Swordsman* films, in *The Terracotta Warrior* and more recent films, such as *An Empress and the Warriors* (which features a lengthy romantic idyll).

Tony Ching Siu-tung said he liked to try new ways of approaching storytelling, and he enjoyed taking on fantasy forms. Why? – 'Because I'm not a normal person. I think it's fun to shoot something different, something unusual'.

When he was asked what the secret was of being a good action director, Tony Ching Siu-tung replied:

> The secret is to stay young. Your ideas can't age with you – although we're getting older, what we film has to feel young. It's not okay to be outdated.

Tsui Hark on action:

> Action is not just by itself; action always comes with a story, it also comes with a style, it comes with extra information about what the director wants to show to the audience. These sorts of things are always with me. (2011)

Tony Leung Siu-hung noted that action choreographers have to imprint their style on a scene:

> All comes from your mind, your imagination. You then have to share it with your assistant. It's the same with Tony Ching Siu-tung; after he's finished working on a choreographed scene, it's eventually Ching Siu-tung's imagination which appears at the end. (A. Lanuque, 2006)

When he's directing, Tony Ching Siu-tung is amongst the actors and crew, not hiding in a video village off to one side. He is interacting directly with the cast, including all of the principals, showing them how to perform the action, often at a micro, beat-by-beat level. (That's partly because an action director can't hide behind a bank of monitors and assistant directors, they have to be in the thick of things). Ching also operates the camera himself, so we are often seeing Ching's own compositions and camera moves in his films.

One of Tony Ching's early assistants, Tony Leung Siu-hung, remarked: 'I really admire some of his creations. He's got no limitations! He really knows how to use camera angles and camera movement' (A. Lanuque, 2006).

One of the hallmarks of Tony Ching Siu-tung's form of action cinema is excessive, fantastical violence, action so quick, intense and extreme it borders on the comical. Such as Ching's penchant for warriors being ripped in half by swords in mid-air, or bodies being sliced apart from head to toe and the two halves falling away. In a Ching swordplay flick, victims are decapitated with a single swish of the blade and the heads spin thru the air.[3] It all happens so rapidly, and without showers of blood, it seems 'unrealistic'. But how can you test 'realism'? – like, when was the last time you saw a warrior in full battle armour being torn to pieces by a slashing swordsman – while both of them were in mid-air, at night, in a forest?

Wire-work: the signature image of Tony Ching Siu-tung's cinema is a swordsman flying through the air, sword arm extended, robes fluttering in the breeze. Ching has several motifs in his wire-work which recur: one is flying several characters at the same time, in groups (a great example occurs in the *Chinese Ghost Story* movies. What you don't see are forty guys off-stage hauling on the ropes and cables,[4] and the enormous cranes).[5] Another is a gentle, romantic flight over a long distance (often it's two lovers, embracing and smiling at each other. Sometimes they're on horseback). Another is the rapid exit from a interior scene by zooming upwards, smashing through the roof. When a swordsman enters or exits a scene of combat, they always spin quickly in the air, and also dive and tumble (these moves are very Peking Opera-ish, emulating the way that performers make their entrance on stage. A flashy entrance is a big deal in Peking Opera). Halfway thru a sword fight, a warrior will disappear – then they materialize far above the opponent, and descend swiftly, sword arm stretched out.

Inanimate objects: the wire-work in Hong Kong action movies is puppeteering the environment extensively: walls topple, tables spin, benches are smashed apart, ladders, columns and logs fly thru the air as weapons, and entire buildings collapse. In a Hong Kong action flick, the whole environment can come alive. Special wire-work in Tony Ching Siu-tung's output includes his penchant for very extravagant deaths – victims are torn apart by sword slices or magic.

While we're celebrating the outrageous stunts and wire-work of Hong Kong action directors, we must also remember that they have whole teams of very clever engineers and talented craftsmen who can build all of those rigs, cable systems, scaffolding, cranes and all the rest (and a bunch of burly guys to hang into the wires and the ropes). Stunt gags require plenty of prep work – building breakaway sets or props, for ex, or manœuvring the cranes into the right position. It's one thing you *don't* see in any 'making of' documentaries – just how those complex rigs work. (Partly, perhaps, because sometimes film crews like to keep one or two tricks of the trade secret).

Ninjas! No other film director, in the West, the East, the North, the South – or on Mars – has been so crazy about ninjas and putting them on

---
[3] Pre-dating *Sleepy Hollow* (1999) by many years.
[4] It requires several people to fly one actor.
[5] Photos or detailed descriptions of just how Ching and his crews achieve their effects are hard to find – because they want to keep it secret.

film (outside of Japanese *anime*). Tony Ching just adores those mysterious, black-clad warriors of stealth and cunning. If there's a chance to include some tumbling, running, super-soldiers in a scene, Ching will take it. (And Ching is especially fond of inventing all sorts of incredible gags for the *shinobi* to perform). It's a pity, perhaps, that Ching hasn't (yet) directed a whole movie about *shinobi*. (If you were going to produce a live-action version of a Japanese ninja tale, such as *Naruto*, Ching is definitely your man).

One of Tony Ching's talents is to make actresses look fantastic when they're in action. Hong Kong cinema has a long tradition of female fighters, but most of the actresses in Ching's films (and others of the 1970s through 2010s) are not professional or trained martial artists (and neither are most of the men). But Ching can make them look incredible: Maggie Cheung, Anita Mui, Sharla Cheung, Fennie Yuen, Zhang Ziyi, Kelly Chen, Michelle Reiss, Brigitte Lin, Flora Cheung, Meng Meiqi and Tang Yixin.

Although the Hong Kong film business is male-oriented and masculinist, like all film centres around the world, some of the movies of Tony Ching and his contemporaries have been written by women. Sandy Shaw Lai-king, for instance, wrote *The Heroic Trio, The Executioners* and *Dr Wai* (Shaw's other credits include *Once a Cop, My Father Is a Hero, The Mad Monk, Justice, My Foot!, Twinkle Twinkle Little Star* and *It Runs In the Family*. Some of those movies were directed by or starred John Woo and Stephen Chow).

Many of the movies that Tony Ching works on are cast young – film producers often have an eye on attracting a young audience. Being young, the actors don't have much – or any – experience with complicated stunts, or doing wire-work, or co-operating with visual effects (effects that are created in front of the camera or added later in post-production).

Thus, one of Tony Ching's jobs on any new movie production is training – to teach the young actors how to work with cables and rigs and visual effects. (This is a key reason why some film directors like to work with the same people, who're often veterans of many movies, precisely because they *don't* have to go through the explanations and training each time. But others welcome it).

If you look at the movies that Tony Ching has chosen to do as an action choreographer, you can see that he is one of those people who thrives on new challenges and working with young people. As he says, films and filmmakers have to stay up to date.

All of Ching Siu-tung's movies as director, and most of those as action director, climax with a giant battle. No matter what the movie has been about, the ending is always a massive sequence of incredible action.

Tony Ching Siu-tung doesn't employ slow motion nearly as much as some of his contemporaries. And some of the directors he's worked for as an action choreographer over-use slo-mo, which spoils the sequences he's devised. (However, having said that, I've just watched the group of movies made in the early 2000s again – *Invincible, Hero, Naked Weapon* and *Belly of the Beast* – which do employ a good proportion of slo-mo per fight).

Many Chinese action movies employ slow motion, and also step-motion. Indeed, step-motion (a.k.a. step-printed film) occurs just as much as slow motion. True slow motion is of course filmed on the set, with the camera running at higher speeds (48 frames per second or 96 f.p.s. being typical speeds). But step-motion is created after the fact, in the editing room and by optically treating the celluloid in the processing lab (where you can also select different kinds of step-motion). Sometimes Chinese action movies play whole beats of an action scene in step-motion, but with heightened sound effects (and usually a big music cue). Incidentally, Tony Ching often films action scenes slightly under-cranked (at 22 f.p.s.), to give them an extra ziiip.

Let's not forget, either, that *comedy* and *humour is absolutely fundamental* to the action direction of Tony Ching Siu-tung. Oh yes, Ching is not a dour, old curmudgeon who never cracks a smile, who never allows a smidgen of humour to infect movies with wall-to-wall grimness and frowningness.

In fact, many of Tony Ching Siu-tung's finest works in action are comedies, or feature comedy as a key ingredient, like *Shaolin Soccer*, *A Chinese Ghost Story*, *City Hunter*, *Krrish*, *Jade Dynasty* and *Heroic Trio*. And his two famous series – the *Swordsman* series and *Chinese Ghost Story* series – are stuffed with humour. Ching has worked many times with comedy directors and actors such as Wong Jing and Stephen Chow.

For some critics, the emphasis in the marketing of Chinese and Hong Kong movies in the West on action, violence, energy and weirdness has put it back into a pigeon-hole, which ignores many other kinds of cinema coming out of Hong Kong, Shanghai or Beijing.

Comedy is certainly one of the staple (and lucrative) genres of Hong Kong cinema, often ignored or derided by Western critics. For instance, between 1950 and 1970, 25% of films from Canton were comedies (of the 3,000 films produced). An industry like Hong Kong only produces that many comedy movies if it knows they are going to find an audience. And they do.

In the West, in the U.S.A., martial arts films, action films and art films are the biggest financial successes (and with the film critics), but in Hong Kong, it's *comedies* that have ruled the local box office. Nine out of the ten bestsellers in the 1980s and 1990s in Canton and Taiwan were comedies. Often they are combined with other genres: vampire comedies, *kung fu*/ martial arts comedies, cookery comedies, gambling comedies, historical comedies, detective/ thriller comedies, etc. (But comedies, as we know, are hampered by problems of translation, dubbing, and cultural specificity. So that giant stars in Asia like Stephen Chow or Michael Hui are still largely unknown in the West. Instead of Adam Sandler or Ben Stiller, try some Stephen Chow for a change).

❂

Tony Ching Siu-tung is not a screenwriter, other people write the scripts that he directs (Ching has only two credits as screenwriter – *Duel*

To the Death and *Wonder Seven*). He is also not a film producer (he has only 4 producer credits). Ching comes to cinema from the practical, organizational side of things, graduating from acting and stuntwork to action choreography and direction.

Tony Ching is thus not an *auteur*, in the manner of filmmakers who write and direct (and also produce) their own material. Much of the time, Ching is a director for hire, someone who's offered scripts and projects – which's how most directors operate (the proportion of film directors who write their own material *and* originate it *and* it's not based on any existing property is *very* small).

Yet Tony Ching Siu-tung's stamp is all over the movies he directs, and his action choreography is instantly recognizable when he works on other productions (especially his style of fantastical swordplay). Certainly, Ching is as natural a filmmaker as any in film history. And tho' not an *auteur* with issues he explores in film after film, he does have recurring themes and motifs. Romance is uppermost, as is action. If something can be expressed in choreography (not always action or military choreography), Ching will try it. This is the Peking Opera form of filmmaking, where gesture and movement, alongside costume and make-up, do the storytelling. In Peking Opera, as soon as an actor steps onto the stage, the audience knows who they are by their clothes, accessories and make-up – and their movement and gestures. Applied to movies, the Peking Opera approach is all over Hong Kong cinema (and Chinese cinema), and informs much of Ching's work (he trained in it for seven years).

Tony Ching Siu-tung is not known for being a firebrand political filmmaker, tho' there are numerous, self-conscious political statements throughout his work.

He's not known for delivering complex narrative structures, but his films are, like many movies, actually more complex narratively than they first appear. This applies to so many movies: film critics routinely call a plot 'simple', when it clearly isn't. Parts of a plot may seem simple (revolving around single words like 'revenge' or 'romance'), but how the plots are portrayed is seldom simple (even in Hong Kong cinema, where the quality of the screenplays is derided in Western film criticism).

Many actors and crew are happy to work with Ching Siu-tung, partly because they know that their work will be seen potentially by millions of people. Which's what it's all about. They also know that Ching is one of the great talents in action cinema, and that working on a Ching movie raises their own profile. And Ching will make them look very cool.

Also, movies directed by Ching Siu-tung will get released, a lot of people will see them, they won't be re-cut by studios or backers (or censored – usually), and there's a good chance that the marketing and promotion will be effective, and that they will be reviewed, and that they will have an after-life on TV, cable, DVD, etc. (All actors, East, or West, have been in or know about projects that were sat on for years, or never got released, or were distributed poorly, or were hacked about by distributors or studios.)

ASPECTS OF CHINESE ACTION MOVIES.

The following items are some of the aspects of Chinese and Hong Kong action movies, compared to Western (North American and European) action cinema:

• Acrobatic and athletic: one of the most obvious differences between Chinese and Western action cinema is the emphasis on acrobatic movement, on portraying the body in movement in space, on action like dance choreography and ballet, and action like circus performers, trapeze artists, jugglers, and street entertainers. (In Western choreography, acrobatics is part of the 'flash').

• Naturalism/ realism vs. fantasy: even the most 'realistic' of Chinese action movies contains more fantasy than most Western fantasy movies! Chinese action filmmakers never feel constrained to stick to notions such as 'realism' or 'naturalism'. A Chinese action scene can fly off in all sorts of directions.

• Humour: even in the grisliest and nastiest and most violent scenes in a Chinese action movie there might be humour. This is one aspect of Asian cinema that really jars with Western audiences, who like their serious moments to stay serious. Asian filmmakers (and Japanese animators in particular) are happy to mix in humour with drama, to pop melodramatic bubbles with laughs.

• Editing: Chinese action movies tend to be cut faster than Western action movies; but they don't resort to four angles of the same action (an irritating recent trend in Western cinema and TV).[6]

• Pacing: Chinese action movies are *much* faster, in terms of storytelling and pacing, than Western action movies. Yet there are many scenes where moments are expanded way beyond the requirements of the drama (emotional moments, for example, or, most famously, big action scenes which go far beyond the dramatic requirements of the scene).

• Cutting: the cuts occur in a different place in a Chinese action movie compared to its Western counterparts, and there is a different emphasis of the flow of movement, rhythm and of timing.

• The camera is very wild in Chinese action cinema: it doesn't stay on the horizontal, it is often tilted, it is often continually moving, and it is often at a low angle.

• The freedom of the camera: Chinese action filmmakers emphasize a feeling of total freedom to put the camera *anywhere* on the set.

• Framing: Chinese action movies tend to compose each shot for a specific movement.

• Shots: Chinese action cinema tends to construct its action scenes using short, individual shots, each one tied to a specific beat or movement or gesture, rather than master shots. In the West, master shot filmmaking is a standard approach, with the crew then moving in for close-ups, medium shots and inserts.

• The Chinese action team will film each individual moment, then turn around the camera and the lights to shoot the reverse angles, then go

---

[6] One reason is they haven't got *time* to film four shots of someone raising a glass to their mouth to drink.

back again to continue with the first side.
- Whole body shots: Chinese action movies typically include all of the body in their action scenes, rather than chopping it up into bits (a frustrating tendency in Western action cinema).
- Some shots are set up to be wildly over-the-top.
- Slow motion is everywhere (and at times filmmakers have had to slow down the martial arts performers because they are too fast for the camera to record their movements).
- Movement and reaction: Chinese action cinema is absolutely brilliant at evoking the impact of hits, the reactions of bodies in movement, the thud of a stunt guy on the ground. In Chinese action cinema, you see people *really* slamming into each other or the wall or the floor. There is always time taken for the reactions and the consequences of a particular movement or gesture.
- Visual effects: most Chinese action movies are filmed live, on the set, without resorting to post-production techniques. By contrast, since the 1990s, Western movies often include a lot of post-production technology. Budgetary reasons are key here, because Chinese action movies have a far lower budget than North American action movies (and visual effects are *very* expensive).
- In front of the camera: Chinese action movies recreate everything in front of the camera, and emphasize atmospheric elements, such as wind machines, smoke machines, fire, explosions, candles, and a host of wire effects and practical effects.
- Wirework: Chinese action filmmakers are without question the masters of using cables and movement of any cinema anywhere.
- Movement is much bigger and freer in Chinese action cinema compared to Western action cinema: bodies float, spin, leap and contort to an extraordinary degree in Chinese action cinema.
- Props: no filmmaking centre uses props as imaginatively as Hong Kong film crews (with a star like Jackie Chan, one of the all-time masters at deploying props in a fight scene).
- Weapons: in a Chinese action movie, anything in the immediate surroundings can be used as a weapon (including clothes and props like hats and umbrellas).
- Sound: Chinese movies tend to be filmed without live sound. The sounds that are added later mix punches and whooshes very high, but only use a few channels of sound; the movies also deploy sound effects in a different, highly stylized and definitely non-realistic manner. Western action movies, if they have the time and budget, often cram action scenes with large quantities of sounds, which tend to promote 'realism'/ 'naturalism' (sound fx fight with the music).
- Budgets: Hong Kong movies in the 1980s typically had budgets between US $100,000 and US $1,000,000.[7] The New Wave cinema of the early 1990s helped lead to rising costs, sometimes up to US $4 million (which was regarded as big budget), tho' around US $1.2 million was

---

[7] The budget for *The Big Boss*, a 1971 Bruce Lee picture, was $50,000.

typical (as was $650,000 – which was the budget of *A Chinese Ghost Story*). Needless to say, these are *very* low budgets compared to Western and Northern American budgets (similar American movies would cost 20 or 30 times more. When you see what Hong Kong filmmakers can do with 1.2 million US dollars, it is simply astounding).

SCRIPTS.

Almost all Hong Kong movies employ conventional narrative structures, including those of Ching Siu-tung. Altho' a common view among Western critics is that Hong Kong movies ignore conventional script structures, and focus on, say, action at the expense of narrative form, in fact they adhere to conventional structures. First acts climax just where you'd expect, for instance, and the finales begin right on cue.

Instead of applying the three-act model to all movies, a better way of thinking of acts in film scripts is to see them as 25-30 minutes narrative units (following Kristin Thompson in her book *Storytelling In the New Hollywood*). Thus, a two-hour movie will have *four*, not *three* acts (otherwise, you'd have a middle act lasting an hour). However, in Hong Kong, the industry usually releases films of 85-90 minutes, so that, yes, they are *three-act movies*. (And thus, for the action movies of Hong Kong, the *second act* is the big challenge – because any decent action movie can deliver a couple of great action scenes in the first act, and a Big Finale for the third act. But coming up with something in the middle which keeps the movie (and the audience) afloat is trickier).

One of the pluses of Chinese action cinema is that it tends to come in at 80 or 90 minutes. Whereas Western action movies of recent times tend to add an extra half-act or another whole act (i.e., 15 minutes or 25-30 minutes) to a movie, so they feel bloated and over-blown, Chinese action movies wind up the story in an hour-twenty or an hour-thirty. Because we've got people to meet afterwards, right? And dinner dates! And more movies to see! And *things to do*. Life in Hong Kong, for many citizens, is fast-paced, so a 2h 20m movie is simply *too long*.

Thus, Hong Kong and Chinese action movies are based on a three-act model – with each act running the customary 25-30 minutes. Altho' some critics complain that Hong Kong/ Chinese movies (in any genre) don't have decent scripts or stories, they do. In fact, they conform very much to traditional narrative structures. The first act, for example, is as conventional as in cinema from anywhere else.

MORE ON THE NARRATIVE STRUCTURE OF HONG KONG MOVIES.

Hong Kong movies are generally three-act movies running 80-90 minutes. The first act is typically the regular length (25-30 minutes), but the second act in an action movie is often shorter (20-25 minutes, rather than 25-30 minutes). This is partly because the second act usually explores characterization, back-stories and subplots, which can take a movie too far from action (it's also because the second act is by far the most challenging to write). Thus, the third and final act in an action movie might run for 35-40 minutes – partly because action movies are all about action and climaxes.

An action movie will typically have three big action set-pieces and three additional, smaller set-pieces – this applies to Hollywood action movies as well as Hong Kong action movies:

Act 1 climax
Act 2 climax
Act 3 climax
In addition, there will be further action sequences:
• The opening scene.
• Halfway thru act one.
• Halfway thru act two.

The finale of act three is often a reprise of the first act finale (on a bigger scale, with more at stake). The act two action set-piece might push the heroes back, have the villains triumphant for a moment, with all being staked in the final showdown. (They might steal the MacGuffin, or kidnap one of the heroes).

Action movies which open with an action set-piece sometimes use it to introduce the characters, and sometimes it will be a stand-alone sequence. After it, the exposition is delivered, as well as the narrative set-up or quest. This will be played out in the act 1 climax.

The action sequence halfway thru act one is often a reversal of fortunes for the heroes (it might split them up or injure one of them). If the movie didn't start with action, this is usually the first big action scene.

The action sequence halfway thru act two is often a chase or a raid or a heist – something to bring the heroes and the villains together. But nobody is a clear winner, and no one is sacrificed (sometimes more action scenes are added to act two).

POLITICS.

The social-political backgrounds of many Hong Kong historical pictures (including those of Tony Ching) can be reduced to simple components, like:

Hong Kong	versus	Mainland China
Capitalism		Communism
Westernization		Eastern values
The new		The old
Modernity		Tradition

And a good deal of the political and ideological content of historical Chinese movies boils down to simple dramatic oppositions:

West = technology (bad) ••• East = tradition (good)

West = guns (bad) ··· East = martial arts (good)
West = modern medicine (bad) ··· East = Chinese medicine (good)
West = exploitation (bad) ··· East = mercantile capitalism (good)
West = individualism (bad) ··· East = communities (good)

Thus, in film criticism of Hong Kong and Chinese cinema, the same simple oppositions are often employed:

Hong Kong	People's Republic of China
Hong Kong	Beijing
Hong Kong	North America
Hong Kong	Britain
Capitalism	Communism
Right-wing	Left-wing
Chinese culture	Western culture
Home	Exile
China	Chinatowns around the world
Chinese	Foreigners

So it's not only the *movies* that offer 'simplified' versions of politics, the *critics* do too.

CHING AND CHINA.
As an action director, Ching Siu-tung has overseen the action on many Western and non-Chinese productions; but his movies as director have tended to gravitate towards Chinese or Asian subject matter. Most of Ching's movies as director have been set in China, or are about Chinese characters. (And when he's directing a North American production, such as *Belly of the Beast*, the story is brought to Asia). As with the films of Tsui Hark, there is a celebration of Chinese tradition and culture in Ching's movies as director.

Stephen Teo, one of the better critics on Chinese cinema, pointed out that Tsui Hark's movies employ some of the icons and clichés of Chinese culture (such as acupuncture, martial arts, Peking Opera), in order to help make the movies appealing to outsiders. Yes – but as Tsui himself has noted, in the New Wave of Hong Kong cinema, the filmmakers were producing movies for the *local market*, and *not* for the global market (that came later).

This also applies to Ching Siu-tung's films, which celebrate traditional Chinese culture and practices. It's true that you could see that as a way of presenting the clichés and icons of China back to the home audience (just as every American cowboy flick contains numerous iconic elements which sell the Western/ frontier lifestyle back to the American audience).

Stephen Teo also talks of 'cultural nationalism', more an emotional desire among Chinese people living abroad for Chinese culture. Chinese nationalism, Teo asserts, is found everywhere in Chinese cinema, from *kung fu* flicks to New Wave films, from Mandarin historical epics to

Cantonese melodramas (1997, 110-1). In the *kung fu* movies of the 1970s, Teo identified an abstract nationalism in which *kung fu* heroes were using traditions (often from Shaolin) to fight foreign Manchus to restore the Chinese race (1997, 113).

Ching Siu-tung doesn't go as far as Tsui Hark in celebrating Chinese culture and society (that is one of Tsui's passions), but Tsui has certainly been a huge influence on Ching's form of cinema, and the cinematic nationalism in Tsui's work has definitely inspired Ching, too.

WUXIA PIAN.

Some eleven of Tony Ching's 22 films as director (from 1983-2019) can be classed as swordplay movies or *wuxia pian* (and also a good proportion of his films as action director). Thus, Ching can be regarded as one of the great experts of recent times in depicting swordplay on screen.

Wuxia[8] means swordsman/ martial fighter/ knight-errant (*wu* = military or armed; *xia* = hero, chivalrous. Known as *Mo hap* in Canontese. *Pian* = movies).[9] Thus, *wuxia pian* were swordplay pictures, and they tended to be filmed in Mandarin (shifts in the popularity of Mandarin versus Cantonese have occurred in the industry over the years).[10] *Kung fu* films referred to fist fighting, and were usually made in Cantonese (with the *Wong Fei-hung* movies as the typical local product). There's a North (Mandarin) vs. South (Cantonese) divide, too.

Wuxia movies were regarded as more historical and 'authentic' than *kung fu* movies; their trademarks included fantasy, the supernatural, performers flying,[11] 'Palm Power' (lightning bolts from the hands in the Taoist tradition), and visual effects. David Desser defined swordplay movies as 'period films, historical epics, mythological tales of magic, or action-spectaculars with colorful costumes' (2002, 31). *Kung fu* movies (from Canton) tended to be more 'realistic', emphasizing training and the body.

Jiangzhu means 'rivers and lakes': the term goes back at least to the 12th century and *The Water Margin* novel. *Jiangzhu* refers to the 'martial world' (and *wulin* to the 'martial forest'), in which the code of honour, of chivalry, of brotherhood, prevails. It's the code of living honourably that's invoked in the *jiangzhu*.

The *jiangzhu* and the *wulin*, the wandering world of a China that never really existed, is a mythical realm that Tony Ching has explored many times.

---

8 *Wuxia*, according to director Chang Cheh, comes from *wu* = martial arts, and *xia* = chivalry.
9 Some titles of Hong Kong and Chinese movies are vague and generic – you'll see these words crop up time and again: *legend, story, hero, cop, dragon, weapon, dagger, sword, swordsman, warrior, butterfly, gambler*, etc.
10 Martial arts movies shifted in the early 1970s to Mandarin cinema, as Cantonese dwindled to nearly nothing in 1971-72. Martial arts movies, in Mandarin, dominated the box office. (Cantonese cinema declined in the middle to late 1960s, down to nearly nothing by 1972: 35 Cantonese films in 1970... in 1971, only one film... and in 1972, not a single one).
11 The powers of the floating warriors in *wuxia* films come from their martial arts skills, their *chi* – but they're not supernatural or superhuman powers.

MORE ON *WUXIA PIAN*.

The genres of Chinese movies in the 1920s were largely defined by the Shaw Brothers (then known as Tianyi Film Company). Shaws was founded in 1925 by Runjie Shaw. The popular genres of the time were *wuxia pian* (swordplay epics), *guzhuang pian* (classical, Chinese costume dramas), and *baishi pian* (historical movies).

Wuxia pian rapidly became popular in the 1920s: 250+ films were produced between 1928 and 1930. One of the most famous was *The Burning of Red Lotus Temple*[12] (Zhang Shichuan, 1928), regarded as the first martial arts masterpiece, which led to 18 sequels in 3 years. In the 1950s, Shaws was making fifty+ swordplay pictures a year. That meant they were releasing a film a week – incredible productivity – and most were in the martial arts genre.

Wuxia pian are typically set in ancient times, often in dynasties and courts, with chivalrous knights. The swordplay genre was associated with the Mainland, with Shanghai, while *kung fu* was a Southern, Hong Kong form. The *kung fu* genre is more 'realistic', often set in the Qing Dynasty, with foreigners as the villains. The heroes of Southern, *kung fu* movies include Wong Fei-hung and Fong Sai-yuk. When a swordsman is about to perform one of their special techniques, they often announce it: 'Flying Sword!'

COSTUMES.

The films of Ching Siu-tung are costume dramas even when they're set in the present day. Chinese, historical movies, historical martial arts movies and *wuxia pian* foreground *clothes* and *costumes*. Outlandish costumes are pretty much mandatory in a Chinese, historical movie, and of course this is also a big part of the Peking Opera tradition. Bright colours, tons of red and gold, rich blues and the brilliant yellows of Buddhism, are everywhere in Chinese, historical movies. And when it comes to depicting royalty or wealth, out come the luxurious frocks, the braid and embroidery, with an obsessive attention to detail (and as many action movies focus on guys, the costume, hair and make-up people seize upon the one or two female actresses with enthusiasm, lavishing attention on them). Purely as displays of costume design, Chinese, historical movies (and many action flicks), are sumptuous. And the films of Ching are some of the finest – one of his hallmarks is a feeling for flowing clothing flapping in the breeze as a swordsman (or swordswoman) makes yet another flying leap.

The wardrobe is also a significant ingredient in the action in a Chinese, historical movie: sometimes characters use clothing to attack opponents (Wong Fei-hung rushing thru a street brawl, for instance, using his jacket to whack people, in *Once Upon a Time In China 3*). In flying scenes, clothes're whipped by high wind, with the sound of flapping, twisting clothing mixed high (the sound of the wind is one of the fundamental sounds of the mysterious and the supernatural – not only in cinema, but

---

[12] It was adapted from the martial arts novel *Legend of Strange Heroes*.

anywhere). The shapes that the clothing makes are beautiful (especially in slow motion). The layers of loose, richly-hued clothing recalls the costumes that the Virgin Mary wears in Renaissance paintings in the West: painters in Europe in the 1400s-1600s had to learn how to depict robes and cloaks with deep, shadowy folds; it was part of the mythology of Christian art. And angels in Renaissance art also had billowing robes, emphasizing their spiritual energy as they descend from the heavens down to Earth).

Clothes are part of the stances and motion of martial arts, of course: flying scenes feature clothes flapping and billowing; in fights on the ground, clothes are grabbed, or they twist around bodies, or're used as weapons; when Jet Li's Wong Fei-hung prepares to battle, he flicks his outer garments back around his right leg, to leave room for movement.

And along with costumes, the hair and make-up in Chinese, historical movies is technically dazzling, but often also extravagant. There's no holding back in some of the fantastical, historical movies, which take place in the *jiangzhu*, the mythical China of yore. Then beards become so long you can trip over them, and wigs become so hairy they become a character in themselves (in fantasy flicks like *The Bride With White Hair* series, hair is a series of weapons in itself).

TEXTURES.

It's common in Hong Kong cinema to add textures in front of the camera, using practical effects: smoke is everywhere, for instance. Smoke in Hong Kong cinema is not a pretty effect that drifts in the background of a scene to enhance the lighting – it is used as a setting in itself, a real, physical presence in the scenes. Sometimes smoke provides the whole environment of a scene (and, yes, sometimes that billowing smoke is used to hide things). Items such as dust, earth, and leaves are thrown in front of the camera just before a take (sometimes petals, feathers, and dripping water). On a Tony Ching set, electric fans are always near the camera – clothes must flap and billow. And if it's a calm night, those fans will add the essential movement. (All sorts of fans – handheld, desk fans, larger fans, fans blowing down tubes to get the air close to the actors, etc.)

Hong Kong cinema developed the Akira Kurosawa School of Filmmaking – plenty of natural, elemental material on screen – rain, fire, smoke, wind, leaves, torchlight, candlelight, and more fire and more rain. Creating those textures also means filming outdoors in sometimes tough conditions (plus many night shoots). It means leading the production team up mountains and across rivers. And for the actors it means quite a bit of hardship (luxurious trailers are *not* usually part of a Hong Kong film production!).

To achieve those Kurosawan effects requires stamina, determination, and, perhaps above all, patience[13] (plus the resources of a fully-equipped studio with its technical staff). This is perfectionist filmmaking, getting

---

[13] Patience may be the number one requirement for a film director – the dogged determination to wait until you get what you're after.

every detail right, composing scenes and frames teeming with incident and gesture.

AVAILABILITY

A *major* problem with approaching the cinema of any Hong Kong or Chinese film director is availability. You will stumble into the issue of availability as soon as you try to see anything other than the movies released in the Western world. Most of the films (and TV work) directed or action directed by Ching Siu-tung were produced for a Chinese market: the markets of Hong Kong and Mainland China are absolutely crucial.[14] This doesn't mean, tho', that the movies travel outside of China, either in their original form or in dubbed versions.

The language issue – Cantonese, Mandarin, English, whatever – is a minor one compared to general availability (subtitling is yet another issue). It's true that some of the key works directed by Ching Siu-tung are easy to obtain in the West – the *Swordsman* series, for instance, or *An Empress and the Warriors*.

But many movies are not easily available in the West, such as: *The Witch From Nepal, The Terracotta Warrior, The Longest Day, Conman In Tokyo* and *Belly of the Beast*. And gems of China cinema that Ching action-directed, like *Peking Opera Blues,* should be available in supermarket racks like Disney cartoons.

Even some of movies featuring big stars such as the two Chows – Chow Yun-fat and Stephen Chow (Chow Sing-chi) are not easily obtainable in the Western world. You should be able to find *Royal Tramp* or *Fight Back To School* anywhere.

That means that plenty of Tony Ching's films as an action director of the 1970s are not widely available, nor his films as an actor. Consequently, some movies directed by Ching Siu-tung, have not been explored fully in this study, including many released before 1980.

The issue of availability affects many celebrated filmmakers – you simply can't find many of their key works. The issue of quality is another consideration: many movies are only available in substandard prints, with bad soundtracks, or in butchered versions (some Hong Kong movies look like they were copied from beat-up release prints that have been kicking around Central for years, then re-dubbed onto video and back again). Despite new distribution systems like the internet, or streaming, or DVD and Blu-ray (or older ones like video, or broadcasting on television), it's amazing how many jewels of cinematic art remain in limbo, or are lost, or can only be bought in poor versions from dodgy, one-eyed former Buddhist monks in the scuzzy end of town (for extortionate prices).

---

14 Hence, Hong Kong films are usually released with a Cantonese and a Mandarin soundtrack, which's the norm in Chinese cinema.

Another issue is that the international and Western versions of Hong Kong and Chinese movies sometimes change the following: the music; the dialogue; the scripts (scripts are rewritten during dubbing); add new sound mixes; and whole scenes are dropped.

Thus often the Western/ international cuts of Asian movies are *not* in the form the filmmakers preferred. Tsui Hark, for instance, has complained many times that distributors have altered his movies for releases overseas.

The practice of dubbing the sound on afterwards in Chinese movies also extends to the stars: it was many years before Chinese movie audiences heard the real voices of Jackie Chan and Jet Li, for instance. Another consequence of dubbing is that the same group of actors tend to be heard in every movie. For international releases, scenes are often added, or cut, and music is altered, as is dialogue.

For research online, the Hong Kong Movie Database and Hong Kong Cinemagic are excellent (they have photos of the cast and crew, for instance – very helpful when Chinese movies are filled with unusual names (and many alternative names and spellings) in both Mandarin and Cantonese). Love Hong Kong Film has useful reviews.

Some of Tony Ching's movies as director

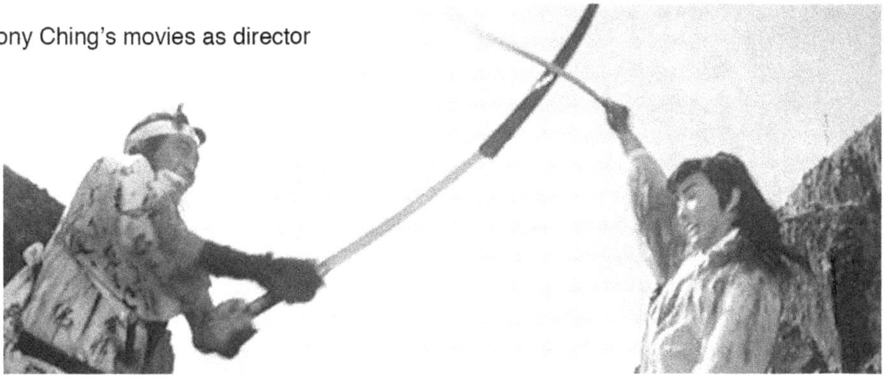

Duel To the Death (1983).

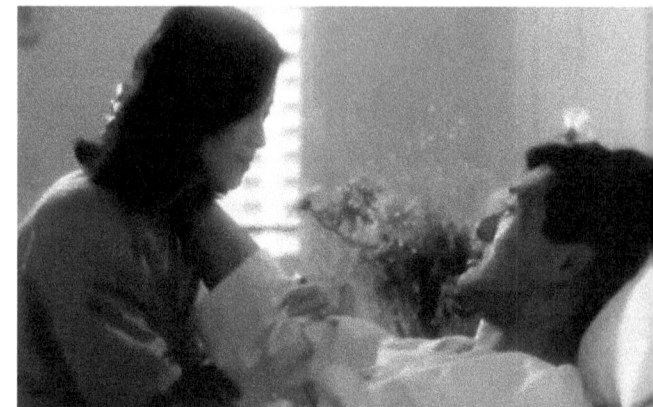

The Witch From Nepal (1986).

A Chinese Ghost Story (1987).

The Terracotta Warrior (1989).

The Heroic Trio (1993).

Dr Wai (1996).

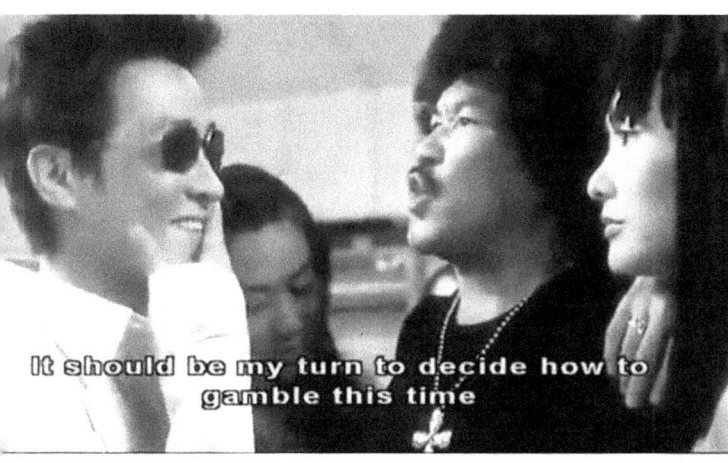

Conman In Tokyo (2000).

Naked Weapon (2002).

Belly of the Beast (2003)

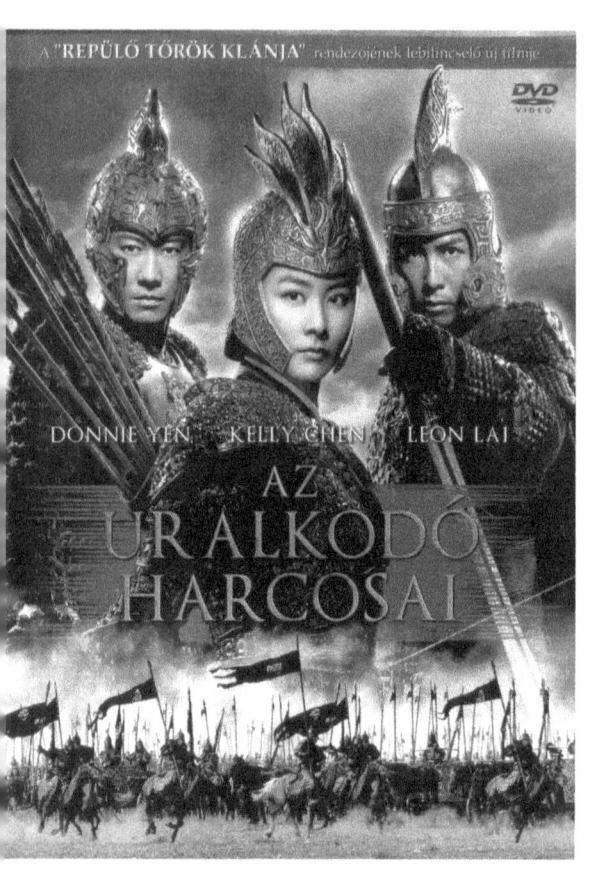 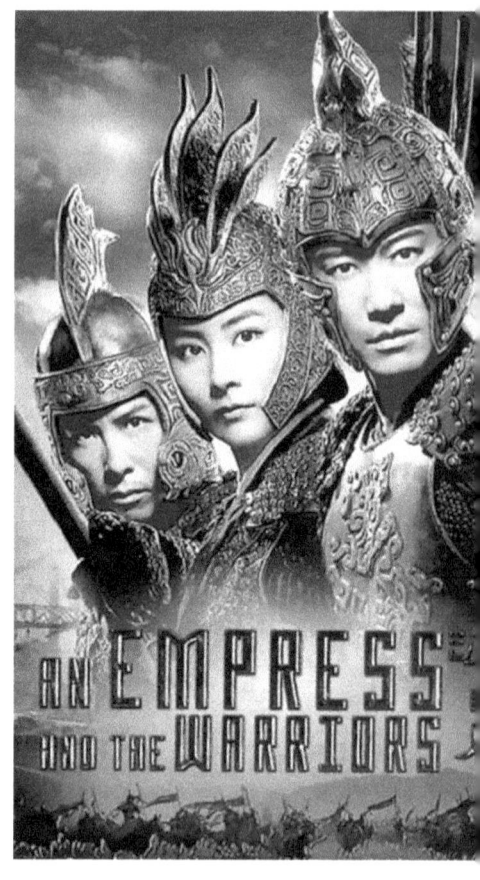

An Empress and the Warriors (2008).

The Sorcerer and the White Snake (2011).

Jade Dynasty (2019).

3
TSUI HARK

INTRODUCTION

Tsui Hark is the dragon master of Chinese cinema (Stephen Teo calls Tsui a 'lion dancer among film directors' [173]). Yes – a master, a lion dancer, a *sifu*, a wizard, a dragon.

Tsui Hark is a one-man film industry – as a glance as his list of credits will show, along with setting up his own film company in 1983, Film Workshop.

Tsui Hark directs movies like a force of nature. The *energy* coming off the screen is stupendous! He is a fearless filmmaker, willing to try *anything* to get a good shot. And I do mean *anything*! That feeling of fearlessness, and wildness, coupled with imagination and technical brilliance, makes Tsui an incredibly *formidable* filmmaker. There are very few filmmakers on the scene today with those qualities in such abundance.

When you come back to a Tsui Hark picture after looking at other movies for a while, you realize, wow, this guy is *so* passionate about cinema, *so* willing to try anything, to experiment, to push the boundaries of what cinema can do, of what cinema can *be.* I've never felt, for example, that Tsui is a 'director for hire', unengaged with the material, or that he is merely punching through the shots as if he's on a factory floor.

No, this man is *on fire*.

BIOGRAPHY

Tsui Hark was born on January 2, 1951 (or February 15; some sources say 1950), in French Cochin China (Saigon, Vietnam). His name was originally Tsui Man-kong (he has also been known as Mark Yu). In Cantonese, his name is Chui Hak; in Mandarin, it's Xu Ke (Xu2 Ke4). He had sixteen siblings (from three marriages). His father was a pharmacist. Tsui changed his name from 'Tsui Man-kong' to 'Tsui Hark' because he thought it was too soft, and for his 'King Kong' nickname (1997, 136). It's pronounced 'Choy Hawk'. Tsui grew up in Saigon until the family moved to Hong Kong in 1966 (Tsui said he migrated around the age of 13, which makes it 1964; Lisa Morton says he was 14).[1]

Tsui Hark is a truly international filmmaker, as well as being a thoroughly Chinese/ Vietnamese one. After going to Hong Kong, he studied filmmaking in the U.S.A., at Southern Methodist University, Dallas in 1969 (for a year) before transferring to the University of Texas in Austin (Austin is a minor filmmaking centre in North America, with its own film culture, where filmmakers such as Richard Linklater are based). He also travelled around the U.S.A.

Tsui Hark graduated in 1975 (he studied for 2 years in Austin, where he was known as 'King Kong'). Tsui later worked in New York City: his first jobs were in television, not cinema: he gravitated from TV to film, as so many filmmakers have done (and as his fellow Hong Kong New Wave filmmakers did). His first jobs in Gotham were as a reporter for a Chinese TV cable station; he was a Chinese newspaper editor; worked with a community theatre group (New Art Drama Group); and helped to make a documentary about Chinatown (as a DP) called *From Spikes To Spindles* (Christine Choy, 1976). Tsui moved back to Hong Kong in 1976 (when he was 25).

Tsui Hark's film career got off to a roaring start with three outstanding pictures. Tsui's first theatrical movie as a director was *The Butterfly Murders* (1979), which combined martial arts, horror, sci-fi, comedy and romance. This was followed swiftly by *We're Going To Eat You* (1980) and *Dangerous Encounter of the 1st Kind* (1980) – both released in 1980.[2]

Directors often work in contrasts – if they've just done a comedy, they might fancy a drama next. Tsui Hark wanted to do something silly after his first three movies, which were 'very serious and very depressing' (LM, 47). Hence *All the Wrong Clues,* which was his first commercial hit (in 1981). And since then, Tsui had rarely let a year pass without releasing a movie as a director or producer (sometimes two! Sometimes three!). By 2014, Tsui had directed around 43 feature films.

As a producer, Tsui Hark has been responsible for masterpieces including: the *A Better Tomorrow* series, the *Chinese Ghost Story* series, the *Swordsman* series, *New Dragon Gate Inn* and *The Killer,* plus a host of

---
[1] Some accounts have Tsui coming to Hong Kong at the age of thirteen; others at fifteen (Tsui's year of birth is usually given as 1950 or 1951). It was in 1966 that Tsui's family moved to Canton.
[2] After *We're Going To Eat You*, Tsui Hark became 'very disappointed in myself', and considered giving up filmmaking.

hugely enjoyable films, such as: *Once Upon a Time in China 4, Once Upon a Time In China 6, Vampire Hunters, The Climbers* and *Black Mask*.

Tsui Hark is much more than a film director. Many directors do the job and go home afterwards. That's it. Some offer to produce other people's projects. Some form their own companies to develop and produce items they might direct themselves, or they might bring in colleagues they know. But only a few opt to take on numerous producing jobs, to the point where their career as a producer is as significant as their directing work. Tsui thus is not only a film director, *and* a film producer, he is also a movie mogul. (To do that amount of work, you have to *really* be committed).

In the press interviews for *Detective Dee and the Mystery of the Phantom Flame*, Tsui Hark was described by the cast and crew as brilliant, stern, tough, sweet, a free spirit, a teacher, boundlessly imaginative, and someone who lives in a different world from the rest of us.

Like many film directors, Tsui Hark has also filmed TV commercials (tho' not as many as some directors). They include *China Motion* (1998), for a telecommunications company on the Mainland (which was likened to the 1984 Apple ad); and *Singapore National Day* (1998).

Change and transformation are key elements in survival in the Hong Kong film industry, Tsui Hark asserted: if you don't change rapidly, you won't survive (LM, 22).

> For me, being commercial is very basic because you need the box office record in order to keep the investor surviving in this industry. But then, you need to be different. You need to be outstanding in terms of film. (2011)

Over the course of his film career, Tsui Hark has worked with practically every big star[3] in the Chinese film industry, as well as every action choreographer,[4] every DP and every major player in film production. (The Hong Kong film industry is small – everybody knows everybody else).

Tsui Hark's energy is legendary. Does he ever sleep? Can he survive on two or three hours sleep a night when he's shooting? (according to rumour). It does seem like that (it seems as if the last time that Tsui slept was in 1978). Tsui is one of those filmmakers who doesn't sit down on set, and is running at a high level of intensity as he's filming.

For instance, in more recent times, Tsui Hark has directed an enormous film production each year! *Detective Dee and the Mystery of the Phantom Flame* (2010), *The Flying Swords of Dragon Gate* (2011), *Young Detective Dee: Rise of the Sea Dragon* (2013) and *Taking Tiger Mountain*

---

[3] As a producer, Tsui Hark has been influential on the careers of Brigitte Lin, John Woo, Chow Yun-fat, Jet Li, Tony Ching Siu-tung, and many others. Jenny Kwok Wah-Lau noted that 'in Hong Kong, most people realize that it is Tsui Hark, the *producer* of *A Better Tomorrow*, who almost single-handedly revised and modernized the action genre and thus directly or indirectly launched the Hollywood careers of John Woo and superstars Chow Yun-Fat (through the same film) and Jet Li (through *Once Upon a Time In China*, which Tsui directed).' (in J. Geiger, 739).

[4] Tsui Hark has worked with practically every celebrated action choreographer in the Hong Kong film business: Sammo Hung, Jackie Chan, Yuen Bun, Yuen Woo-ping, Tony Ching Siu-tung, Yuen Wah, Lau Kar-leung, Xiong Xin-xin, etc.

(2014). Plus directing other movies, such as *Catching Monkey 3-D*.

There are times in the writing of this book (starting 2013-14), that I couldn't believe just how much Tsui Hark has achieved. Even compared to other workaholic film directors and producers, Tsui stands out. He really is a one-off. (Sometimes I wonder if 'Tsui Hark' is really a conglomerate of writers, producers, directors and visual effects mavens which uses the person we know and love, Tsui Hark, as their spokesman).

Tsui Hark's films have earned numerous awards. 1992 was one of Tsui's best years for awards – 21 nominations at the Hong Kong Film Awards – for *Once Upon a Time In China 2*, *New Dragon Gate Inn*, *The Swordsman 2* and *King of Chess*.

It's usually the same movies from Tsui Hark that feature in top ten lists – *Zu: Warriors From the Magic Mountain*, *Once Upon a Time In China*, *A Better Tomorrow*, *The Killer*, and occasionally the early, angry films: *We're Going To Eat You* and *Dangerous Encounters of the First Kind*. Tsui Hark has 7 films in the Top 100 Hong Kong Films in *Time Out*.

Some observers reckoned that Tsui Hark's film career stalled somewhat in the late 1990s and early 2000s, and that his movies didn't seem to find an audience during that time. Tsui said, yes, he had been trying different things; but he had also been doing the same thing he always did – make movies. It's all relative, tho', and box office success doesn't always match up with critical praise, or what a filmmaker regards as his best work. We all know filmmakers who produced much better movies than the ones that made the most $$$$$. However, commercial success *is* important if you want to produce movies on an ambitious scale (which Tsui often does).

A filmmaker of Tsui Hark's astounding abilities might be expected to go to Hollywood, as some of his Chinese contemporaries have done (notably John Woo, Tony Ching Siu-tung, Jet Li and Yuen Woo-ping). Tsui could've worked in Europe or Hollywood for all of his career following the big success of *Aces Go Places*. But Tsui's career in the U.S.A. has been patchy and somewhat disappointing. For example, instead of being hired by a film studio to helm a historical epic or a contemporary fantasy blockbuster (*Memoirs of a Geisha*, *X-Men*, *The Avengers* or *Pirates of the Caribbean*, say – Tsui would be perfect for *Pirates*!),[5] Tsui was hired to direct two Jean-Claude van Damme actioners. While John Woo directed *Mission: Impossible* and *Face-Off*, and Ringo Lam Ling-tung and Ronnie Yu made *Maximum Risk* and *Replicant* (Lam) and *51st State* and *Fredy vs. Jason* (Yu), high budget action movies, Tsui helmed a couple of van Damme movies which nobody has seen (altho' Woo also directed a Muscles From Brussels picture, *Hard Target*, 1993, as did Ringo Lam – *Maximum Risk*. Everyone in Hong Kong, it seemed, worked with van Damme at one time or another).[6]

Altho' the three Hollywood pictures helmed by Tsui Hark – *Knockoff*, *DoubleTeam* and *Time and Tide* – were fascinating (and *Time and Tide* was

---
[5] And he delivered his own version in the *Detective Dee* series.
[6] The deal seemed to be: you can make an American production, but only if van Damme is the star.

as good an action thriller as has ever been made), the first two were still below the potential and talents of a director like Tsui. (All three were pointedly *not* filmed in the United States of America, however, but in Europa and Asia).

The anti-American politics in some of Tsui Hark's movies may have contributed towards his lack of success in the U.S.A (LM, 14), even tho' his movies are steeped in Hollywood/ Western cinema.

Following his uneven spree in Tinseltown, Tsui Hark has remained devoted to *Chinese* subjects – nearly *all* of his movies as director and producer have had Chinese settings, Chinese stories, Chinese themes and Chinese characters.

❁

Tsui Hark has gained a reputation for arguing with his collaborators, for taking over from other directors, or for directing when he should be producing. Or for being 'difficult'. Tsui doesn't understand it himself, but there are too many stories for there to be nothing in it! (Yet when actors meet him, expecting a difficult or irritable guy, they find someone very different).

When Tsui Hark is involved in a production, whether as producer, director, writer or backer, you know it's going to be interpreted as 'a Tsui Hark movie' (the same thing happens with filmmakers such as Steven Spielberg or George Lucas – they are such big, influential names in the movie business). Tsui is like that – he's the gorilla in the room that nobody talks about.

But one look at Tsui Hark's filmography, and you see an *enormous* amount of work, containing quite a few classics, plenty of ambitious works, and also several landmark movies in Chinese film history. Any history of recent cinema will have to include an entry on Tsui.

Tsui Hark is not a martial artist, and doesn't practise martial arts. He is not, as are Steven Spielberg, John Milius, Masamune Shirow and Mamoru Oshii, a gun nut.[7] For him, martial arts and guns are part of creating a fantasy.

Stephen Teo likens Tsui Hark's role in Hong Kong cinema to the Taoist priest in *A Chinese Ghost Story*: 'although he's not the hero, the Doaist plays the role of a *deus ex machina* in putting things right and making sure that the natural order is not disturbed' (1997, 228).

That Tsui Hark is a workaholic goes without saying. Tsui could've retired ages ago, or found a much easier way of making a buck than producing movies. Everybody who works with Tsui attests to his boundless energy. On the set, Tsui seems to wear everyone out with his relentless determination to get what he's after.[8] Tsui may come over in interviews as a slim and affable Asian guy who's happy to discuss any toplc, but on the set[9] he must be a tough task-master at times.

---

[7] Tsui Hark doesn't know much about guns, or martial arts, and relies on other people for that. Instead, Tsui says that he's a fantasist, he imagines things that're the opposite of his real life.
[8] According to rumours, actors would bring their toothbrushes and pyjamas to the studio, because sometimes filming wended on for 48 or 72 hours.
[9] According to onlookers, the mood on a Tsui Hark set is pretty serious; not much goofing around, but getting on with the job.

When it comes to work, Tsui Hark's philosophy is simple: *if you see an opportunity, take it!* It sums up Tsui's incredible drive and ambition: this is a filmmaker with a truly extraordinary level of energy.

Hong Kong filmmakers are not known for their integrity: they have to survive, so, as Tsui Hark noted, 'they will do anything' (LM, 27). So it's the worst, because the filmmakers don't have integrity, but it's also the best because they are always looking for the next thing, for change.

Tsui Hark is happy to be interviewed and there are many interviews available of Tsui. Among the pieces on video and television about Tsui (apart from the usual 'making of' pieces on home releases), I would recommend *Action et Vérité* (2006), about the production of *The Blade*, a short but illuminating interview on *The Butterfly Murders*, *The Incredibly Strange Film Show* (1988-89), and *Yang ± Yin*, a documentary on gender in Chinese cinema directed by Stanley Kwan (1997).

Among Western movies, Tsui Hark has cited Orson Welles (*Citizen Kane*), Francis Coppola, John Ford, Roman Polanski (*Macbeth*), and Frederick Wiseman. The Marx Brothers have certainly influenced Tsui's comical style – not the speedy quips of Groucho, but the surreal bickering, and the silent comedy of Harpo.

You can see Tsui Hark's influence in many places: in movies like *The Stormriders* (Andrew Lau Wai-keung, 1999), *Initial D, He's a Woman, She's a Man, Ashes of Time*, and in filmmakers such as Wong Kar-wai, John Woo, Daniel Lee, Tony Ching, Peter Chan, Andrew Lau, Ang Lee, and Wong Jing. And the many Hong Kong movies which have emulated the Tsui Hark approach are easy to spot.

The *Once Upon a Time In China* series, as Jeff Yang put it, 'single-handedly revived the *kung fu* genre,[10] re-energized the Hong Kong film industry, and launched Mainland *wushu* master Jet Li's career into superstardom throughout Asia, and eventually, the world' (2003, 97). Tsui Hark called Jet Li a 'very special person'.

To make so many movies, as producer and director, means that Tsui Hark must *really* ♥ movies and filmmaking. Hooked on it, perhaps. Obsessive, even. Tsui is simply a natural filmmaker, like Jean-Luc Godard, Ingmar Bergman and Akira Kurosawa, filmmakers who seem to be live and breathe cinema. Tsui seems happiest when he's deep into production on a wild adventure in the archaic *jiangzhu*, or exploring a little-known corner of Chinese history.

Some have dubbed Tsui Hark the 'Asian Steven Spielberg', while others have noted that Spielberg should be so lucky.[11] Because Tsui goes beyond Spielberg in some respects. But they share numerous affinities: they are film buffs, they enshrine cinema of the past, they remake and update old classics,[12] they have taken on a wide variety of genres, they prefer storytelling with music and images above all, they are workaholics,

---

10 Certainly *Once Upon a Time In China* was a key movie in reviving the *kung fu* and martial arts genre – to the level of an artform.
11 Tsui has remarked: 'I don't know – it's unfair to him, I think. It's unfair to me too: he's so rich' (1997, 136).
12 Altho' Tsui Hark has gone back and remade the movies he enjoyed as a kid, he also knows that sometimes those movies one enshrined turn out to be silly and disappointing (LM, 23).

they work very fast on set, they make 'movie-movies', they are both moguls with their own companies, they have worked as film producers extensively, they adore visual effects and the artificiality of cinema, and they are master showmen.

Tsui Hark is also a movie and television generation filmmaker, like the 'movie brats' of the 'New Hollywood' era, such as Steven Spielberg, Brian de Palma, George Lucas and Jonathan Kaplan. There's no doubt that, like his N. American counterparts, Tsui is also remaking and updating many of the movies and TV shows he enjoyed as a youth. There is certainly a strong baby boomer aspect to Tsui's cinema, and a postmodern reworking of earlier forms and genres.

Stephen Teo calls Tsui Hark 'Hong Kong cinema's one genuine prodigy', a filmmaker who's 'primitive, even brutish', whose movies are too fast and too cluttered for some and remain indigestible. Teo reckons that the super-fast Tsui doesn't really have a counterpart in the West.

Stephen Teo:

Tsui Hark has what Hong Kong critics call a "devil's talent" (*gui cai*), a talent so broad and brilliant that it does not seem human. He is one of the prime movers in the industry and an original New Wave director who pushes his commercial instincts to the limit. (1998, 157)

Lisa Morton summed up Tsui Hark in her 2001 study:

Tsui Hark is unique in world cinema, a prolific filmmaker (Tsui has directed, written, produced and/ or acted in more than 60 feature films since 1979) who is also a master stylist; a political auteur and a populist; an artist with an obsessive private vision who is also commercially successful; and a filmmaker who seems to revel in deconstructing genres even while celebrating their tropes. (6)

Jeff Yang described Tsui Hark as 'one of the most reliable box office breadwinners of the eighties', a conceiver of new trends, a developer of new technologies and new cinematic techniques, a filmmaker who 'has generally beaten a path for the rest of the industry to follow' (2003, 95).

THE FILM CREDITS OF TSUI HARK

MOVIES AS DIRECTOR

The Butterfly Murders, 1979
We're Going To Eat You, 1980
Dangerous Encounters of the First Kind, 1980
All the Wrong Clues, 1981

Zu: Warriors From the Magic Mountain, 1983
Search For the Gods, 1983
Aces Go Places 3, 1984
Shanghai Blues, 1984
Working Class, 1985
Peking Opera Blues, 1986
Spirit Chaser Aisha, 1986
The Master, 1989
A Better Tomorrow 3, 1989
The Swordsman, 1990
Once Upon a Time in China, 1991
The Banquet, 1991
The Raid, 1991
Once Upon a Time in China 2, 1992
Twin Dragons, 1992
Once Upon a Time in China 3, 1993
Green Snake, 1993
Once Upon a Time in China 5, 1994
The Lovers, 1994
The Chinese Feast, 1995
Love In the Time of Twilight, 1995
The Blade, 1995
Tristar, 1996
Double Team, 1997
Knock Off, 1998
Time and Tide, 2000
The Legend of Zu, 2001
Black Mask 2: City of Masks, 2002
In the Blue, 2005
Seven Swords, 2005
Triangle, 2007
Missing, 2008
All About Women, 2008
Detective Dee and the Mystery of the Phantom Flame, 2010
The Flying Swords of Dragon Gate, 2011
Young Detective Dee: Rise of the Sea Dragon, 2013
Catching Monkey 3-D, 2013
The Taking of Tiger Mountain, 2014
Journey To the West: Conquering the Demons, 2017
Detective Dee and the Four Heavenly Kings, 2018
The Battle At Lake Changjin, 2021
The Battle At Lake Changjin: Water Gate Bridge, 2022

MOVIES AS PRODUCER

All the Wrong Spies, 1983
A Better Tomorrow, 1986
The Laser Man, 1986
A Chinese Ghost Story, 1987
A Better Tomorrow 2, 1987
The Big Heat, 1988
Gunmen, 1988
Diary of a Big Man, 1988
The King of Chess, 1988/ 1992
The Master, 1989
A Better Tomorrow 3, 1989
The Killer, 1989
Just Heroes, 1989
The Terracotta Warrior, 1989
The Swordsman, 1990
A Chinese Ghost Story 2, 1990
A Chinese Ghost Story 3, 1991
Once Upon a Time in China, 1991
New Dragon Gate Inn, 1992
The Swordsman 2, 1992
The Wicked City, 1992
Once Upon a Time in China 2, 1992
Once Upon a Time in China 3, 1993
Green Snake, 1993
The Swordsman 3: The East Is Red, 1993
Once Upon a Time in China 4, 1993
Once Upon a Time in China 5, 1994
The Lovers, 1994
Burning Paradise, 1994
The Chinese Feast, 1995
The Blade, 1995
Shanghai Grand, 1996
A Chinese Ghost Story: The Tsui Hark Animation, 1997
Once Upon a Time in China and America, 1997
Time and Tide, 2000
The Legend of Zu, 2001
Old Master Q, 2001
Tsui Hark's Vampire Hunters, 2002
Black Mask 2: City of Masks, 2002
Xanda, 2004
Seven Swords, 2005
The Warrior, 2006
Triangle, 2007
Missing, 2008
All About Women, 2008

Detective Dee and the Mystery of the Phantom Flame, 2010
The Flying Swords of Dragon Gate, 2011
Young Detective Dee: Rise of the Sea Dragon, 2013
Christmas Rose, 2013
The Taking of Tiger Mountain, 2014
Sword Master, 2016
The Thousand Faces of Dunjia, 2017
Journey To the West: Conquering the Demons, 2017
Detective Dee and the Four Heavenly Kings, 2018
The Climbers, 2019
The Battle At Lake Changjin, 2021
The Battle At Lake Changjin 2, 2022

By any standards, that list of film credits is completely remarkable! And it's a selective list, which doesn't include everything that Tsui has done.[13] You have to add writing credits to that list, and entries in anthology films, plus several TV series, as well as plenty of acting and cameos. And design work, editing and visual effects.

Up to 2013, Tsui Hark had writing credits on 36-42 movies,[14] story credits for 10 films, director credits for 43-45 movies, producer credits for 58-62 productions, and actor credits for 26 films.

Tsui Hark has writing credits on most of the movies he's directed, and he has producer credits on most of them, too. Which means that Tsui can properly be regarded as an *auteur*. The key production credit in many respects, in relation to the cinema of Tsui (and most cinema), is *producer*, more even than director or writer. (But Tsui is also more than a producer, director and writer, he is also a movie mogul with his own production company and visual effects company).

Among the movies directed by Tsui Hark, the following are masterpieces: *Once Upon a Time In China 1*, *Once Upon a Time In China 2*, *Once Upon a Time In China 3*, *Seven Swords*, *Detective Dee and the Mystery of the Phantom Flame*, *Young Detective Dee*, *Zu: Warriors From the Magic Mountain*, *The Flying Swords of Dragon Gate*, *The Taking of Tiger Mountain*, *Shanghai Blues*, *Peking Opera Blues* ,and *The Swordsman*. Many other movies directed by Tsui are fantastically enjoyable cinema: *Green Snake*, *The Blade*, *The Master*, *Detective Dee and the Four Heavenly Kings*, *The Legend of Zu* and *Time and Tide*. Only one or two movies with Tsui at the helm are disappointing: *Triangle* (co-directed with To and Lam), and *All About Women*.

One striking aspect of Tsui Hark's output is that fully half or more of his movies as director and producer have been historical pictures, a much greater ratio than most other filmmakers. Tsui is a specialist in costume films, and most of his masterpieces have also been historical movies. Notice, too, that in the more recent part of his career, the 2000s and 2010s, Tsui has been focussing on history – going back to the mid-20th

---
13 *The Legend of Famen Temple* (*Fa Men Si Mi Ma*), another historical fantasy, was rumoured in 2016-2017, based on a novel by Huang Shang Jin-yu, and starring Kenny Lin, Chen Kun, Zitao Huang and Xun Shou.
14 44 films to 2016, at Internet Movie Database.

century in the war pictures (*Tiger Mountain, Lake Changjin*) or Ancient China (*Detective Dee*). The last feature films set in the contemporary era was in 2008 (*All About Women* and *Missing*).

The production roles are important, because we know that Tsui Hark is a very hands-on producer. The role of a producer varies widely, from someone way back in a project's history who oversaw one of the numerous script rewrites to a producer who oversees every aspect of the production.

Well, we know that Tsui Hark has performed second unit direction on some movies he's produced, and also co-directed some of them. And when Tsui insists that he *didn't* direct some of the movies (such as those directed by Tony Ching Siu-tung), his influence as writer or co-writer and of course as producer can felt everywhere in those movies.

TSUI HARK AS FILM PRODUCER

The movies that were produced by Tsui Hark can be regarded as part of his *œuvre* to a greater degree than many films which other directors have acted as a producer on – because Tsui is a hands-on producer.

But what is a film producer? Critics don't really know, yet the Western/ Hollywood film industry is a producer-led, producer-based business, and in the Hong Kong industry, too, producers lead the way. Among the many functions a good film producer does is: (1) buying and developing material; (2) hiring writers; (3) putting together deals; (4) approaching investors, and finding backing/ money/ resources; (5) hiring directors and other personnel; (6) over-seeing the all-important pre-production, which includes 100s of elements; (7) casting; (8) over-seeing shooting; (9) over-seeing post-production (again, this involves 100s of ingredients); (10) music, selecting composers; and (11) publicity, marketing, advertizing.

Tsui Hark has performed all of those tasks many times, and there's no doubt that as a film producer he is right in there, selecting and developing projects, and shepherding them to pre-production (that's when a movie is really made). If he's sometimes a dictator, well, he replies, the creative process needs that.[15]

Among Tsui Hark's numerous production credits, apart from acting as the producer on the movies he's directed, are (Tsui also has writing credits on most of these movies):

• *All the Wrong Spies* (Teddy Robin, 1983), a sequel to *All the Wrong Clues* (dir. by Tsui Hark). Written by Raymond Wong Pak-min, it starred George Lam, Teddy Robin, Paul Chun Pui, Brigitte Lin, Shing Fui-on, Joe Junior, Tsui Hark and Anders Nelsson. Tsui and his wife Nansun Shi Nan-sheng are credited as production designers.

---
15 Is he a dictator? Yes, he admits, 'But the creative process needs that'.

- The two *A Better Tomorrow* movies[16] (1986 and 1987).
- *The Laser Man* (1986), was executive produced by Tsui Hark and Sophie Lo, written, directed and co-produced by Peter Wang, and starred Marc Hiyashi, Peter Wang, Tony Leung and Sally Yeh.
- *Gunmen* (Kirk Wong, 1988),[17] starring Tony Leung, Adam Cheng, Elvis Tsui, Waise Lee and Carrie Ng.
- *The Big Heat* (Johnny To & Andrew Kam, 1988), written by Gordon Chan, starring Waise Lee, Philip Kwok, Paul Chu-kong, Stuart Ong Sai Kit, Michael Chow Man Kin, Ken Boyle and Joey Wong. Tsui Hark appears in some credits as the co-director in this very troubled production.
- *Diary of a Big Man* (1988) was produced by Tsui Hark, directed by Chor Yuen, and starred Chow Yun-fat, Joey Wong, Sally Yeh, Waise Lee and Kent Cheng.
- *A Chinese Ghost Story* (Tony Ching Siu-tung, 1987), starring Leslie Cheung, Joey Wong and Wu Ma.
- *A Chinese Ghost Story 2* (Tony Ching Siu-tung, 1990) starring Leslie Cheung, Joey Wong, Michelle Reiss, Jacky Cheung and Waise Lee.
- *A Chinese Ghost Story 3* (Tony Ching Siu-tung, 1991), starring Tony Leung Chiu-wai, Joey Wong, Jacky Cheung and Nina Le Chi.
- *I Love Maria* (a.k.a. *Roboforce*, 1988), was a Hong Kong version of *RoboCop* (1987), co-produced by Tsui Hark with John Sham, directed by David Chung Chi-man,[18] starring Sally Yeh, Tsui Hark, John Sham and Tony Leung.
- *The Killer* (John Woo, 1989), starring Chow Yun-fat, Danny Lee, Shing Fui-on and Sally Yeh.
- *Deception* (a.k.a. *Web of Deception*, David Chiang, 1989), starring Brigitte Lin, Joey Wong and Pauline Wong.
- *The Terracotta Warrior* (Tony Ching Siu-tung, 1989), starring Zhang Yimou, Gong Li and Yu Rongguang.
- *Just Heroes* (a.k.a. *Tragic Heroes*, 1989) was a benefit movie for the Hong Kong directors' union. It starred a host of names, including David Chiang, Danny Lee, Chen Kuan-tai, Stephen Chow, Lo Lieh, Ti Lung, Cally Kwong, Wu Ma, Shing Fui-on, James Wong Jim, Bill Tung, Zhao Lei and Tien Niu.
- *Spy Games* (David Wu Tai-wai, 1990) was a spy movie spoof directed by Wu, who's edited many of Tsui's movies. It was written by Ng Man-fai, Philip Cheng, Lam Kee-to and Lau Tai-mok, and starred Joey Wong, Kenny Bee, Noriko Izumoto, Waise Lee and Shut Yam.
- *The Raid* (Tony Ching Siu-tung and Tsui Hark, 1991) was a 1930s adventure comedy co-written by Tsui Hark and Yuen Kai-chi, and starring Jacky Cheung, Dean Shek, Tony Leung, Paul Chu, Fennie Yuen and Joyce Godenzi.
- *The Swordsman* (King Hu *et al*, 1990), starring Sam Hui, Cecilia Yip, Yuen Wah, Jacky Cheung and Cheung Man.

---

16 The *Better Tomorrow* movies inevitably inspired cash-ins – such as *Return To Better Tomorrow* (Wong Jing, 1994).
17 Critics have discerned the influence of Tsui Hark in *Gunmen* (which he produced), in the romantic atmosphere, and in the action.
18 Tony Ching Siu-tung was 2nd unit director.

- *The Swordsman 2* (Tony Ching Siu-tung, 1991), starring Jet Li, Brigitte Lin, Rosamund Kwan, Michelle Reiss and Fennie Yuen.
- *The Swordsman 3: The East Is Red* (Tony Ching Siu-tung & Raymond Lee, 1993), starring Brigitte Lin, Yu Rongguang, Joey Wong and Eddie Ko.
- *Dragon Inn* (a.k.a. *New Dragon Gate Inn*, Raymond Lee, 1992), starring Tony Leung, Brigitte Lin, Maggie Cheung and Donnie Yen.
- *The Wicked City* (*Yiu Sau Do Si*, dir. Peter Mak Tai-kit, 1992), a live-action version of the Japanese *animé* (1987), staring Leon Lai Ming, Jacky Cheung Hak-yow, Michelle Reiss and Tatsuya Nakadai.
- *Iron Monkey* (Yuen Woo-ping, 1993), co-written by Tsui Hark with Tang Pik-yin and Lau Tai-mok, and starring Donnie Yen, Yu Rongguang and Jean Wong.
- *The Magic Crane* (Benny Chan, 1993), co-written by Tsui Hark (with Jobic Chui Daat-Choh), and starring Anita Mui, Tony Leung Chiu-wai, Rosamund Kwan and Damian Lau.
- *Burning Paradise*, a.k.a. *Red Lotus Temple* (Ringo Lam Ling-tung, 1994), starring Willie Chi, Wong Kam-long and Carman Lee.
- *Once Upon a Time In China 4* (Yuen Bun, 1993), co-written by Tsui and Tang Pik-yin, was released only four months after the third *Once Upon a Time In China* movie, and starred Vincent Zhao, Jean Wong, Xiong Xin-xin, Max Mok and Lau Shun.
- *Shanghai Grand* (Poon Man-kit, 1996), was a period gangster tale co-written by Sandy Shaw, Matthew Chow Hoi-kwong and Poon Man-kit. It starred Andy Lau Tak-wah, Leslie Cheung and Lau Shun.
- *Black Mask* (Daniel Lee Yan-kong, 1996) was a wild superhero adventure co-written by Koan Hui-on, Teddy Chan Tak-sum and Joe Ma Wai-ho, and starring Jet Li, Karen Mok, Lau Ching-wan, Francoise Yip, Moses Chan and Anthony Wong.
- *Once Upon a Time in China and America* (Sammo Hung Kam-bo, 1997), was co-written by Roy Szeto Cheuk-hon, Shut Mei-yee, Sharon Hui Sa-long, Philip Kwok and So Man-Sing, and starred Jet Li, Rosamund Kwan, Xiong Xin-xin, Chan Kwok Pong, Richard Ng and Jeff Wolfe.
- *Old Master Q* (2001) was co-written by Tsui Hark with Roy Szeto Cheuk-hon, Herman Yau and Man Choi-lee, exec-prod. by Charles Heung and Tsui Hark, and dir. by Herman Yau.
- *Tsui Hark's Vampire Hunters* (2002) was produced and written by Tsui Hark, and dir. by Wellson Chin Sing-wai.
- *Xanda* (*Sanda*, 2004) was wr. by Kai-Cheung Chung, Derick Lau, Ask Lee, Xiao-Long Lin and Tsui Hark, exec-prod. by Satoru Iseki, Nansun Shi Nan-sheng and Le Qun Song, prod. by Tsui Hark, and directed by Marco Mak Chi-sin.
- *The Warrior* (literal title: *Wong Fei-hung: Brave Into the World*, 2006) was a Wong Fei-hung movie as an animation, directed by Tiger Fu Yin and Chen Yue-Hu and produced by Yang Yong.
- *Sword Master* (Derek Yee, 2016) was a 3-D *wuxia pian* produced by Tsui Hark and co-written by Tsui with Derek Yee and Chun Tin-nam.

Another aspect is immediately obvious: there were years when Tsui Hark was directing not one but two movies! And in some years, even more! In 1995: *The Chinese Feast, Love in the Time of Twilight* and *The Blade!* (In the North American film industry, it's typical for a film director to direct every three years).

TSUI HARK AS WRITER

Among Tsui Hark's writing for cinema credits are: *Di yu wu men, Dangerous Encounters of the First Kind, All the Wrong Clues, A Better Tomorrow 2*,[19] *Tit gaap mou dik maa lei aa, The Master, A Better Tomorrow 3: Love and Death in Saigon, A Chinese Ghost Story, A Chinese Ghost Story 3, Once Upon a Time in China, The Banquet, Twin Dragons, The Swordsman, Once Upon a Time in China 2, New Dragon Gate Inn, Once Upon a Time in China 3, The Swordsman 3: The East Is Red, Once Upon a Time in China 4, Iron Monkey, Ching Se, Yiu sau dou si, The Magic Crane, Once Upon a Time in China 5, The Chinese Feast, Love In the Time of Twilight, The Lovers, The Blade, Da san yuan, Black Mask,* the animated *Chinese Ghost Story, Time and Tide, Old Master Q, The Legend of Zu, Black Mask 2: City of Masks, The Era of Vampires, Xanda, Seven Swords, Missing, All About Women, Flying Swords of Dragon Gate, Young Detective Dee: Rise of the Sea Dragon, Sword Master, Detective Dee and the Four Heavenly Kings, The Thousand Faces of Dunjia* and the two *Battle of Lake Changjin* movies.

Tsui Hark has also worked uncredited as a writer, sometimes helping out pictures that are in trouble. For ex, Tsui contributed (along with Gordon Chan) to *Dr Wai* (Tony Ching Siu-tung, 1996), a Jet Li actioner.

Lisa Morton noted that Tsui Hark has only made one proper sci-fi movie – *I Love Maria* (a.k.a. *Roboforce*). Actually, the two *Black Mask* movies are science fiction. But Tsui has acknowledged that he hasn't done much in sci-fi – he prefers Ancient Chinese fantasy and mythology.

However, Tsui Hark has certainly directed movies which portray savage realms that come across like post-apocalyptic worlds: the brutish martial arts world (*jiangzhu*) of *The Blade*[20] and *Seven Swords* come to mind.

---

[19] *A Better Tomorrow 2* (1987) was written and directed by John Woo, produced by Tsui Hark, with action direction by Tony Ching Siu-tung, and starred Chow Yun-fat, Dean Shek, Ti Lung, Leslie Cheung and Emily Chu.
[20] Paul Fonoroff reckoned that 'if movies were judged on visuals alone, *The Blade* would certainly rank as one of the decade's most stunning motion pictures' (527).

TSUI HARK AND TELEVISION

> I went to film school simply because I like to express my feelings on certain issues through film, which was a pretty popular medium during the 1960s. We spent a lot of time in movie theaters. At that time I was already thinking how to make Chinese cinema more interesting.

Tsui Hark first worked in television in the late 1970s; his first TV shows were *Golden Dagger Romance* (1978), made for C.T.V., adapted from a novel by Gu Long (during Tsui's 6 months there) and *Aries, Scorpio, Aquarius* (T.V.B., 1978). Tsui was also one of five directors (Ringo Lam Ling-tung was another) of *The Family* (1978, at T.V.B.), a 104-episode soap opera ('people die, get rich, get divorced', as Tsui summed it up [1997, 133]). Tsui came back to television several times – for the *Wong Fei-hung* and *Seven Swordsmen* TV series, for example.

For Stephen Teo, Tsui Hark's cinema is a vivid embodiment of the maturation of the New Wave, and the postmodernism of commercial cinema:

> Using Tsui as a yardstick, the postmodern phenomena grew from a ragbag of causes and effects: new wave æsthetics mixed with Cinema City-style slapstick, anxiety over 1997 and the China syndrome, the assertion of Hong Kong's own identity as different from China, and a new sexual awakening arising from an increasing awareness of women's human rights and the decriminalisation of homosexuality. (1997, 246)

CINEMA CITY

Tsui Hark was part of the group of filmmakers at Cinema City (from 1981). A new studio, Cinema City wasn't independent – it was owned by Golden Princess. It had been founded by Raymond Wong Pak-min, Karl Maka (b. 1944) and Dean Shek in 1979 (as the Fun Dao Film Company). The so-called 'Gang of Seven' at Cinema City were Tsui, Maka, Wong, Shek, Teddy Robin Kwan, Eric Tsang and Tsui's wife Nansun Shi Nan-sheng. As Tsui recalled, they would consider everything, go thru scripts at length and discuss them.

All the Wrong Clues... For the Right Solution (1981) was Tsui Hark's first Cinema City production: it was produced by Karl Maka and Dean Shek, written by Roy Szeto Cheuk-hon (a regular collaborator with Tsui) and Raymond Wong Pak-min, and starred George Lam, Teddy Robin Kwan, Maka and Wong Tso-sze (for some critics, this movie announced the end of the Hong Kong New Wave).

Aces Go Places 3 (a.k.a. *Mad Mission 3,* 1984) was another installment in the successful *Aces Go Places* franchise from Cinema City (the earlier films were released in 1982 and 1983. The movies were the top films of each year (the first *Aces Go Places* grossed HK $26 million[21] when ticket prices were HK $15 (= U.S. $1.95).) It was produced and written by Raymond Wong Pak-min, and starred Sam Hui, Karl Maka and Sylvia Chang. According to Stephen Teo, 'Tsui's own dynamic style of filmmaking initiated a level of structural experimentation which was to be highly influential' (153).

The 'Cinema City style' emphasized comedy above all, stunts, visual effects, big budgets, and movies constructed by a creative team. For a period in the 1980s, Cinema City cornered the market for theatrical comedies. About 17% of films were comedies between 1985 and 1997 in Hong Kong.

FILM WORKSHOP

In 1984 Tsui Hark founded Film Workshop with his wife, Nansun Shi Nan-sheng (he had decided to create a company during post-production of *Zu: Warriors From the Magic Mountain*; it was partly because Cinema City were only interested in making comedies). Film Workshop is based in Kowloon Bay.

Terence Chang[22] worked as general manager at Film Workshop in the 1980s (at Nansun Shi Nan-sheng's invitation). Following Tsui Hark's dispute with John Woo over *The Killer* and *A Better Tomorrow 3*,[23] Chang left with Woo. Chang described his time at Film Workshop thus:

> The first year was really exciting. The company was new, vibrant, and a lot of great films came from that time. Tsui Hark was very idealistic. He wanted to round up the best directors in Hong Kong and put them under one roof. He wanted to create an environment where all the directors, under his leadership, could be given the opportunity and nourishment to make artistic, yet commercial pictures.

The productions of Film Workshop include: *Shanghai Blues* (1984), *The Master* (1989), *King of Chess* (1992), *The Swordsman 2* (1992), *Wicked City* (1992), *New Dragon Gate Inn* (1992), *Once Upon a Time in China 2* (1992), *The East Is Red* (1993), *The Magic Crane* (1993), *Iron Monkey* (1993), *Once Upon a Time in China 3* (1993), *Once Upon a Time in China 4* (1993), *Green Snake* (1993), *A Chinese Ghost Story: The Tsui*

---

21 There are typically 7.75 Hong Kong dollars to the U.S.A. dollar. (So when a movie makes HK $30 million in theatrical release in Hong Kong, that equals US $3.87 million).
22 John Woo's regular producer, Terence Chang (b. 1949), had studied in New York and Oregon before working at Golden Harvest and in TV before joining Film Workshop. Chang also worked at D. & B.
23 He rushed his own sequel to *A Better Tomorrow* into theatres, for instance (which he had co-produced), to beat John Woo's sequel (altho' Woo doesn't like doing sequels).

Hark Animation (1997), Knockoff (1998), Time and Tide (2000), The Era of Vampires (2002), Xanda (2004), Seven Swords (2005), Triangle (2007), All About Women (2008) and the Detective Dee movies.

Tsui Hark has worked with Golden Harvest for much of his career; they have enjoyed many successes. However, they have also fallen out – over the release of Zu: Warriors From the Magic Mountain, for instance. And in the late 1990s, Golden Harvest sued Tsui for over-runs on 8 films (and Tsui's lawyers responded with a counter-suit for revenue from the Once Upon a Time In China pictures).

SOME GREAT MOMENTS IN TSUI HARK'S WORK

- Avoiding the cannibals in We're Going To Eat You
- The finale of Zu
- Meeting under the bridge in Shanghai Blues
- Backstage in Peking Opera Blues
- Chow Yun-fat versus the tank in A Better Tomorrow 3
- Maggie Cheung in New Dragon Gate Inn
- The first act of Once Upon a Time In China
- The ladders duel in Once Upon a Time In China
- Leslie Cheung in the haunted inn in A Chinese Ghost Story
- Wu Ma's Taoist dance in A Chinese Ghost Story 1
- Jet Li versus Donnie Yen in Once Upon a Time In China 2
- The Lion Dance competition in Once Upon a Time In China 3
- Jet Li in a clinch with Brigitte Lin in The Swordsman 2
- The watery finale of Green Snake
- The musical/ romantic montage in The Lovers
- The final duel in The Blade
- The motorcycle chase in Black Mask
- The market chase in Knock-Off
- The apartment fire-fight in Time and Tide
- The arrival of the warriors in Seven Swords
- Jet Li vs. Gordon Liu in Flying Swords of Dragon Gate
- Andy Lau and Jinger in Detective Dee
- The sea monster in Young Detective Dee
- The snow tiger scene in The Taking of Tiger Mountain
- The Battle of the Buddhas in Journey To the West
- The monster battle in Detective Dee 3

On the set of Flying Swords of Dragon Gate (above).

Tsui Hark on the sets of the Detective Dee films.

PART TWO

THE SWORDSMAN

1

THE SWORDSMAN
Siu Ngo Gong Woo

The *Swordsman* movies[1] were adapted from *The Smiling, Proud Wanderer* by Jin Yong (Louis Cha, 1924-2018), which have been used for five or so TV series (and a Shaw Brothers movie of 1978). So the *Swordsman* films are by no means the only interpretations of the novels of Jin Yong, one of the best-known authors of *wuxia* stories. In fact, a TV series is a probably more fitting form for adaptation, because Jin Yong's stories contain a huge cast of characters and numerous events. Those depicted in the *Swordsman* movies are but one small segment (and a loose adaptation at that).

The film is usually credited to Raymond Lee (but in fact six directors are known to have worked on it, including the original director, King Hu, and Tsui Hark and Ann Hui).

The Swordsman (Cantonese = *Siu Ngo Gong Woo,* Mandarin = *Xiao Aoi Jianzhu* = *Laughing and Proud Warrior*), was produced by Tsui Hark, Tommy Law Wai-Tak and Chu Feng Kang for Film Workshop.[2] It was written by six people: Kwan Man-Leung, Daai Foo Ho, Huang Ying, Tai-Mok Lau, Yiu-ming Leung, and Jason Lam Kee To; costumes: Cheung Sai-Ying, Cheung Kam-Kam, Lui Siu-Hung, Shing Fuk-Ying, Edith Cheung Sai-Mei, and Bo-Ling Ng; hair by Sam Biu-Hoi and Lee Lin-Dai; A.D.: Kuo-Han Yuan (and 8 other A.D.s); music by Romeo Diaz and James Wong Jim; the DPs were Andy Lam, Lee Tak-Wai, Joe Chan Kwong-Hung, Horace Wong Wing-Hang and Peter Pau; art direction by Leung Wah-sang; make-up by Lau Gai-Sing, Poon Man-Wa and Cheung Bik-Yuk; editing by Marco Mak Chi-sin and David Wu Tai-wai; the action choreographers were: Tony Ching Siu-tung, Lau Chi Ho, Bruce Law, and Yuen Wah. It was released on Apl 5, 1990, and grossed about HK $16 million.[3] 115 mins.

---
[1] For more information on the *Swordsman* movies, see my companion book.
[2] According to Tsui Hark, the investor backing *The Swordsman* was not convinced about the movie, because it had been done before, and failed. Tsui insisted that he could make it work (LM, 24).
[3] *The Swordsman* series was parodied in *Royal Tramp* (1992), directed by Wong Jing and Gordon Chan and starring Stephen Chow.

The production apparently wound on for 2 years (LM, 172). It boasts 9 assistant directors, six costume designers, five DPs, etc – and six writers. At around 115 minutes, *The Swordsman* is significantly longer than many Hong Kong action pictures (which're usually 80-90 mins, tho' this length might be not sanctioned by the filmmakers).[4] It won Hong Kong Film Awards for Best Action and Best Song and the Golden Horse Award for Best Film and Best Supporting Actor (Jacky Cheung).

✦

The Swordsman was completed by Tsui Hark after King Hu walked out (after ten days of filming), and other directors (such as Ann Hui, Andrew Kam Yeung-Wa and Raymond Lee) were tried; Tsui co-directed the remainder of the movie with action director Tony Ching Siu-tung. (Nothing remains in the film of Hu's footage, according to Lisa Morton [LM, 172]). *The Swordsman* was credited as being co-directed by Tsui Hark, Raymond Lee, Tony Ching Siu-tung and the two directors who left: King Hu and Ann Hui (Andrew Kam also appears in some credits).

Raymond Lee Wai-man was born on Aug 10, 1949 in Hong Kong; like many of his generation (including Tsui Hark and the Hong Kong New Wave), Lee first worked in local television (at Commercial Television until 1978, then Asia Television to 1981, then Hong Kong Television Broadcast, Ltd.). Among Lee's movies as director are *The Last Conflict* (1988), *Tour of Revenge* (1989), *Rebel From China* (1990), *Blue Lightning* (1991), *Once a Killer* (1991), *New Dragon Gate Inn* (co-directed, 1992), *The Swordsman 3* (co-directed, 1993), *Fatal Obsession* (1994), *The Other Side of the Sea* (1994), *Police Confidential* (1995), and *To Be No. 1* (1996), along with TV series such as *Assassinator Jing Ke* (2004), *The Shaolin Warriors* (2008) and *Invincible Knights Errant* (2011). Lee's producer credits include *Farewell 19, Running On Empty, Deep In Night,* and *The Treasure Hunter.*

For filmmakers of the Hong Kong New Wave, King Hu was a key figure, a pioneer of the martial arts movie (and of making *wuxia pian* artistic and poetic as well as visceral and commercial). Hu's swordfighting films were typically set in the Ming Dynasty, 1368-1644 (like this one), featuring swordsmen (and women) and eunuch villains (emissaries of the oppressive Dongchang, the Imperial authorities). Hu was known for treating action as choreography as something lyrical and abstract, and stylized.

By inviting King Hu to work on *The Swordsman,* Tsui Hark and co. were expressing their appreciation for a veteran of the kind of cinema that they loved (and grew up with). However, Hu's health was failing, which didn't make the disagreements between him and the filmmakers easier (Hu died in 1997, aged 66).

✦

Sam Hui Koon-kit (who had worked with Tsui Hark in 1984's OTT *James Bond* spoof *Aces Go Places,* and in *Working Class* in 1985), plays the lead role in *The Swordsman,* Linghu Chong, the Hua Mountain student

---

[4] It's true that some of the scenes in act 3 of 4 do meander somewhat, with maybe a subplot too many.

and swordsman.5 Hui's Linghu is confident and calm, one of the most easy-going figures in movies of the *jiangzhu,* played with a light-hearted charm by Hui. (Jet Li continued with that light touch in the *Swordsman* sequel).

Among the supporting cast in *The Swordsman* were a bunch of Hong Kong regulars (this is a terrific cast), including: Cecilia Yip as Yue Lingshan (a.k.a. 'Skinny Boy'), Linghu Chong's sidekick (another of the many crossdressing charas in Hong Kong cinema, and another of Tsui Hark's cute tomboys); Yuen Wah plays one of his customary nasty bruisers,6 Zuo Lengshan, a practitioner of 'dark' martial arts (Wah was also one of the action directors); Jacky Cheung Hok-yau is Ouayang Quan, eunuch Gu Jinfu's ambitious, cunning henchman; Sharla Cheung is Ren Yingying, leader of the Sun Moon Sect; Fennie Yuen is Blue Phoenix a.k.a Lan Fenghuang (Ren Yingying's aide); Wu Ma is Liu Zhengfeng, one of the retiring Sun Moon warriors; and the ever-dependable Lau Shun is Gu Jinfu, the eunuch villain from the Eastern branch of the Imperial forces. (*The Swordsman* casts three beautiful actresses to counter-balance the masculinist bias of martial arts movies: Fennie Yuen, Cecilia Yip and Sharla Cheung. Placing two women as leaders of the Sun Moon Sect – Cheung and Yuen – is very much part of Tsui Hark's project of re-instating roles for women in movies. And it's typical of a Tsui-produced *jiangzhu* movie that the sidekick of the hero is a boy played by a girl).

The casting of *The Swordsman* is marvellous, and each of the principals embodies their characters as well as popping out of them – there is always a feeling in Chinese, historical action movies of this kind that it's all a pantomime, that it's pure entertainment, and should be taken as just that – a wild show. Actors aren't allowed to wink at the camera (rightly), but the movie does. The cast play it straight – but also with plenty of Peking Operatic over-acting. They don't need to nod at the audience, because the situations are so outlandish.

The Swordsman is a gorgeous *mix* of elements: comedy, romance, spectacle, music, characterization, history/ mythology, Chinese culture – and of course action and martial arts. *The Swordsman* is also a truly inspired vision of the *jiangzhu,* the martial arts world, which Tsui Hark explored many times (in fact, *The Swordsman* marks the first major entry in evoking the *jiangzhu* in the 1990s became home-from-home for Tsui and his contemporaries in Hong Kong); and, of course, Tsui had dived into the *jiangzhu* in his very first feature film as director, *The Butterfly Murders,* while Tony Ching had lived in the cinematic *jiangzhu* since the 1960s (working on his father's films at Shaws).

The editing of *The Swordsman* – by Marco Mak Chi-sin and David Wu Tai-wai (regulars in the Tsui Hark Cinematic Circus) – is fiendishly intricate. Tracking the ensemble cast and their subplots with sword-sharp precision, the cutting weaves a story stuffed with incidents and bits of business.

---

5 It might've been tempting, tho', to play up to Hui's comical persona.
6 Yuen Wah was an actor and martial artist, who doubled for Bruce Lee at Golden Harvest; he was one of the 'Seven Liittle Fortunes' from *sifu* Yu Jim Yuen's Peking Opera school. Yuen appeared countless times as heavies in Hong Kong movies (such as *Eastern Condors, Kid From Tibet, Dragons Forever* and *Iceman Cometh*).

The theme song of *The Swordsman*, 'Chong Hoi Yat Sing Siu', was composed and written by James Wong Jim; Sam Hui performed it (several times – the film fully exploits Hui's pop star status). Like the theme music of *Once Upon a Time in China*, 'Chong Hoi Yat Sing Siu' has a sad, lyrical tone which enhances the atmosphere of nostalgia and history (and you'll be humming it immediately).

✦

The Swordsman helped to create many of the staple scenes of the 'New Wave' of historical action movies in Hong Kong – the *jiangzhu;* the nighttime attack on the inn or palace; the sword fight in the trees (again at night); *ronin* warriors; the gratuitous, nude bathing scene involving a beautiful woman (plus crossdressing comedy); a wild brawl on a boat; inter-clan rivalries; a musical interlude; rebellion against oppressive/corrupt regimes, etc.

The sequels to *The Swordsman* continued with most of the same elements and characters. Much of the cast was changed for the sequels, however, tho' returnees included Fennie Yuen as Blue Phoenix, and Lau Shun (it's not a Tsui Hark-produced movie unless Lau Shun is in it).

✦

The Swordsman teems with plots and counter-plots. Much juice is elicited, for instance, from disguises: so Ouyang Quan acts as Lin Pingzhi, Skinny Boy is a girl, an old man (Feng Qingyang – Han Ying-chieh) is really a master martial artist, and Gu Jinfu and the Imperial guards are forced to pretend to be Lam's bereaved family.

Clans and communities are a very prominent feature of *The Swordsman* (as in many Chinese, historical movies), and they're pitted against each other: the Mount Hua clan, the Sun Moon Sect, the emissaries of the Imperial Court, etc. Meanwhile, Linghu Chong and the *Sunflower Scroll* are at the centre of the tussles for power. Each group is vying for the upper-hand, imagining that the secret techniques of the *Sunflower Scroll* will give them the advantage. Within the strict hierarchy of each group (where the authority of the leaders or the *sifus* must never be questioned), there are traitors (such as Ouyang Quan). But Linghu Chong, being the hero, is of course good and straight and true (he embodies the element of righteousness that is a primary issue for Tsui Hark).

The MacGuffiin in *The Swordsman* is that old chestnut of Chinese *jiangzhu* stories, the sacred scroll (the *Sunflower Manual* contains martial arts secrets, including telekinesis and the ability to walk thru walls). In the opening scene, it is stolen from the Imperial Palace. The (nighttime, rooftop) theft kickstarts the narrative of *The Swordsman*, with the Imperial Court ordering the return of the scroll to the Imperial Library. (As is customary in Chinese, *wuxia* films, the Imperial Court scenes are placed upfront, to offer some spectacle, to orientate the movie in time and place (it's the Ming Dynasty), and to provide the impetus for part of the narrative – an Imperial order, a move against rebels, a kidnapping, or the theft of something important. But those Imperial Court scenes soon fulfil their dramatic function, and movies tend to shift rapidly to the *jiangzhu*, the martial arts world).

And the *Sunflower Scroll* is a martial arts manual which's confused in the finale for a music manuscript (a telling comment on what is important in life). The M.S. is a scroll called 'Xiao-ao Jianghu', the 'proud and laughing martial arts world' (which's the song that Liu Zhengfeng and Qu Yang sing on the boat).

The pursuit of the thieves thought to possess the *Sunflower Scroll* provides the first part of act one of *The Swordsman*, with Gu Jinfu leading the Eastern forces of the Chinese Empire. Exposition is woven into these scenes but, as the audience in this movie is chiefly a Chinese-speaking one, it contains far less exposition than movies aimed at an international market. We are thus introduced to the villains and the narrative engine that ignites the plot first, before moving on to the heroes.

We first meet the heroes Linghu Chong and Yue Lingshan (a.k.a. 'Skinny Boy') when they visit the den of Lin Zhennan, to deliver messages from the Mount Hua Sect (yes, once again a buddy duo is set up in a Tsui Hark movie, but with a lovely actress playing one of the guys). The tone of *The Swordsman* is set out here, deftly combining comedy and action, with Sam Hui's Linghu Chong played casually and humorously. For instance, to prove who he is, Linghu launches into an elaborate sword dance (the scene also demonstrates that he's an experienced swordsman).[7] (The house is one of those traditional buildings seen in 100s of martial arts movies – a large interior of wood with upper balconies, perfect for staging action all over the place. It could be intercut with the buildings in the *Chinese Ghost Story* flicks or *Once Upon a Time In China*, or the inn in *Crouching Tiger, Hidden Dragon*). Gu Jinfu and his henchmen soon attack, providing one of the first action sequences in *The Swordsman* (the finale also takes place here).

Zuo Lengshan, acting for Gu Jinfu and co., is a malicious piece of work all-round: in a scene of extraordinary barbarity, his heavies torture Lin Zhennan's wife by tearing out her eyes, then her tongue (the gore, including a bloody eyeball, is typical of Hong Kong cinema, but also seems unnecessary and over-the-top). Lin is nearby, listening to Zuo's taunts, and unable to retaliate because he's injured.[8] All of this takes place in long grass at night where no one can see what's going on. As if Gu Jinfu and his army aren't enough, Zuo and his thugs up the threat even more.

✦

One of the stand-out sequences in *The Swordsman* is a delightful musical interlude that occurs at the start of act two – 'Xiao-ao Jianghu' ('Hero of Heroes' or 'A Laugh At the World'), by James Wong Jim and Tai Lok-man, a song about the 'proud and laughing martial arts world' (the *jiangzhu*). Finding refuge on a boat, Linghu Chong and his sidekick Skinny Boy meet some fighters from the Sun Moon Sect, Liu Zhengfeng (Wu Ma) and Qu Yang (Lam Ching-ying), who are retiring. They sing and play the

---

[7] Using flames flicked from candles on the sword blade; the dance goes slightly wrong (Linghu Chong invents some of his own moves); later, there are huge explosions when gunpowder is accidentally set off.
[8] By Linghu Chong and co. – as if Linghu unconsciously realizes that Lin Zhennan is not all he seems.

song 'Xiao-ao Jianghu', which acts as a pop promo within the movie (a not-uncommon practice in 1980s cinema, and songs and pop stars are common in Hong Kong movies). It's moving, too, that Liu and Qu are fatally wounded in the giant action scene that follows, and opt to go out in style: Liu dies, as they play the song of the *jiangzhu* one last time, then Qu sets fire to the boat, and they expire in flames on the sea. (*The Swordsman* is partly concerned with the passing of the *jiangzhu*, in common with many *wuxia pian* in this period – it's a gesture towards nostalgia, it's a swansong for the movies of a generation's youth, nostalgia for the movies that the filmmakers grew up with, nostalgia for a vanished world (that never existed in the first place, but *should* have), it's a pæan to historical as well as mythical China, plus a commentary on the state of modern China. And it's also a passing of the torch from the older generation to the younger generation).

Indeed, music is one of the most direct methods for accessing those historical, mythical, romantic realms, as filmmakers know well (the *ronin* Feng Qingyang tells Linghu Chong that emotions are more powerful than martial arts). The composers of *The Swordsman* (Tsui Hark regulars Romeo Diaz, Tai Lok-man and James Wong Jim) employ many traditional musical forms; and there's a *qin* (stringed instrument) which Linghu carries (and plays). The 'proud and laughing martial arts' song is reprised several times (including in the midst of the action finale, when Linghu sings it again, and when he is recovering from being poisoned).

Linghu Chong encounters another older, wiser figure, in the guise of Feng Qingyang (mid-way thru the movie, in the second half of the second act): as the Imperial heavies close in, a fierce battle ensues (again staged at night). Feng turns out to be a master swordsman, despite his age (at first he seems to be a weak, old man who's only interested in cooking some food): this is one of the outstanding action scenes in *The Swordsman*, definitely directed by Tony Ching Siu-tung, with its miraculous feeling for wire-work and speed and practical effects. Feng defeats one of Gu Jinfu's most vicious henchmen and his crew, with some help from Linghu; the non-stop stunts include the lightning-fast passing of swords from hero to hero, Ching's penchant for airborne swordsmen slicing through dust, and Feng and Linghu working together, culminating in the extreme (and very Chingian) physical gag of a body in flight being sliced in half. (And the sequence offers another master-pupil relationship, with Feng showing Linghu the 'Nine Swords of Dugu'. Feng also tells Linghu that all is not well in the *jiangzhu*, and that Yue Buqun (Lau Siu-ming – the Tree Demon in *A Chinese Ghost Ghost Story*), the leader of the Mount Hua Sect, is also corrupt. In the final fight of *The Swordsman*, Linghu uses the 'Nine Solitary Swords' moves to defeat the crooked leader, Yue Buqun).

✦

In the third act (using a 4-act model), *The Swordsman* travels to the exotic realm of the Sun Moon Sect in Miao: their HQ is an inn[9] in a bamboo forest. This part of *The Swordsman* is very reminiscent of the central

---

9 The bamboo inn is exploited to the max.

section of *New Dragon Gate Inn* (the latter film is almost a remake of *The Swordsman*) – you've got several groups travelling in disguise, numerous cat-and-mouse manœuvres (as each group tries to gain the upper hand), creeping about at night, evocations of erotic desire (including lesbianism), eating and carousing, a powerful female leader, etc.

Each of the *Swordsman* movies comes even more to life when it depicts the Sun Moon Sect – out come the scarlet[10] costumes and sets, the wonderful headdresses[11] (the costume design by Cheung Sai-Ying, Cheung Kam-Kam, Lui Siu-Hung, Shing Fuk-Ying, Edith Cheung Sai-Mei, and Bo-Ling Ng is outstanding), the use of wood and bamboo, the exaltation of superstition and ritual. One imagines that Tsui Hark and the teams could create whole movies around the Sun Moon Clan – a band of warriors led by a beautiful, young woman who oppose corrupt regimes seems to inspire them (Tsui is especially fond of evoking ancient traditions and beliefs). But, like many exotic and unusual communities, they have a greater impact when they're set against regular, everyday folk. (However, there aren't many communities that are 'normal' in the *Swordsman* movies!).

In the Sun Moon Sect sequence, suspicion and distrust play out in the primary plot, while the secondary plots include some romantic comedy; disguises/ crossdressing; and the poisoning of Linghu Chong. Our heroes arrive, but are treated suspiciously; Ouyang Quan appears in disguise as the dead Lin Pingzhi; and there are tussles for supremacy.

Altho' critics continually deride Hong Kong action movies for what they see as their poor scripts, the characters and their relationships are carefully worked out in *The Swordsman*: for ex, in the Sun Moon Sect section of *The Swordsman*, the antagonism between Ren Yingying and Blue Phoenix (over the leadership of the clan), between Linghu Chong and Yue Buqun (whom he now distrusts), over the secret messages from Lin Zhennan, between Linghu and Blue Phoenix, and many other charas are all evoked clearly.

Historical Chinese movies often squeeze a *lot* of dramatic mileage out of rivalries, loyalties, betrayals and disguises. The issue of loyalty and doing the right thing is vital. *Where* you put your loyalty is absolutely crucial here: are you for the Eastern branch of the Imperial Court or for the Sun Moon Sect? Or, like Ouyang Quan, are you out for yourself?

In the Sun Moon Sect part of *The Swordsman*, the struggle for the superior position politically is played out visually and dramatically in a marvellous series of kinetic scenes, with charas sneaking about, leaping thru open windows, hiding, spying, over-hearing, and occasionally fighting.

The Swordsman happily and nimbly switches genres and moods, moving from deadly serious statements about doing the right thing and opposing corrupt regimes to goofy comedy (Linghu Chong sits on Blue Phoenix when she's hiding and sings), romantic farce (Blue Phoenix

---

10 Red is the signature colour of this film.
11 The Miao (a.k.a. Hmong) are known for their elaborate embroideries (for wedding attire); and their jewellery – silverwork, coil necklaces, spiral earrings, and headdresses.

seducing Skinny Boy), and mystical healing montages.

In the midst of it all, our hero, Linghu Chong, is poisoned (the filmmakers employ a lengthy three-shot, as poisoned cups of wine are passed back and forth in an elaborate, well-rehearsed dance). But this time, instead of the cup being knocked out of the hero's hand by accident, or something distracting the drinkers, Linghu is poisoned. Luckily, there are experts in Ancient Chinese medicine on hand (thus, Tsui Hark and the filmmakers shoehorn some more traditional, Chinese culture into a movie – altho' scenes of restoring the hero via magical and medical means are a standard trope in Chinese, historical movies).

In *The Swordsman*, Linghu Chong experiences a rough regime of healing via worms – yes, wriggly worms, administered thru pipes (by Blue Phoenix) into the nostril (ugh!). In his fever dream, Linghu thinks back to the Sun Moon Sect Elders he met, and here the footage of the song on the boat and the subsequent battle is recycled in a montage. But the recycling is not wholly shameless padding, because Linghu's visions seem to be apprehended by Ren Yingying, proving Linghu's trustworthiness (two beats before this, Ren was all for dispatching Linghu).

◆

Tsui Hark is fond of creating buddy duos, but subverting them by having the counterpart to the hero (or top-billed star) being played by an actress. The ruse works on several levels: the masculine relationship of the buddy set-up is maintained (they are 'men' in a man's world, or 'men' in public); being men, the characters can interact in the strictly patriarchal society of historical China; there's inevitable erotic attraction/ teasing between the two; and there's crossdressing and disguises (which're eventually uncovered); the crossdressing also provides opportunities for misunderstandings, embarrassments, and farce.

The quasi-lesbian scene in *The Swordsman* is pure Tsui Hark – it combines crossdressing with lesbianism. So, Blue Phoenix is given a lusty characterization (dropped from the later *Swordsman* films): she takes a shine to Yue Lingshan, Linghu Chong's companion (Skinny Boy), who travels as a man. Blue Phoenix flirts with Lingshan (who's drunk), then carries him/ her into a side room and is about to have her wicked way with her/ him, only to discover that she's a woman as she rips apart her clothes. It's not the first time (nor the last!) where Tsui teases audiences with some woman-on-woman action.[12]

Further romantic elements in *The Swordsman* include Yue Lingshan's unspoken affection for Linghu Chong (witness her dismay at being ordered to marry Lin Pingzhi), and the erotic, quasi-lesbian undercurrent in the antagonism between Ren Yingying and Blue Phoenix.

One of the issues tackled in *The Swordsman* is the Sins of the Fathers, and the troubled relationship between the older generation and the younger generation: this is a staple of martial arts movies, and is always featured in Tsui Hark's interpretation of the genre. Thus, both Gu Jinfu and Yue Buqun are corrupt patriarchs (and are duly punished in the

---

[12] The comic goofing around, when Linghu Chong sits on Blue Phoenix's head when she's sneaked into his room, is another example of Tsui Hark's brand of erotic but ditzy comedy.

finale). Meanwhile, a good and true patriarch, Liu Zhengfeng (Wu Ma), is killed by the Imperial bruisers. The lust for power is loudly scorned in *The Swordsman*, with the crooked Elders and Ouyang Quan hungering for the *Sunflower Scroll*.

◆

With some great directors of action involved (Lee, Hu, Tsui), plus Tony Ching Siu-tung, Lau Chi Ho and Yuen Wah as action choreographers, *The Swordsman* doesn't disappoint as an action movie. Among the delights in *The Swordsman* are a fierce bust-up on a boat; several nighttime duels in smoky forests; an attack on a house; a brawl in an inn; and duels involving flying snakes and bees. The action is of the swordplay variety – fantastical and exaggerated, with much use of cables, rigs and flying, the manipulation of props, and intensely acrobatic movements out of Peking Opera. The *wuxia* genre is presented here via action which emphasizes energy and magic – there are numerous stunning evocations of high energy, and different forms of energy, in conflict with each other. (Several scenes are Chingian: the nighttime display of special swordsmanship by the hermit Feng Qingyan; the battle on the boat; and the final duel between Linghu and his *sifu* Yue Buqun, which shows Linghu Chong using the sword forms on Yue).

In the boat sequence, most of the vessel is destroyed as our heroes beat off Yuen Wah's Zuo Lengshan and his henchmen. Linghu Chong and Skinny Boy are travelling by sea with the retiring Sun Moon Sect members. Following the lovely song scene, Zuo's boat rams the ship, and an all-out battle ensues. The boat offers plenty of opportunity for stuntmen to go crashing into sails, for masts to topple, and – a Chinese speciality – characters to fly up out of the water. This is a beautiful sequence of flowing movement and inventive stunts, with a poetic use of water and light.

Yuen Wah suffers a nasty (but well-earned) death: attacking the Mount Hua house, he is set upon by Ren Yingying's bees as well as Blue Phoenix's snakes. In a disgusting, nightmarish image,[13] Zuo Lengshan's face and shoulders are crawling with bees (a call-back to *The Butterfly Murders*, perhaps). This occurs after a wonderfully staged fight in amongst the long grass once again, where Blue Phoenix and Ren are pushed to the limit against Zuo (while carrying a comatose Linghu Chong, whom Ren is trying to resuscitate even as she flies thru air, fleeing from Zuo).

As all trails lead back to the Lam house, there's the delightful sight of the Imperial eunuch and his underlings having to don disguises, and pretend to be the grieving family of *sifu* Yue Buqun. The film exploits the reversal of political power as Gu Jinfu is forced to kowtow repeatedly. The tables are turned once more, before the finale, when Yue Buqun is brought to his knees and Gu Jinfu holds court again.

The action in the finale of *The Swordsman* is remarkable for its physical and technical complexity. In the small, enclosed space of the interior of the Lam household, with its upper balconies and pillars, the

---

[13] I've had nightmares like this with bees! I can't watch this scene again!

filmmakers stage a series of fierce battles. There's barely any room to swing a sword, let alone fly a stuntman thru the air in that building, but Tony Ching Siu-tung, Lau Chi Ho and Yuen Wah and the team deliver absolutely outstanding choreography.

Prior to the demise of the villains, the MacGuffin of the *Sunflower Manual* scroll is brought into play several times; it's repeatedly confused with the 'proud and laughing martial arts world' music scroll (and Linghu Chong gets to sing the catchy tune once more).

The Imperial eunuch, Gu Jinfu, is set upon by pistols and a rifle (brought by clever Blue Phoenix), plus swords (from Linghu Chong) and finally Ren Yingying adds the last touch, tearing the guy apart with her whip. And Linghu, in the closing duel, brings the over-bearing *sifu* Yue Buqun down a notch or two (including cutting his meridian points), using the 'Nine Swords of Dugu' forms he learnt from Feng Qingyan. Only the intervention of Skinny Boy stops the hero running her father thru with his sword.

The duel is a very Chingian swordplay scene – to portray the deadly *chi* emanating from *sifu* Yue Buqun, the environment is puppeteered – wooden fences split apart, for example, and the ground is sliced with energy lines. Tony Ching's penchant for very extravagant aerial spins and somersaults, complete with flapping clothing, is much in evidence. Ching would later make this kind of highly romantic action choreography famous in the West in the 2002 film *Hero*.

The Swordsman closes with what became one of Tsui Hark signature motifs (which he used many times): the heroes riding off into the sunset on horses under a big sky in the countryside (this time in slo-mo), as if the producers have decided to go for the most clichéd ending they can imagine. Thus ends one of the great Hong Kong action movies.

The Swordsman (1990), this page and over.

Classic Tony Ching imagery – flying swordsmen.

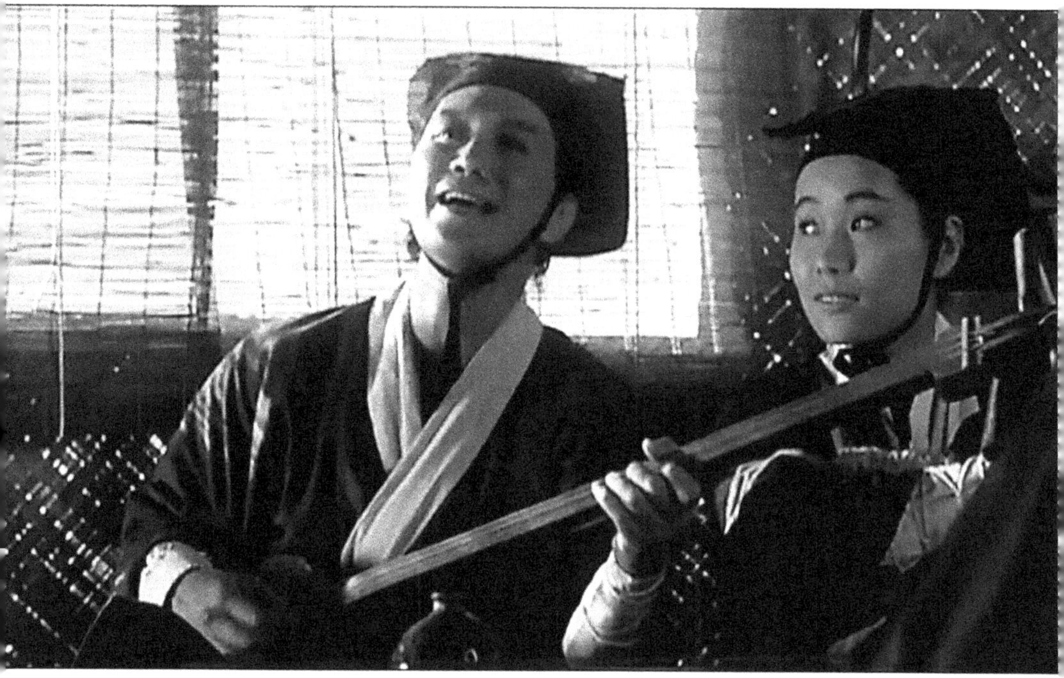

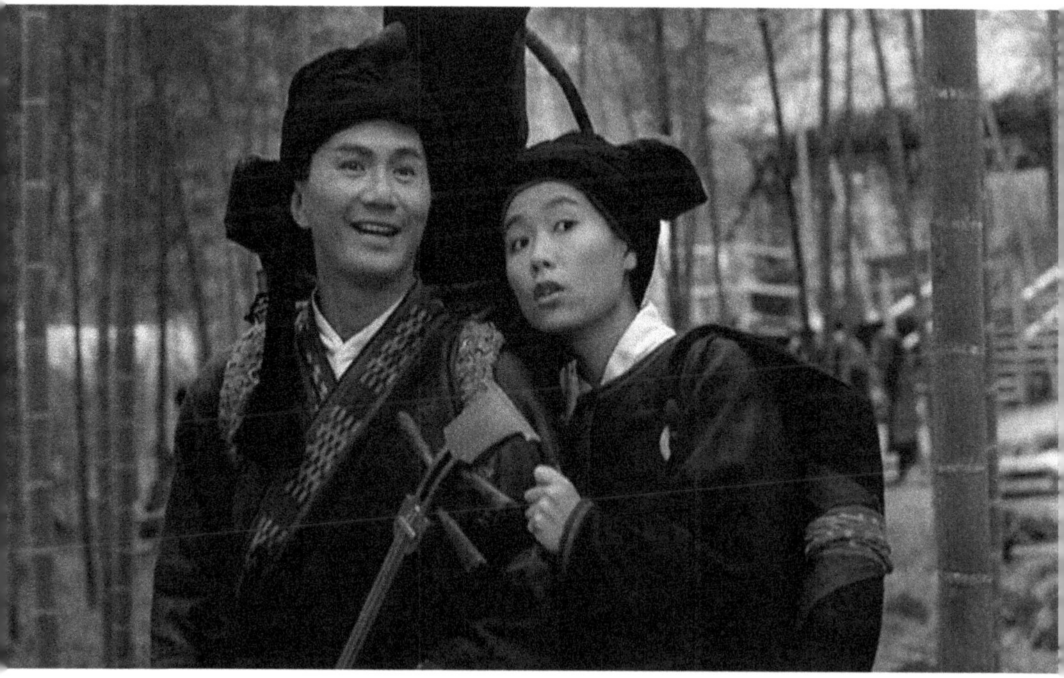

2

THE SWORDSMAN 2

Siu Ngo Kong Woo II Dung Fong Bat Baai

THE PRODUCTION.
Jet Li plus Brigitte Lin plus superstar action director Tony Ching Siu-tung with Tsui Hark as producer and an outrageously over-the-top story combine to produce one of the great fantasy swordplay movies of recent times. It starts at full speed and doesn't let up! The prologue alone contains a horse being sliced in half, flying horses and warriors, decapitation, a swordplay battle in an Imperial palace, and a god-like being in scarlet who declaims from the tops of trees.

The Swordsman 2 is a work of genius. It's a masterpiece of pure popcorn movie fantasy, and can stand beside any of the great action movies in the history of cinema. 'Ecstatic cinema', 'giddily demented', 'eye-popping', and a 'gender-bending, gravity-defying, mystical-surreal fantasy beyond your wildest dreams' (F. Dannen, 339), are some of the critical assessments of *The Swordsman 2*.

The Swordsman 2 (Cantonese: *Siu Ngo Kong Woo II Dong Fong Bat Baai*; Mandarin: *Xiao-ao Jianghu II Dongfang Bubai = Laughing and Proud Warrior: Invincible Asia,* 1992) was directed by Tony Ching Siu-tung, and starred Jet Li, Brigitte Lin, Rosamund Kwan, Michelle Reiss (Lee), Waise Lee, Lau Shun, Chin Kar Lok, Yen Shi Kwan, Candice Yu On-on, and Fennie Yuen (that's one of the best casts in a 1990s Chinese movie). *The Swordsman 2* was a re-thinking of the first *Swordsman* movie, with the major roles being re-cast. (Others in the ensemble included: Kwok Leung Cheung, Kwok-Ping Choi, Man-Kwong Fung, Choi-Chow Hoh, Kwok-Kit Lam, Yeung-Wah Kam and Chi Yeung Wong).

Tsui Hark was producer, Chi-Wai Cheung and Wai Sum Shia were assoc. producers, Hanson Chan, Elsa Tang Pik-yin and Tsui Hark wrote the script, Tom Lau Moon-tong was DP, Marco Mak Chi-sin was editor, music was by Richard Yuen, action directors were Tony Ching Siu-tung,

Yuen Bun, Ma Yukshing, Bruce Law and Cheung Yiu-sing (plus 6 assistants), costumes: Bruce Yu Ka-on, Kwok Mei-Ling, Shiu Ching-Yee, Chan Bo-Guen, Yeung Lin-Mui and William Chang, make-up by Man Yun-Ling and Lai Ka-Pik, hair by Chau Siu-Mui and Wan Yuk-Mui, prod. des.: Yee-Fung Chung and Wah-Sang Leung, sound rec. and ed.: Kam Wing Chow.

It was produced by Film Workshop/ Long Shong Pictures/ Golden Princess. It was a big hit in Canton, with a gross of HK $34,462 million (great business for any Hong Kong movie, and one of Jet Li's biggest hits in China). Category IIB. Released on June 26, 1992. 108 mins.

The Swordsman 2 has everything – all you could desire from characters, a story, action, visuals, music and film stars. And for film critics it delivers a strong political commentary, while cultural theorists can delight in the transgender play.

Jet Li (Li Lanjie) and Brigitte Lin (Lin Ching-hsia) head up the terrific cast of *The Swordsman 2* : both have never been better, and both were at the peak of their powers. With *Once Upon a Time In China* and *The Swordsman 2*, Li established himself as a major force in Chinese cinema (*The Swordsman 2* and *Once Upon a Time In China 2*, another masterpiece, were both released in 1992). Li is at his winsome, charming best[1] in *The Swordsman 2* – yes, and he moves like a dream! He really is one of the most beautiful creatures ever put on film. (Western cinema has many male babes, pin-up stars, and great actors who're charismatic, talented and beautiful – but can they *move like that*?!).

JET LI.

Jet Li was born on April 26, 1963 in Beijing, China. (In Cantonese, Li's name is Lei Lin Git; in Mandarin, it's Li Lanjie). Li is short (5' 6"), but can take on anyone in movies. Li won the first national *wushu* competition in China since the Cultural Revolution (aged 9); he was the Chinese Men's All-round National Wushu Champion at the age of twelve. (*Wushu* is a form of martial arts as performance, combining Peking Opera, gymnastics, and colourful costumes, developed during the Cultural Revolution). Li moved to San Francisco with a Chinese actress (Huang Qiuyan) in 1988; they married (1987-90) and had two daughters. In the U.S.A., Li received his Green Card. Li later married actress Nina Li Chi (they have two daughters).

Jet Li first appeared in some movies about the Temple of Shaolin.[2] His break-out role was playing Wong Fei-hung in the *Once Upon a Time In China* series. Li appeared in several martial arts movies right after the first *Once Upon a Time In China* film, including *Tai Chi Master, New Legend of Shaolin* (about Hung Gar), the *Fong Say-yuk* films, *Last Hero In China*, and *Kung Fu Cult Master* (a.k.a. *Evil Cult*).

With Ching Siu-tung, Jet Li has appeared in the *Swordsman* films, *Hero, The Warlords, The Terracotta Warrior, The Sorcerer and the White Snake,* and *Dr Wai.*

[1] Jet Li is not serious and dour in *The Swordsman 2*, as some critics complain – he plays a drunken warrior in an appealing manner (he's introduced riding on a horse, drinking). Indeed, Li follows how Sam Hui played the character in the first *Swordsman* film.
[2] Li didn't make much money from his Shaolin pictures (he was paid a State subsidy).

BRIGITTE LIN.

Brigitte Lin is... Brigitte Lin; Lin was born in Sanchong, Taiwan on Nov 3, 1954.[3] (She is Lam Ching Hsia in Cantonese and Lin Qinhxia in Mandarin; she is also known as Venus Lin). Lin was in many Taiwanese films (beginning in 1973) before appearing in Hong Kong films such as *Zu: Warriors From the Magic Mountain, All the Wrong Spies, Police Story, Peking Opera Blues,* the *Bride With White Hair* films, the *Royal Tramp* films, *New Dragon Gate Inn,* some Wong Kar-wai films such as *Chungking Express* and *Ashes of Time,* and the *Swordsman* cycle.

Brigitte Lin is one of the most remarkable of all recent Asian stars. She 'must certainly be one of the most fearless performers in the world' (Lisa Morton, 101). Lin, tho' straight, is known for playing lesbian and crossdressing women in pictures such as *All the Wrong Spies* (a lesbian disguising herself as a guy), *Fantasy Mission Force* (she shoots the clothes off a tied-up woman), *The Swordsman 2* and *3* (she's a lesbian, transsexual superhero), *New Dragon Gate Inn* (she steals another woman's clothes for herself), *Peking Opera Blues* (she wears men's military uniforms), *Boys Are Easy* (she's a lesbian cop), *Ashes of Time* (she plays both a brother and a sister), *Eagle Shooting Heroes* (she's a butch princess), and *Fire Dragon* (she's a masked male warrior).

Brigitte Lin's crossdressing or trans-gender character in the *Swordsman* movies (as Dongfang Bubai = Asia the Invincible) draws on the Peking Opera tradition (where actors can be both warriors and princesses. Indeed, the Tsui Hark movie *Peking Opera Blues* explores issues of gender[4] at length).

Brigitte Lin, according to Bey Logan, was one of the few bankable female stars in Asia: 'basically, all the ageless Ms Lin has to do is wave her arms and smile enigmatically and local audiences will pay to watch' (166).

Tsui Hark has tried to entice Brigitte Lin back to acting – for the remake of *Zu: Warriors From the Magic Mountain,* for instance, and to play the Empress Wu in *Detective Dee and the Mystery of the Phantom Flame.* Lin retired from acting in 1994, when she married businessman Michael Ying and had children.

Brigitte Lin delivers a career high with her powerful and unforgettable turn as a human-becoming-a-god in *The Swordsman 2*, Asia the Invincible. In a cinema jammed with truly insane villains/ monsters/ crime lords and all-round psychos, Lin manages to fashion a transgendered character all of her own in the world of Hong Kong movie-making. Of course, let's not forget that the role of Asia/ Dawn was actually created by the writers and the filmmakers (plus the costume designers, the hairdressers and the make-up artists. The film won the Hong Kong Film Award for Best Costumes and Make-up). But, as directors and producers and writers know all too well, they can only go *so far* in putting a character together: because, ultimately, an actor needs to embody that character on screen.

---
[3] Some sources say 1957.
[4] Peking Opera had a huge impact on the young Tsui Hark – including the play with gender.

And Lin achieves that magnificently.5

Tsui Hark said he had the idea for the character of Asia the Invincible when he was filming *Zu: Warriors From the Magic Mountain* – it was a chara tailor-made for his friend Brigitte Lin6 (LM, 90). The character came out of Jin Yong's book, but was considerably expanded from the ten pages in the novel. Tsui told Lin not to read the book, but to read the script; he also wanted to dub her voice; Lin agreed. (However, as Tsui recalled, 'virtually everyone, including the author Jin Yong (Louis Cha) was vehementaly against' casting Lin).

After *The Swordsman 2*, the character of Dongfong Bat Baai became a popular gag in movies – and the next *Swordsman* movie acknowledged the popularity of the character, by building the entire plot around him/ her.

It's a wonderful fantasy of Imperial, political oppression – and if you're going to be oppressed, at least Asia the Invincible is charismatic and beautiful (if also insane and brutal). Brigitte Lin's Asia makes a change, too, from the usual Imperial tyrants in Chinese, historical movies, who tend to be twisted, eunuchized sickos.

✦

The Swordsman 2 also conjures kick-ass roles for the other women in the cast: the lovely Rosamund Kwan, as Ren Yingying, leader of the Miaos (taking over from Sharla Cheung in the first film), gets to wield whips and daggers with an impressive confidence (and she rips assailants to shreds, too!). Michelle Reiss/ Lee is cute, naïve, playful and charming as Yue Lingshan (Kiddo), the hero's sidekick (replacing Cecilia Yip). She's the familiar tomboy woman in Chinese cinema (and a recurring motif in Tsui Hark's films), dressing like a man, and joining the Wau Mountain Sect as one of the boys. The character of Blue Phoenix (Lan Fenghuang), played by Fennie Yuen again, is intriguing: another tomboy, who looks up to her chief, Ren Yingying (Kwan), with hints of distant, unrequited lesbian desire (tho' Blue Phoenix subsumes her emotions into the goals of her group, the Miaos).

The rest of the supporting cast of *The Swordsman 2* is very fine: Candice Yu On-on is suitably attractive and tender as Asia the Invincible's concubine Snow (a.k.a. Cici),7 adding a running commentary on the transformation of Asia from male to female (and finding Asia becoming more diva-like and difficult as the magic of the sacred scroll takes hold). Among the guys, Lau Shun, one of the great character actors of this period of Chinese cinema (who seems to have appeared in everything, and was certainly a favourite of Tsui Hark's), is superb (as always) as Swordsman Xiang Wentian (a.k.a. Zen), part of the Sun Moon Sect. Yen Shi-kwan plays the imprisoned former chief of the Miaos, Ren Woxing (a.k.a. Master Wu), with a cackling intensity. Waise Lee, another actor who is everywhere in Chinese cinema, was impressive as the *ronin* leader Fubu Qianjun (a.k.a. Hattori), who aligns himself with Dongfang Bubai.

---

5 Tsui Hark said he didn't include Asia the Invincible in the first *Swordsman* movie, because her character would've upset the balance (LM, 90).
6 Brigitte Lin as Asia may not look masculine, but her presence, her attitude and the expression of her will persuade us to accept her as male.
7 The name of one of the only two Empresses of China.

Cheung Kwok-leung was Eunuch Hong (whose fate is to be another of Asia's victims – decapitated), and Chin Kar-lok was another mad cackler, as Yuanfei Riyue (a.k.a. Saru), Hattori's henchman.

THE CRITICS.

The Swordsman 2 has everything going for it, *and then some*. The action is completely spell-binding, with the 39 year-old Tony Ching Siu-tung, the king of wire-work and flying actors and stunt people everywhere, at the top of his game.[8] Once again, one is struck by the feeling of total freedom that Ching's films as director or action choreographer possess. The sheer beauty and grace (and speed) of the movement thru the frame is gorgeous to contemplate. *The Swordsman 2* is one of Ching's finest outings – as the fantastical and exotic elements are allowed to run riot. Ching explained the approach:

> We tried something new in every action scene, like Brigitte Lin's *zhang feng* [palm power]. In other films *zhang feng* causes only an explosion, but I tried disintegrating an entire person.

Barry Long on *The Swordsman 2* noted:

> Bordering on expressionism, this contains all of the classic elements of a Tsui Hark Film Workshop production – crisp action choreography, an ensemble of A-list performers, a visual flair that is always eye-popping, and plenty of gender confusion.[9]

Lisa Morton adds:

> one of the most giddily demented films ever made... This is gonzo filmmaking, with a complexity of vision and a surety of skill that are continually jaw-dropping. (LM, 87)

Stokes and Hoover describe *The Swordsman 2* thus:

> Ching plays it over the top with Dionysian abandon, creating 'ecstatic cinema' captured by multiple cameras dramatically careening at all angles and sundry color schemes of permeating blues, reds, and browns. The wire stunts come fast and furious... (104)

THE SCRIPT.

Check out the script of *The Swordsman 2*. So often critics complain about the quality of the scripts in Hong Kong cinema, insisting that they are patchy, don't make sense, and are ignored in favour of action and spectacle. Sure, many times, yes (but you try writing scripts for five or more movies per year!).

Actually, the screenplay for *The Swordsman 2* (by Hanson Chan, Tang Pik-yin and Tsui Hark) is as neatly worked-out as any good film script: the

---
8 'The physical effects are genuinely amazing', Lisa Morton said (LM, 88).
9 Quoted in F. Dannen, 36.

structure is rock-solid, heading from an initial crisis (Asia the Invincible taking over the Sun Moon Sect), through the reactions of the Mountain Wau Sect to the problem, up to the bloodshed and multiple deaths in the finale, as everybody converges on Asia in her/ his Imperial stronghold. Like a tragic play, the narrative in *The Swordsman 2* has an unstoppable inevitability about it – a continuous descent into turmoil, you might say. The writers make sure, for instance, that the opponents and obstacles are piled up high for our heroes: not only the Imperial court, and Asia the Invincible, and the Sun Moon Sect, and Japanese ninja/ *ronin,* but even one of their own – Master Wu, Ren Woxing (who, upon his release from prison, turns out to be something of a psychopath,[10] and once Asia is (apparently) vanquished, Wu embarks on a cruel programme of elimination).

Also, the script for *The Swordsman 2* is tightly-plotted and mixes up the tempo: it's not all slambang action; not only are there character-led scenes, there are musical and nostalgic interludes, humorous scenes, and a series of seduction/ flirtation scenes. There are moments, for example, when the characters stop and reflect on what it all means, and on the passing of time. (Tsui Hark said he put all of the characters onto a white board, to work out with the production team what to do with them [LM, 90]). 'What makes *Swordsman II* a great film (instead of merely an interesting curiosity) is that the emotions are as intense as the action (and the warped morality)', remarked Lisa Morton (LM, 89).

The Swordsman 2, set in 1572, continues to use the same narrative ingredients of the first *Swordsman* movie of 1990, but the new cast and the new approach makes it feel like a different story with different characters (there are rival clans, Imperial heavies, a magical scroll, a wandering warrior and his sidekick, etc). There's no doubt that Jet Li blossomed into a huge star at this time, filling the role of the drifting, drinking warrior with a wonderful, self-deprecating humour, as well as of course the agility and grace of a dancer. As Linghu Chong, Jet Li (taking over the role from Sam Hui in the first film) is a delight from his introduction onwards (swigging at a bottle on a horse, accompanied by his sidekick, Kiddo, played with sweet charm by Michelle Reiss/ Lee. So, yes, Li is evoking another version of the drunken swordsman, a staple of many a *kung fu* flick. And that wine flask crops up repeatedly – and is also part of the flirtation scene between Linghu and Asia the Invincible – staged, with typical eccentricity, with both characters waist-deep in the sea).

The Swordsman 2 is also a companion to the first *Once Upon a Time In China* movie, released in 1991: there's a similar romance, for instance, between Jet Li and Rosamund Kwan (there's no doubting that, in this period, Li and Kwan made a gorgeous couple – and both exude a fresh-faced, rosy-cheeked innocence that only exists in movies. If people were really like this, Earth would be Heaven!).[11]

The Swordsman 2 has time for character scenes, for love scenes, for

---
10 In the jail, Master Wu reveals his nasty side when he kills five guards – and Linghu Chong remarks that it's not necessary.
11 And yet Earth *is* Heaven – we just don't realize it.

humorous scenes, and for musical scenes: there are several musical montages: music is a key component in this 1992 movie (Linghu Chong plays a *qin*, to charm Kiddo),[12] the Wau Mountain Sect sing the 'Hero of Heroes' song repeatedly round the fire, and music provides the springboard for nostalgic and poetic interludes.[13] There's even a *Count of Monte Cristo* prison sequence, when Linghu's captured by Asia the Invincible's mob, and discovers that Master Wu is chained up in the cell opposite his (with an inventive use of rats to carry messages between the cells).

STYLE AND LOOK.

Technically, *The Swordsman 2* boasts an all-round cinematic brilliance, some lavish and intricate costumes, a battery of visual and practical effects, and incredible cinematography. This is a very, very beautiful film. The lighting is truly magical, with firelight, flaming torches, moonlight, stormlight, smoke-filled nights,[14] candles and natural light deployed with absolute mastery and lyricism. The textures and atmospheres are beyond even the celebrated Hong Kong films. *The Swordsman 2* is I think one of the greatest movies to come out of Hong Kong, and certainly one of the finest movies anywhere for lighting and photography.

Look at the use of locations in the New Territories, for instance. Even tho' fans of Hong Kong cinema will have seen some of these locations before (many times, some of us! – that same beach, that same piece of cliff and rocks, that same forest, etc), DP Tom Lau Moon-tong lends them a delightfully heightened, lush look, as if China were being re-invented all over again. The ocean, forests, mountain roads, roadside inns, and Imperial palaces – *The Swordsman 2* creates a magical dream of a China that never existed (but *should* have existed!).

The extensive night shoots out-of-doors enhance the 1992 movie with atmospheric scenes lit by burning torches and campfires. You get the impression that if the electrical power was suddenly cut for the lighting rigs, the cinematographers and the sparks would find a way of lighting the entire movie using wood fires, candles and oil-fuelled torches.

The Swordsman 2 is also a giant visual effects movie, in the Hong Kong New Wave tradition of never letting the limitations of the budget hold you back. Smoke billows thru every scene (indoor or outdoor), and the air is full of leaves, fire, kicked sand, flying snakes, branches, logs, and swords. Wind machines, rain machines, smoke machines, full-body burns, explosions, pyrotechnics, optical super-impositions, special make-up, models, animation, puppetry, and of course lots of wire-work – is there a visual effect that *The Swordsman 2 doesn't* use? Not really – and yet all of the effects are deployed in the service of the story and the characters. Or

---

12 He sings a James Wong Jim song, 'Jek Gei Gam Woo Siu'.
13 Linghu Chong, with his irrepressible charisma, leads the singing of the theme song ('Xiao Hongchen') of the movie in act one, at the Mountain Wau Sect's hide-out in an inn; *The Swordsman 2* seamlessly segues into the Sun Moon Sect also singing the song, as the musicians sway, while Ren waits for Linghu's return. That's clever screenwriting.
14 By this time, Hong Kong camera and lighting crews had enough lamps and electrical power to really make outdoor night scenes work.

put it like this: *The Swordsman 2* is such a great visual effects movie because the script is solid. And most of the effects occur in front of the camera. (Again, altho' Tsui Hark is known as a master of visual effects, Tony Ching Siu-tung employs them just as brilliantly).

The Swordsman 2 is edited by Tsui Hark's regular editor, Marco Mak Chi-sin, a genius editor if ever there was one: one of the chief reasons for this movie being a masterpiece is the brilliance of the editing (which's true of many classics). Contrasts are made by cutting on visual rhymes (from one set of characters sitting around a camp fire at night to another, for example, or by cutting from one group singing a song to another). Mak doesn't simply join one scene to another: he conjures up several incredible montages – and not only poetic montages over music, but also parallel action. The most melodramatic slice of action in parallel occurs when the hero Linghu Chong is making love with Snow (Candice Yu – thinking she's Asia the Invincible), while the *real* Asia is out and about wasting all of his cohorts! Wow!

How do you portray a god or demi-god on screen? The solution in *The Swordsman 2* is inventive, to say the least. Verticality and height is emphasized – Asia the Invincible stands on top of trees,[15] or in their branches,[16] as if s/he is nature itself. When s/he talks, her voice echoes around the landscape everywhere, as if the Earth is speaking.[17] Characters are rushing upwards into the sky or the branches of a tree, or diving downwards following their swords onto an opponent, or leaping into the ground. And a vast battery of practical effects are deployed to dramatize the powers that the god-like Asia possesses.[18]

ASIA THE INVINCIBLE.

In *The Swordsman 2*, Dongfang Bubai, Asia the Invincible (sometimes called Dawn), is using the sacred scroll to achieve great power. The cost? His masculinity, his male identity – or, as Master Wu chortles, his penis – he has to castrate himself (when Wu reads the sacred scroll, he roars with laughter). There's more: the characterization of Asia the Invincible not only uses the cliché of eunuchs, he is transforming into a woman (the movie tracks the change bit by bit, so that, in the finale of *The Swordsman 2*, Asia is making himself/ herself up as a woman in front of a mirror, and his/ her voice changes (in most of the movie Asia seems to be dubbed by a male actor; halfway thru, his voice becomes hoarser, and when the change is nearly complete, it seems to be Brigitte Lin's voice). The 1992 film plays with how people perceive leaders and political power – Asia's followers notice that his/ her voice has altered, but they still follow the commands).

The Swordsman 2 is a movie where a flirting scene between the two main stars is played waist-deep in water off a sandy beach in the late

---

15 Meanwhile, Ren Yingying and Master Wu also spend time on the roof of the inn.
16 In one amazing shot, Brigitte Lin stands in the branches of a huge tree, as Dawn converses with Master Wu in the distance.
17 But Asia doesn't move her mouth in her first encounter with Linghu.
18 Using wind machines, smoke machines, special make-up, puppetry, models, optical printing, and of course wires.

afternoon. A mysterious scene, with the threat of antagonism (and violence) being put aside momentarily when Asia the Invincible finds him/ herself being instantly intrigued by this bold trespasser on his/ her realm. A scene where the anti-hero alters the weather and kills birds[19] out of the sky with his/ her new-found magical powers. A scene where the hero, in his drunken, youthful energy, spins in the air for sheer joy, flying out of the water.[20] Remarkable – it's like no other flirtation scene in cinema (especially when we know that Asia the Invincible is a demi-god, and is transforming from a man to a woman. In this scene, s/he seems to reveal herself/ himself as an attractive heterosexual prospect to Linghu Chong). And of course, the scene is performed by two of the loveliest stars in Hong Kong cinema, Brigitte Lin and Jet Li (both of whom have blurred the categories of gender, and have also played gender-bending roles). So that if the issue of homoeroticism is raised by the ruse of Asia the Invincible finding Linghu attractive, it is offset by having Asia played by a woman. So the film producers cover all bases (which they always prefer to do!).

Most of the love scenes btn Linghu Chong and Dawn the Invincible are played with Dawn staying mute, so his/ her voice doesn't give him/ herself away (it's a wry commentary on the relation between power and communication, on identity and expression, and also on gender roles – how Dawn acts the coquettish lover when s/he is still partly a man, how s/he laughs exaggeratedly, like Harpo Marx,[21] at Linghu's jokes). When Asia finally speaks to Linghu, in his/ her womanly guise, the first thing s/he says is Linghu's name.

The gender-bending in *The Swordsman 2* (which continued in the sequel of 1993, of course), fascinated Western critics. Of *The Swordsman 2,* Raymond Murray commented in *Images In the Dark:* 'the film's ultimate plot twist involves Jet spending the night in Brigette's bed, before realizing it means he's had sex with a eunuchized man!' (373). And yet, of course, he doesn't – we see Linghu Chong in a clinch with Snow (a.k.a. Cici), Dawn's lover (tho' they haven't made love for 6 months, according to Snow – that is, when Asia was still a guy). Linghu Chong is not sure – he demands that Asia tell him the truth in the finale, but s/he remains, of course, a mystery.

Men meant to be men but played by women, and vice versa, and men pretending to be women, and vice versa, and the voices of men or women being dubbed by their opposite, are staples of Chinese cinema (also drawing on the theatrical tradition of all-male troupes), but seem to titillate Western film critics. Well, there *is* a tradition in the West of men playing women's roles, which Western critics keep forgetting (the history of theatre going back to Ancient Greece, for example, where everybody, male or female, on stage was played by a guy). But in North American and Western cinema, characters that're meant to be men are almost always played by men (and vice versa). However, in Chinese cinema (and

---

19 And notice how Linghu Chong and his Mountain Wau chums don't waste those dead birds! If they fell on many places around the world, they'd be cooked immediately! And the lads do just that.
20 The phallic aspects of Linghu's delight are obvious.
21 Brigitte Lin doing Harpo Marx?! Why not?!

Japanese cinema), having women play guys, but not in a disguise or as a gender switch, is a convention.

With the *Swordsmen* movies, the fact that Brigitte Lin was doing the gender-bending added immensely to the tease for Western film critics – because Lin is a fantastically attractive woman (and also already possesses a masculine/ tomboy appeal even before she steps into men's clothes). And, in portraying three other women in strong, kick-ass roles – Michelle Reiss/ Lee, Fennie Yuen and Rosamund Kwan – *The Swordsman 2* was adding to the gender reversals (a running gag, for instance, has the boys in the Mountain Wau Sect joking about Kiddo being a woman).

◆

In act two of *The Swordsman 2*, there are seduction scenes between the hero and the heroine who's still partly the anti-hero. Linghu Chong opts to investigate Asia the Invincible's quarters (along with Swordsman Zen). This is one of several mid-film action sequences: Linghu doesn't simply sneak into Asia's palace, or knock on the front door: this is a flamboyant section of *The Swordsman 2*, involving much flitting about at night on rooftops, hanging from rafters, battling guards who erupt from underneath the ground (a classic Chingian motif), and a complex duel between Linghu and Asia the Indivisible in his/ her chambers. The editing is as nimble and swift as one of Asia's flicked needles or pebbles, and the choreography is some of the finest in a Tony Ching Siu-tung movie (notice how both characters are moving very close to the floor, never more than waist high).

To illustrate just how venal Asia the Invincible could be, Chimp (Chin Ka-lok) had already been cornered and executed earlier: Asia controls his body with a well-aimed needle at a pressure point. In a grotesque moment (which also doesn't make sense), the shape of Chimp's body is imprinted on the wall of Asia's chambers in blood (and Chimp collapses on the ground soaked in blood and very dead).

Butterflies or moths fluttering inside a paper lamp (likely a Tsui Hark addition)[22] are one of myriad details in this sequence, and in the follow-up seduction (of course, the insect is nailed by a flying needle). Yes, those flying needles do a lot of work in *The Swordsman 2*. How wonderful is Chinese cinema in being able to turn something so domestic and 'feminine' (and *small*) – embroidery and needlepoint – into fearsome weaponry which can control the victim's pressure points. (The flying needles are reprised several times in *The Swordsman 2* – during the Linghu Chong and Asia the Insatiable seduction scenes, Linghu gets entangled in the threads,[23] a terrific *femme fatale*-as-spider motif; and in the finale, Master Wu is ensnared by a battery of needles which Asia unleashes in her/ his fury.)

And yet this elaborate scene, which displays the bodies of Brigitte Lin and Jet Li in an inventive, very graceful and tangled choreography, is only one of many packed into this part of *The Swordsman 2*, which also includes a scene of Swordsman Zen versus Hattori and his guards, Linghu Chong and his cohorts in disguise as gypsies, and Linghu carrying Asia

---
22 A reference to his first film.
23 And there are playful jokes – like when Linghu tears the embroidery, so there are two dragons. (A reference to the movie *Twin Dragons*).

the Invisible away from the palace, to drink with his buddies round a fire. And in this frenetically-paced movie, there is a moment where Linghu speaks longingly of a time outside of war and politics, a time when he can just drink (these anti-war, anti-oppression interludes are a recurring motif in Tsui Hark's cinema).

(This sequence also contains one of the signature romantic motifs in *wuxia* pictures of this era: the hero and the heroine flying side by side through the tops of trees, accompanied by a lush music cue – moments that become iconic, and are tailor-made for the trailers).

WOMEN IN ACTION.

The Swordsman 2 is full of women, too: there are not one, not two, not three, but four prominent female roles in *The Swordsman 2* (plus Snow). The clever script gives them all things to do,[24] plus goals and motivations, and none of them are simply 'girlfriend of the hero', or 'stay at home mom', or 'girl next door'. *The Swordsman 2* is a movie which foregrounds women in action – as only Hong Kong action cinema can! Each actress has her own scene (actually several scenes) in which to shine: Rosamund Kwan[25] explodes flying warriors with her whip; Michelle Reiss takes on numerous swordsmen, spinning like a top; Fennie Yuen is an incredible snake-handler and martial artist;[26] and Brigitte Lin is, well, simply astounding as the demi-god Asia the Invincible.

Ah, how happy for Jet Li! – because each of the women in *The Swordsman 2* is in love or half in love with Linghu Chong. Thus, *The Swordsman 2* has not one romantic subplot, but several (Linghu has four admirers – a harem). And the 1992 film carefully tracks each of the women's feelings for Linghu – consider how the numerous looks and quips are integrated into the scenes (yet again negating the common view among critics that the scripts and dramas of Hong Kong movies are not carefully worked out). How, for ex, Kiddo looks at Linghu hugging Ren Yingying enviously, and how Blue Phoenix notices that (Fennie Yuen is great at sly smirks). The barely-suppressed jealousy is a delight to see in characters such as Ren (Kwan) and Kiddo (Reiss) as they squabble in the background over Linghu. (Kiddo, for instance, is keen to primp up herself to attract Linghu – the film includes humorous scenes where Kiddo's new hairstyle[27] causes surprise and pratfalls, and when her make-up is switched with ingredients for the soup. Kiddo's scene at the mirror depicts another gender reversal: Kiddo has been dressed as a man, and here feminizes herself with the aid of make-up and a new hairstyle. The comedy thus plays into the central theme of gender confusion).

Indeed, the love/ romance elements are no mere subplot/s in *The*

---

[24] Presumably Tsui Hark, as co-writer, had some say in bumping up the roles of the women in *The Swordsman 2*. Because it doesn't really need five women – it could get by, as many action movies do, with one or two.
[25] It's great to see Rosamund Kwan's demure Aunt Yee from *Once Upon a Time In China* as an action heroine. And she's given a whip! In one scene, she's pulling along a swordsman with her whip snagged on his foot, while he holds himself up with his sword, which sparks as it's dragged thru the dirt.
[26] 'One of the most non-traditional martial arts films ever made', opined Lisa Morton (LM 87).
[27] The buns on the side of the head are a classic, Chinese hair-do, but also might be a *Star Wars* joke.

Swordsman 2, but bear upon the main plot of clan/ political rivalry many times. Dawn the Invincible's feelings for Linghu Chong, for instance, prevent her/ him from slaying Linghu's countrymen (well, for a moment, at least!).

Jet Li and his women! – because there's another woman for Li, when Asia the Invincible coerces her lover Snow to seduce Linghu Chong (thus neatly circumventing the notion of the (apparently) straight hero of an action movie having sex with a man who's castrated himself and is transforming via magic into a woman.[28] But when that 'man'/ 'woman' is played by the incandescent Brigitte Lin, what's the problem?!).

Even more remarkable, in a movie stuffed with remarkable sequences, while Linghu Chong is taking the lovely Snow at Asia the Invincible's place, his cohorts are embroiled in to-the-death battles with Asia and his/ her crew. Yes, the action hero is having sex while everyone is getting slaughtered left, right and centre! (Thus, when the lights go out in Asia's chambers, and the switch of Asia for Snow occurs, it's not played for farce. It's an erotic scene, but played straight, because editor Marco Mak intercuts it with Asia demolishing Linghu's colleagues. Another detail in this sequence has Asia sensing what Snow is feeling, and perhaps regretting it).

ACTION SCENES.

It's pure pleasure all the way in *The Swordsman 2*: among the many delights are the action scenes. First up, in the prologue, there's a sword battle and escape in an Imperial palace, and a battle between Linghu Chong and Kiddo on a mountain trail with Asia the Invincible. The Japanese ninja-style attack on the inn is the highlight of act one of *The Swordsman 2* – it boasts a sophistication and invention with wire-work and movement beyond even 99% of Hong Kong filmmakers. Scenes where the warriors spin flying blades and then hop on them to soar into the building are simply astonishing. (Nothing in Western cinema has ever come close – right up to today).

There are many points in this 1992 Hong Kong movie which seem miraculous – as if we are witnessing the Birth of Cinema all over again. To achieve that (or even attempt it) is absolutely amazing. And this occurs many times in Hong Kong cinema. (This is not a pompous or pretentious statement: it *feels* like this is the Birth of Film because the filmmakers take such delight in their work; they are artists in their child-like mode, where making art has a significant and very appealing sense of *play*).

But then our heroes fight back with – what? – *snakes*. And that means snakes, Chinese-style! Draped all over the actors, whizzed on wires, and sliced to pieces by flying swords (in a huge cascade of snakes, in slo-mo). Blue Phoenix shines in this part of *The Swordsman 2* (check out the *physical* acting here, the rapid changes of pose as Blue Phoenix trills on her high-pitched whistle to call up the serpents. Tony Ching has a brilliant feeling for bodies in movement, and how the camera can frame and follow

---
[28] But why does castration equate with becoming a woman?!

that movement). The Japanese *shinobi* respond with scorpions – so it's scorpions vs. snakes. And Linghu Chong later takes up a scorpion and puts it in his flask of wine, to enhance the flavour – this is one of the numerous comical touches woven into the slambang action sequences in *The Swordsman 2*).

The exploitation of space in *The Swordsman 2* is also exceptional – the Chinese filmmakers use every inch of the inn, upper and lower levels, including having characters (like Kiddo) crash thru the floor, hurtle thru windows, fall from upper to lower levels, and fly up to the roof.[29] The attack on the inn continues into the forest outside, with Ren Yingying and Blue Phoenix duelling swordsmen using snakes, whips and flying swords (in *The Swordsman 2*, the participants announce their martial arts techniques before they use them, as often in swordplay films: 'Flying Sword!').

Oh, this is glorious cinema, so self-assured, so inventive – and so silly! As if being human is simply not enough for mere humans – they must be able to zoom up into the trees on cables, or disappear into holes in the ground, with their swords leaving an energy line of sparks.

The assault on Asia the Invincible's palace is another outstanding sequence: the traditional, Chinese rooms, with their veils and patterned screens, provide tight, enclosed spaces where the action choreography at times emulates lovemaking (after all, this is Linghu Chong entering Asia's chambers). The editing (by Marco Mak Chi-sin) is especially fine in this sequence, combining extreme close-ups of flying needles with shadowy rooms and partially-lit close-ups of stars Jet Li and Brigitte Lin.

The penis – the sword – the needle – the canon – so many phallic tropes; there's no need to tease out the sexual subtext in *The Swordsman 2*, because the movie deconstructs itself for your pleasure in front of your eyes. Yes, this is a movie stuffed with Freudian, castration imagery, too – guys have their heads torn off, Dawn castrates himself, and both Swordsman Zen and Hattori cut off their own arms!

In a movie which reinvents fantasy swordplay yet again, as if from scratch, and also pushes what has already been achieved in *wuxia* movies even further, the Swordsman Zen versus the Mountain Wau warriors sequence is remarkable. Zen is the lone swordsman, mysterious and super-powerful (later, he's revealed to be a member of the Highlanders who's disfigured himself to elude capture. He's played by the ever-dependable, awesomely versatile Lau Shun).

So it's one man against seven or so, including Linghu Chong, and *everyone* is flying on cables (set in, of course, a smoke-filled forest at night). This is a ballet of ferocious energy and high speed. The photography and framing is another object lesson in filmmaking, the editing and rhythms have a mesmeric flow, and it's quite, quite beautiful (and details like the spinning swords, the swords rotating around the wrists, in and out of the grasp, has the vertiginous ecstasy of Japanese animation. Yes – in Chinese action cinema, it's as if all inanimate objects

---

[29] Several characters spend time on the roof – Wu, Ren and Blue Phoenix. Indeed, roofs are a major location in many Chinese action movies – filmmakers can't resist taking the action upwards.

become alive, and the environment too is a force that can't be ignored).

In the climactic love scene in *The Swordsman 2*, where Linghu Chong arrives at Asia the Invincible's quarters and discovers that s/he has flattened many of her/ his underlings, the filmmakers orchestrate space and light with a deft, skilful ease. How, for instance, Asia rapidly douses the lamps so that s/he can slip away and have Snow stand in for her/ him in the love scene. How Linghu stands some way off, so he doesn't see Snow (she's behind the door).

Martial arts that can reverse the flow of blood, or momentarily paralyze the victim, is a recurring motif in the *Swordsman* series, and in many Hong Kong action pictures (in *The Swordsman 3: The East Is Red*, Koo has his blood flow reversed by Asia the Intractable, and in *The Swordsman 2*, Blue Phoenix immobilizes Kiddo during the massacre, so she can take on Asia alone[30]).

Not simply killed – victims are torn to pieces in *The Swordsman 2* in grotesquely over-the-top ways. In the massacre by Asia the Invincible in the outdoor, nighttime battles at the start of act three, the demi-god uses his/ her magic to shatter the survivors of the Wau Mountain Sect into pieces. Like a tragic play (and like many a Chinese action movie), the finale becomes wholesale slaughter – most of the Wau Mountain Sect are killed, Hattori is decimated by Master Wu, and Snow poisons herself (staying alive long enough to gloat at Asia when s/he returns).

The Swordsman 2 is stuffed with gross-out moments, too – not action, but pure horror: Master Wu's 'essence-absorbing' stance provides a few. Like, in his duel with Hattori, Wu withers Hattori's arm, and then shrinks his head to rubbery goo (while Hattori's headless corpse staggers about). To rejuvenate himself, in the impressive prison sequence, Master Wu sucks the life out of the guards, compressing the hapless victims down to football-size bundles of clothes. At the end of the movie, Swordsman Zen cuts off his own arm (in order to save face and not return to Master Wu empty-handed, so to speak, when he's sent to accost Linghu Chong and his chums, as they leave on a ship).

Asia the Invincible on her/ his nighttime rampage is the first part of the finale of *The Swordsman 2*, and at times bests the action sequence in the Imperial palace. It contains some thrilling duels – such as (1) Master Wu against Hattori (ending in Hattori's head being shrivelled then simply yanked off Hattori's body); (2) Blue Phoenix against the Japanese ninjas; (3) Kiddo taking on the ninjas single-handed; (4) Kiddo and Ren Yingying battling more *shinobi*; (5) Asia the Invincible as a one-woman-man army, slaughtering the Mountain Wau brothers; and (6) Blue Phoenix taking on Asia using snakes and poison.

The sequence, one of Tony Ching Siu-tung's finest as a director, is freighted with many memorable images, such as Asia the Incredible against a burning building... the Japanese ninjas riding on spinning throwing stars pursing Blue Phoenix crawling on the ground... and the Mountain Wau lads being literally ripped to shreds by Asia's magic...

---

[30] Eventually, it wears off, and Kiddo returns to the fray.

The strength of the imagery here is far more than making pretty pictures: every single camera angle and camera set-up is designed not only to express exciting action, and to tell the story (tho' that's enough), but to create mysterious, magical events.

The sequence has a powerful dramatic countdown added to it, too – Blue Phoenix has been attacked with one of Asia the Invincible's needles, and is ailing fast (despite managing to halt the damage temporarily using pressure points). So there's a girl to save on top of everything else. (This is a reprise of the scene where Linghu Chong was poisoned in the first film.) Incredibly, Blue Phoenix has enough strength to attack Asia the Inflexible with a flying snake; when that doesn't work, she simply eats a snake and spits the poison back at Asia.

Yet *The Swordsman 2* is *not* wall-to-wall action in the finale (tho' it feels like that). In fact, there is a touching scene where Linghu Chong and his pals bury their Mountain Wau colleagues in graves (in pouring rain, of course). Linghu scratches their names on the wooden posts. Kiddo hurries back to the grave of her horse, where she left her sword, now determined to have her revenge on Asia the Invincible.

Most action-adventure movies don't have time for lengthy burial scenes – often it's just three shots lasting four seconds each for maybe two of the main characters, and then we're back to the rushing around, the yelling, the motorcycles and the explosions.

The Swordsman 2 also has time in the final act for a key scene, also between Master Wu and Linghu Chong: beside a bonfire at night they discuss the sacred scroll. Linghu is stunned to discover that to master the magic you have to lose your penis; Wu, of course, continues to laugh and laugh. (Linghu is also confused now about just who – or what – he had sex with at Asia's digs[31]).

✦

The second half of the finale of *The Swordsman 2* is set back in the Imperial palace at Black Cliffs, with Asia the Invincible single-handedly taking on the heroes. Among the many, many fantastic gags in this sequence is one where, having launched a spinning, flaming cauldron at the heroes, Asia simply turns back to work on his/ her embroidery! It's very seldom you see the master villain in any action movie doing some needlework[32] right in the middle of a giant action scene! S/he sits there and ruminates pensively in voiceover, as if it's a sleepy afternoon of falling cherry blossom, while our heroes battle balls of fire in the air (once again, Linghu Chong rushes to Kiddo's aid).

The finale of *The Swordsman 2* features a vast battery of props that're spinning, flying and exploding across the screen – cauldrons, hooks, needles, wooden pergolas, even whole buildings. Linghu Chong of course attacks first (Jet Li is the star, after all), and manages to wound Asia the Invincible; s/he responds with multiple flying needles, as each of the heroes launches themselves at her/ him. Master Wu's life essence

---
[31] If this was a Wong Jing or Stephen Chow movie, that part of the plot would be much cruder!
[32] One of her needles wraps around Linghu's sword and pierces it.

absorbing skill is used on Asia the Invincible repeatedly, until blood gushes out from the sword wound made by Linghu (as weapons, in an inventive touch, he brings along the metal hooks that Asia used to string him up in prison. But Asia is able to stop them with her/ his flying needles).

The battle includes almost every gag and stunt you can think of, yet the psychodrama isn't forgotten (as when Asia the Invincible foxily lets slip that s/he and Linghu Chong have had sex – much to the distress and outrage of both Ren Yingying and Kiddo fighting alongside Linghu. They make catty remarks about it during the tussle). The action continues up onto a building at the end of the court, which crumbles and crashes down a cliff, topped by several more flying gags, where Linghu can't help saving Asia, even though s/he's killed his comrades (he also rescues Kiddo and Ren).

✦

Serious points are made in *The Swordsman 2*, even tho' this is very much a popcorn movie. For instance, at the end, Master Wu becomes the guy sitting on the throne in the Black Cliffs Imperial palace,[33] replacing Asia the Invincible. And what does he do? Only order the ruthless annihilation of anyone who opposes him.[34] And he cackles like a madman while heads are rolling and blood's splashing up the palace walls. So, yes, you replace one brutal head of government (Dawn the Invincible) with another (Master Wu) and, for the populace, and the law, and the nation, what's the difference? (That *The Swordsman 2* is making political comments about modern China seems obvious – but they are there if you want to take them up. After all, the background context of *The Swordsman 2* is the struggle for power in a nation riven by conflicts between warring groups. The vaguely historical context includes references to the Maindlanders, the Highlanders, and the Japanese ninjas brought in to help the Sun Moon Sect. References to the brutality of the Chinese government resonate throughout 1990s Hong Kong cinema, and to events such as Tiananmen Square).

The pursuit of Master Wu's new regime continues to a harbour, where Linghu Chong and Kiddo are preparing to leave (Ren Yingying suggests they find sanctuary for a while in Japan; she remains in China, opting to stay loyal to her father, even tho' he's turned out to be a psychotic tyrant). Zen the Swordsman is sent to bring back Linghu, giving us an unexpected final swordfight on the boat and the dockside. It's here that Zen slices off his arm, so he can return to Master Wu severely injured (and this's after he's already disfigured his face!).[35]

All of which ties up the plots so that the heroes can sail off into the sunset on a ship amidst drifting smoke and the final reprise of the heroic song, 'Hero of Heroes' (Ren Yingying watches from the harbour then a beach; the 1992 film cuts back repeatedly between her and Kiddo and Linghu Chong on the boat, underlining the poignant motif of departure and change, a recurring theme in Chinese cinema).

33 Seen in a low angle shot which tracks into an ugly close-up.
34 Most of the victims (who appear on a list, including Linghu's name), are youngish types – which we can take to refer to students and radicals in modern China.
35 But, as he puts it, he can't fight, can he, with his sword arm amputated?

The Swordsman 2 also performs the familiar work of re-setting the characters back to their default positions: now it's Linghu Chong and his companion Kiddo on their travels again, which's how they were introduced 105 minutes ago. So they're ready for a new set of adventures in the next movie (except *The Swordsman 3* decided to take a different approach, and dispensed with Linghu Chong and Kiddo altogether).

3

THE SWORDSMAN 3: THE EAST IS RED

Dung Fong Bat Baai 2 – Fung Wan Joi Hei

Move over Supergirl. Your days are numbered Wonder Woman. Asia the Invincible, the first transsexual lesbian superhero is now the reigning queen! This spectacular *kung fu* fantasy is 95 minutes of non-stop action featuring awesome special effects and enough flailing bodies and exhilarating fight sequences to keep any fan of the genre enthralled.

Raymond Murray, *Images In the Dark* (373)

The Swordsman 3: The East Is Red[36] (1993, *Dongfang Bùbài – Fengyún Zàiqi* in Mandarin = *Invisible Asia 3: Turbulence Again Rises*), was directed by Tony Ching Siu-tung and Raymond Lee Wai-man, co-written by Tsui Hark, Charcoal Tan and Roy Szeto Chak-Hon, produced by Tsui and Lau Jou for Film Workshop/ Long Shong Pictures/ Golden Princess, and crewed by many of the same people who made *The Swordsman 2* or who were regulars in Tsui's movies of the era, including: music: William Hu and Woo Wai Laap, DP: Tom Lau Moon-tong, editing: Chun Yu and Keung Chuen-tak, set dec.: Chung-Sum Lam, art dir.: Eddie Ma Poon-Chiu, costumes:[37] Kwok-Sun Chiu, William Chang Suk-Ping, Chan Sau-Ming and Pat Tang Yu-Hiu, make-up: Hon-Wan Tung and Chan Kok-Hong, hair: Jane Kwan Yuk-Chan (and 4 others), sound mixers: Wai-Luen Cheng and Kam Wing Chow, and action directors Ma Yuk-shing, Tony Ching and Dion Lam

---

[36] Fans and critics often refer to *The Swordsman 3* as *The East Is Red.* The title comes from an opera written during the Cultural Revolution. And *The East Is Red* is the title of a 1965 movie (directed by Wang Ping).
[37] The costumes in *The Swordsman 3* are outstanding: Kwok-Sun Chiu, William Chang Suk-Ping, Chan Sau-Ming and Pat Tang Yu-Hiu designed the wardrobe. With several Hong Kong stars to dress up, the costume dept go to town with colour and shape (plenty of loose robes for the stars, so they can float in Tony Ching's customary slow motion, aerial scenes).

Dik-On. Category II. Released on Jan 21, 1993 (a Chinese New Year release).[38] 93 minutes.

Swordsman 3 fared less well at the Canton box office (with HK $11.248 million) than *The Swordsman 2* (and it is, in the end, a lesser movie than *The Swordsman 2*, and, in a way, it's a side-story, focussing mainly on Asia the Invincible).[39]

The production of *The Swordsman 3* was 'chaos', Tsui Hark recalled, 'because we ran out of people, we ran out of actors'. Everybody seemed to be working on at least one other movie simultaneously (Tony Ching was working on two other flicks, and Brigitte Lin was shooting another film). Consequently, the picture writes and shoots around actors such as Lin who weren't always available (as well as using doubles, etc). Thus, by now in the *Swordsman* franchise Asia the Invincible has a feared reputation, so s/he can be referred to in dialogue but not seen, because the audience knows that character. And instead of the 'original' Asia, we now have impostors.

As Tsui Hark recalled, it was the backers who asked for a third helping of the *Swordsman* (because, yes, sequels and franchises are originated and orchestrated by studios and financers, not writers and directors, in the East as in the West. Sequels are usually produced in order to make money). Tsui thought he was done already with the *Swordsman* world, and with the character of Asia the Invincible (and s/he seemed to have died. However, a high fall doesn't always mean instant death in Movieland – there's no shot of Asia dead on the ground (or in pieces) in the second *Swordsman* film).

So coming up with a story for a third *Swordsman* flick required some finagling with the mechanics of the narrative: Tsui Hark and his co-writers Charcoal Tan and Roy Szeto Chak-Hon opted for a 'Death of the Costumed Swordplay Movie' concept, in which everybody is trying to cash in on the mythical status of Asia, copying her/ him (a sly dig at the rip-off ethic of the film industry in Canton, and actors playing the same role in multiple movies. The *Swordsman* movies had their own cash-in films, of course, as any box office hit does – in the West as in the East).

The Swordsman 3 is built around the usual three-act model of most Hong Kong movies (which fits an 80-to-90-minute picture). However, the problems in making the film are obvious: it really only has enough decent material for two acts (also, the film recycles both previous *Swordsman* movies in order to bump up its running time). It might've been more honest to deliver a 60-minute movie, but for a theatrical release in Canton and East Asia, that wouldn't satisfy the audience. Several of the great Walt Disney movies are a shade over 60 or 70 minutes. But audiences expect more from a live-action feature.

The Swordsman 3 is a kind of cruder, exploitative version of the previous *Swordsman* movies and of the swordplay genre: it's got sleazy scenes with hookers, gory violence, and gratuitous lesbian scenes.

---

38 To make that release date, *The Swordsman 3* would have been filming not long after the release of the second *Swordsman* movie, in June, 1992.
39 The name Dongfong Bat Baai is on everybody's lips – they repeat it all the time.

The Swordsman 3 lacks a strong story to tell: there isn't an overarching plot which compels the viewer – or compels the characters. For example, what is at stake isn't clearly defined: in *The Swordsman 2*, Asia the Incredible is a major threat because he/ she's destabilizing part of China, breaking up the clans, and ruling with a iron fist.[40] In the first *Swordsman* film, we had the brutal Eastern branch of the Imperial forces, among other villains, intent on demolishing the Sun Moon Sect.

In *The Swordsman 3*, Asia the Inconsolable seems more interested in pretending to be one of the girls in a brothel, or lording it over former lovers (like Snow), or pursuing her/ his impostors (like a multi-national corporation hunting down copyright theft and licensing pirates).

✦

Brigitte Lin Ching-hsia was back as the great, wild, unpredictable and very dangerous Dongfong Bat Baai (who else could it be?!); Joey Wong Cho-yin played Xue Qianxun (Snow), Asia's former lover (the Cici role in the 2nd film, played by Candice Yu On-on), and now an Invincible Asia impostor (and leader of the Sun Moon Sect; however, Snow poisoned herself in *The Swordsman II*); Yu Rongguang was Gu Changfeng (General Koo), the government official tasked with discovering what really happened with Asia the Nasty years ago (he's not a replacement for Linghu Chong, tho' Koo is the main male role in *The Swordsman 3*). The rest of the cast included Lau Shun (playing Asia the Crossdresser in her/ his aged guise, whom we meet first),[41] Eddy Ko (the Chief from *We're Going To Eat You*, and one of the leads in Tony Ching's first directorial effort, *Duel To the Death*), Jean Wang, Lee Ka-ting, Dion Lam Dik-On, Lau Chi-Ming and Kingdom Yuen.

Yu Rongguang (b. 1958), a Peking Opera performer and former martial arts boxer, is I reckon a very fine actor, looks great, moves well, and is often overlooked in accounts of this period of Chinese cinema (where he's overshadowed by stars such as Jet Li, both Tony Leungs, Sammo Hung, Sam Hui, Andy Lau, Chow Yun-fat and Jackie Chan). But in movies such as *Iron Monkey, The Terracotta Warrior, Supercop 2, Rock 'n' Roll Cop* and *My Father Is a Hero,* Yu is a strong leading man, as well as a suitably cruel villain (however, in *The Swordsman 3*, Yu has the tough job of following Jet Li – as with Vincent Zhao in the later *Once Upon a Time In China* movies, that proves a challenge).

Yu Rongguang trained in Peking Opera performance (in Beijing – he is a Mandarin speaker). He had already appeared in movies and TV before starring in Tsui Hark productions; he was the lead in *The Terracotta Warrior*, directed by Tony Ching. Later, he moved into producing and directing.

✦

The principal charas in *The Swordsman 3: The East Is Red* are General Koo and Asia the Incontrovertible, Snow (Asia's lover), and Dai (Snow's lover) – with Koo hoping to humanize Asia (good luck with that!), trying to tame him/ her (or at least to stop her/ him childishly, selfishly, and

---
40 A fist clutching needles and colourful threads, though.
41 In the credits, Shun is known as 'Warden of the Holy Altar'.

rather pointlessly wasting anyone who gets in her/ his way). Yet the 1993 movie wrongfoots the audience with regard to Koo – introducing him as the hero (as he leads the band of Spaniards to Asia's resting place in act one), where the real emphasis is on Asia, Snow and Dai.

The Swordsman 3: The East Is Red is a reworking of the *Swordsman*'s themes and elements: this time General Koo takes up the role of the Swordsman Linghu Chong, tho' his government official is a departure from the conception of the character in the previous movies (and in Jin Yong's stories). Koo doesn't joke around, or drink, like Linghu, for instance, and he's not a heroic swordsman, he's a government employee. Gone too is some of the rivalry between the clans and groups (tho' the Sun Moon Sect is back – and up to their usual decadent antics, with a harsh leader – Snow). And most of the characters from *The Swordsman 2* have been ditched, too, with the focus now on Asia the Insatiable and her/ his clones.

The Swordsman 3: The East Is Red politicizes the myths and legends of the *jiangzhu* by including Spanish conquistadors in the mix, as well as the Japanese military (in the form of samurai and ninja), and referencing attacks from the Dutch Navy (a caption says the film is set in 1595). Thus, once again it seems as if the adventures of swordsmen and beautiful but deadly semi-demons are being presented within a quasi-historical context which refers to the formation of early, modern China in amongst international forces (Japan and Russia on one side, and Europe on the other).

The foreigners are sent up, as usual in a Hong Kong movie (and especially in a Tsui Hark's production): the Japanese are portrayed as humourless – they go to sea dressed in full samurai armour, clad all in black. Their fiendishly clever inventions (flying ninja, a submarine) are no match for Ancient Chinese magic. And their samurai leader is a midget. The Spaniards are fools who don't understand the language, trailing along their witch doctor, the Catholic priest to cleanse the land.

The prologue recycles the climactic ending of *The Swordsman 2* for three or so minutes (helping to bump up the running time of this troubled second sequel): from *The Swordsman 2,* we see Asia the Invincible battling our heroes at the Black Cliffs palace, and Asia falling to her/ his doom. Notice a glaring omission from the recycled footage: no close-ups of Jet Li whatsoever (even tho' he was the most prominent chara in the finale of film two); it would mislead the audience. Sorry, there's no Jet Li in this movie, folks! (This film was released in Jan, '93, seven months after *The Swordsman 2*).

General Koo and his Chinese buddies Ling and Hon Chin (Eddy Ko), for instance, arrive with the Spanish contingent on their ship (and we know that the Spaniards are after something different from the Chinese). The opening sequence takes us 23 years[42] after the end of *The Swordsman 2*), with our heroes landing at the mysterious, foreboding Black Cliffs (where, the last time we saw Asia the Inalienable, s/he was leaping to her/ his ruin). The Spaniards have brought along a Christian priest in order to exorcise

---

42 Or is it 100 years? Or is it 4 months?

the evil land of China – but of course European Catholicism is no match for Oriental magic! So Asia the Unwastable is soon breaking loose from her/ his grave (appearing first as a wizened, slightly sinister woman with wild, white hair, played by the ever-amazing Lau Shun – Lau went from playing the evil, Imperial eunuch in film one to the disfigured warrior Zen in film two to the aged Asia in film three!), before the reveal of Brigitte Lin Ching-hsia in all her glory, as a rubber mask is tossed away – another bit of Chinese Opera business. Asia also dispenses with his/ her silly white fright wig).

Thus, as Asia the Invincible is now one of the two main protagonists, she/ he is given goals to achieve and things to do: when General Koo informs her/ him that there are folk going about impersonating her/ him and debasing her/ him image, s/he flies into a rage, and vows to wipe them out (Koo's sensible pleas of 'no more killing' we know are not going to last long!). Wow! – Asia is a true diva, flying off the handle at the slightest slight (in this pumped-up sort of movie, everything is played at a hysterical level, from the performances of the actors to the visual effects, the costumes and the action). 'One of the most outrageous examinations of feminine power ever committed to film' (Lisa Morton, 99-100).

The introduction of the existence of the fake Asia the Invincibles is a clever gimmick to exploit the now-popular character with multiple versions (as well as playing to Asia's vanity, her/ his hunger for power, and ensuring that Asia's journey back from the wilderness to the centre of the story has some dramatic weight behind it. And it also solves the scheduling issues – if Brigitte Lin isn't always available, other actors can play one of the impostors).

It's a narrative hook that works well enough as a means of stirring up some conflict between the groups – the Chinese, the Spaniards, the Japanese, and the rivals (the Spanish declare that they too are seeking the sacred scroll).

The first Asia-as-impostor sequence features Snow and her Sun Moon Sect cohorts on a ship at sea being attacked by Thunder and his Japanese crew: the scenes of two ships shelling each other, one of the staples of the pirate genre are, in the hands of this group of filmmakers, merely one element in a panoply of visual effects, tricks, stunts and gags – including Japanese ninjas on flying kites, multiple sword fights, the Nipponese vessel turning into a submarine, and Joey Wong going into battle as Snow at her huffiest and fiercest.

Another Asia-impostor sequence (we're still in act one!) has Asia the Indescribable and General Koo weightlessly travelling to a forest where a more primitive, tribal form of ritual and worship is taking place (wild dancing, a roaring fire, ethnic masks, a mad mob, and sacrificial victims who are happy to be burnt as offerings to the deity Asia). Poor Koo isn't able to stand in the way of the real Asia's rage at these heathens (how *dare* they worship a fake Asia?!) – which extends to blasting out the hearts of the soldiers ranged against him/ her (one of numerous *ugghh* moments in the *Swordsman* series – including the willing sacrificial victim having *her* heart yanked out by the head priest). This ridiculous scene, which tops act one of *The Swordsman 3*, is a return of the horror genre for Tony Ching and Tsui Hark, but played for gruesome fun, like the haunted house in the funfair.[43]

✦

So much for the background story of *The Swordsman 3: The East Is Red* – this is 'ecstatic cinema', remember, and traditional/ conventional elements such as 'character' and 'story' and 'theme' are only part of the mix! Yes – because this is an action-adventure movie directed by Tony Ching Siu-tung and Raymond Lee, and it's produced by Tsui Hark, and it's stuffed with action.

Among the numerous ecstasies in *The Swordsman 3: The East Is Red* are the many scenes filmed at sea. This is a maritime version of a *wuxia pian* (it's really a pirate movie in many respects), with ships blasting away at each other, fights in the rigging, stunt people flying about on ropes, masts toppling, and many other of the expected gags in a pirate or sea-based adventure movie (much of the *Once Upon a Time In China* series occurs at harbours – border zones between China and the rest of the world, and also stages fights on ships). But, this being Hong Kong cinema, there are all sorts of eccentric elements added to the mix, like: flying needles; like: Japanese ninja flying from ship to ship on flags like kites; like: fighters holding up cannons in one arm and firing them; like: Asia the Invincible riding a swordfish[44] (!); like: Asia the Inviolable collecting all of the bullets fired by the Spaniards in the air, and flicking them back, to kill them (another version of Chinese using traditional means (i.e., magic), to trump the *gweilo* invaders with their guns and bullets); like: ships running aground and also flying; like: a ship turning into a wooden submarine (yes, of course it's the fiendishly tech-minded Japanese who pull off this trick! This outrageous gag is likely a Tsui Hark idea).

For this version of swordplay-meets-pirates-meets-*kung-fu*-meets-fantasy, the filmmakers have procured some full-size boats (as well as the usual models and scaled-down sets).[45] Filming models on water is a giveaway of scale, of course, so inter-cutting with full-size sets helps a lot. [46]

The sequence where Asia the Invincible in her/ his furious god-like persona attacks Snow and her ship is simply extraordinary – the filmmakers create enormous explosions of water,[47] and place Asia rising up out of the sea on a swordfish, unleashing waves of energy (with the screen filled with sparkling, back-lit waterdrops). And all of this is filmed at night. [48]

It's like seeing a Las Vegas show combined with a Disney theme park

---
[43] Or the second *Indiana Jones* movie.
[44] Almost certainly Tsui Hark's idea – like a stag, of all things, popping as the wise oracle in *Detective Dee*.
[45] The filmmakers happily have some grips manhandling a scale model ship in front of cliffs or against the sky, to stand in for the full-scale vessels they haven't got. Orson Welles did that in *Othello* (1952).
[46] The budget is still stretched, here, though it thankfully doesn't resort to the Hollywood approach of filming boat scenes in the studio, against either panoramas or green screens.
[47] First seen in *The Swordsman*, but here taken to extravagant heights. In one extraordinary shot, water explodes around the whole perimeter of the ship.
[48] This would've be a tough series of nights for everyone involved. Logistically, these scenes are very challenging.

show combined with a Japanese *manga* brought to life. Again and again, Hong Kong cinema reminds us that *anything is possible*.[49] Well, at least in movies it is!

The Swordsman 3 contains action which 'makes John Woo's *The Killer* seem like a Bergman opus', according to Raymond Murray (*Images In the Dark*, 373). 'One of the most audacious works of genius in the history of the fantasy film' (Lisa Morton, 98). '*Swordsman* is a mad, muddled and marvellous 90s update of *wuxia* films', said Stephen Teo (199).

And seeing Brigitte Lin Ching-hsia let rip as a one-womany army is worth the price of admission alone: despite the 1993 movie not fitting together narratively, or thematically, or dramatically, it features some wonderful scenes. Like Joey Wong, Lin's screen persona in many movies is of a gentle, intelligent and somewhat enigmatic actress. But Lin convinces as an arrogant, ultra-violent tyrant (partly because, as with Wong, the contrast is so extreme, and what Lin gets to do is so over-the-top. Similarly, the pert, winsome, rosy-cheeked Rosamund Kwan is dressed in dominatrix black in the *Swordsman* movies and wields a whip).

The mad laugh, the scornful looks, the sudden switches in emotion – Brigitte Lin Ching-hsia has movie villain-dom down pat. And when s/he's standing proudly on the arm of the mast, sweeping her/ his robes to one side, looking down on everyone, Lin's Asia the Infrangible is a memorable image, an Errol Flynn or Burt Lancaster pirate gone very, very bad. Even the *Pirates of the Caribbean* films, much as we love them, with their state-of-the-art visual effects and colossal, 200 million dollar budgets (probably 100 times what *The Swordsman 3* cost), couldn't match this.

✦

For beauty, *The Swordsman 3: The East Is Red* boasts two of the great faces of recent Chinese cinema: Brigitte Lin Ching-hsia and Joey Wong Cho-yin. The filmmakers shamelessly exploit the sexual heat that their starlets generate, too, by putting them together physically as lovers. Both are women impersonating men (Wong's Snow, now pretending to be Asia), or sort-of-women that were once men (Lin's Asia). That Snow is pretending to be Asia the Invincible complicates the erotic subterfuge (and her lover Dai turns out to be a guy) – this is the kind of thing that makes postmodern critics go ga-ga. Gender-bending, transgender and lesbianism – all in one scene! *Sooo* postmodern! *Sooo* radical! Oooh, *sooo* transgressive!

It's staged as a flashback for Snow (a.k.a. Xue Qianxun), who has never stopped loving Asia the Invincible (Snow reprises the role of Cici in the 2nd *Swordsman* picture), when Asia was Dongfong Bat Baai, it seems (i.e., a man). It's intercut with Snow and *her* lover, Dai, in another lesbian, opium-sweet clinch. But on screen we see Joey Wong and Brigitte Lin (and Jean Wang) kissing, sharing opium on their tongues, and pouring wine into each other's mouths (in one of those luxurious boudoir settings, complete with painted screens and candles, exquisitely lit by DP Tom Lau Moon-tong – not forgetting the make-up by Hon-Wan Tung and Chan Kok-Hong,

---

[49] Lisa Morton speaks, *pace The Swordsman II*, of 'the dizzying idea that human beings are capable of anything, whether it's flying or changing sex at will' (LM, 88).

the costumes by William Chang Suk-Ping and others, and the hair by Jane Kwan Yuk-Chan and others. The colours in the boudoir setting are of course red and gold). The camera lingers over the faces of Lin and Wong, and Wong and Wang, in giant, glowing, back-lit close-ups... by Ganesh, these are fantastically beautiful people!

The romantic subplot of *The Swordsman 3* pays off in several ways. For a start, it is one of the few things that can humanize or redeem Asia the Inestimable (tho' not in the end!), it reminds the characters that there are other things at work and worth fighting for/ living for than taking over China as a demi-god, and of course it provides the eye candy of Joey Wong and Brigitte Lin in a Lesbian Kiss Scene, and Joey Wong and Jean Wang in *another* Lesbian Kiss Scene.

Having Joey Wong Cho-yin playing a jilted lover, a spurned and hurt lover, works perfectly (tho' Asia the Inexpiable isn't going to be sucked into a guilt trip! If anyone's going to be ladling out guilt, it's Asia). It plays to Wong's strengths, too, as an actress (Wong can evoke the pain of love perfectly – she can sulk and huff and pout at an Olympic Games level. Wong is terrific in *The Swordsman 3* – her screen persona is so æthereal and gentle, it makes a striking and appealing contrast when she lets fly as a tyrant). And it works well too because this side of Snow's personality is introduced *after* she was depicted as the brutal leader of the Sun Moon Sect (where her followers see her as a man. Once again, there's an important political point being made when Snow is revealed to be a woman, and the soldiers realize they've been ruled by an impostor. Yes, your leaders are never quite what you thought!).

But for an impostor of Asia the Indivisible, Snow is doing pretty well. She has many aspects of Asia down pat: the needles-as-weapons *kung fu*, the imperious, impatient, declaiming tones, the kingly demeanour, and even a devoted concubine. (Unfortunately, Dai the concubine turns out to be a Japanese ninja in disguise – his/ her face's ripped off as a mask, revealing an ugly, middle-aged guy who's near-naked in a loincloth. Snow is, naturally, *very* enraged, and their duel, filmed amid the upper levels of the Sun Moon Sect vessel at night, and then out onto the ocean, is one of the highlights of *The Swordsman 3: The East Is Red*. It includes remarkable images such as Snow flying in slo-mo against a giant, full moon, while slicing the air with her/ his sword, and conjuring explosions out of the ocean. Like the real Asia, when Snow is crossed in love, she is *very* disgruntled!).

Two women, one man – *The Swordsman 3* again turns the tables, gender-wise, and also adds a hysterical, sadomasochistic vibe, so that Snow offers her life to Asia the Indefectible when Asia's fury is unleashed when s/he finds out that Snow has been posing as her/ him, and Koo, who seems to be the hero (and casting Yu Rongguang suggests that), becomes dangerously obsessive.

In keeping with Tsui Hark's ambition to make a 'Last Of' movie (the Last Swordplay Film, the Last Costume Epic, etc), there's a raw, apocalyptic atmosphere to *The Swordsman 3*, which's expressed in the high energy, the multiple deaths, the insanity. (Tsui would take this martial-arts-movie-as-apocalypse even further two years later with *The Blade*).

◆

In its third and final act, *The Swordsman 3: The East Is Red* loses its way somewhat, narratively. There are several sequences which don't do justice to the premise and the themes (or the characterizations), or the goodwill that the *Swordsman* series has generated thus far (for the audience) – so that, when the final smackdown occurs (as we all know it will!), it lacks the full dramatic resonance (altho' it *is* extremely spectacular).

For instance, following the superb dust-up between Asia the Indivisible and Snow (where Snow comes off worst, as expected), the filmmakers spend maybe too much time with scenes that meander a little – like General Koo and his cohorts in a mutinous face-off with the Sun Moon Sect crew on the ship, or arguing amongst themselves, or taking care of an ailing Snow and escaping on the ship's sail like a kite, and later a wooden raft. (Some of these scenes are simply not very gripping: like, the Spanish ships approach the Sun Moon Sect's vessel, but after shelling them, they sort of vanish. Like, the scene where Koo and Snow bond on the makeshift raft runs on too long, and doesn't contain enough dramatic juice).

However, what happens is truly unexpected: the 1993 movie lurches drunkenly into a side alley marked 'Crazy-Weird' (which in Hong Kong cinema is not a tiny alley, of course, but a very wide boulevard lined with neon-drenched skyscrapers and monsters). We follow Asia the Indefinable into, of all places, a harem of prostitutes who serve a military encampment:[50] this is Asia wondering what it's like to be ordinary and human. He/ she impersonates a mysterious woman who joins the camp – the narrative of *The Swordsman 3* is undergoing lots of sudden narrative jumps which don't quite make sense.[51] How, for example, Asia wants to be regarded as just one of the girls, only to immediately subvert that by being antsy and sly and ruthless (s/he just can't help him/ herself taking command of any situation. No one is going to boss Asia around, and Asia simply has to control everything).

So there are scenes where Asia the Inequable challenges the Japanese visitors (including the midget samurai leader, Thunder) to a deadly dice game (where the stake is losing your legs! – very Tsui Hark), and also allowing her/ himself to be captured and imprisoned (and in jail, apparently, Asia realizes that to be an ordinary human sucks just as much as being a demi-god. Anyway, we don't *want* to see Asia as an 'ordinary' person!).[52]

On the plus side, this part of *The Swordsman 3: The East Is Red*

---

[50] The setting of the military encampment at night is skilfully portrayed – it's striking how much time we viewers spend out of doors, at night, where it's always breezy, and a half or full moon shines, amongst campfires, and drinking, carousing soldiers.
[51] The flow of scenes judders a little, suggesting that scenes were curtailed or left out.
[52] But has Asia forgotten what it felt like to be human? Well, it has been a long time since s/he was human!

allows Brigitte Lin Ching-hsia to go all-out with the characterization of Invincible Dawn. And Lin rises to the challenge, turning Asia the Incalculable into an unpredictable force of nature – you don't know what he/ she is going to do next. For instance, nobody would guess that Asia would turn all homey and cosy and folky, when s/he picks up a *pipa* (lute) and sits by the campfire to sing a song (and the movie turns into an MTV pop promo for a minute or two, lit by flickering light, as the whores gather round to wonder who this amazing new recruit could be. It's nothing out of the ordinary, tho', for a Hong Kong movie to include several musical montages).

As wayward as the brothel sequence is, though, Brigitte Lin Ching-hsia looks as if she is enjoying herself here – this is Lin at her most arrogant, cunning, catty and teasing. The scenes where Lin pretends to laugh along with the hookers, or to be best friends and all girls together, are funny but also scary – we've already seen Asia the Intolerable literally tearing people apart in the Highlanders ritual scene. (The brothel madam (Kingdom Yuen) is rightly suspicious of Asia, but when she sees the newbie getting the better of the rough, demanding men, she warms to her/ him).

◆

Meanwhile, the writers – Tan, Szeto and Tsui – struggle to find new obstacles/ complications to the *Swordsman* plot and themes: anyone can spot what *The Swordsman 3* desperately lacks: a strong central plot which'll tie all of the characters together. Or to put it in simpler terms: the screenwriters didn't have a satisfying ending.

So the authors return to the concept of multiple impostor Asia the Invincibles. Thus, now the commander of the encampment, General Tin Kai-wan (an overblown performance by Lee Ka-ting), is also having delusions of grandeur, imagining himself to be another Asia the Invincible (and having his concubines dressed up as a bunch of little Asias in red – this's where *The Swordsman 3: The East Is Red* derails itself in digressions that don't really go anywhere, and also repeat what we've already seen. Yes, it's a *second* encampment of hookers! With a similar atmosphere of drunk, out-of-control guys lurching about, ogling the prostitutes dressed as their arch enemy).

This part of *The Swordsman 3: The East Is Red* becomes Chaos Night, Topsy-Turvy Time, when things go just a little crazeee – so that even General Koo is taken over the mood of power-madness. Generals Tin and Koo are soon coming to blows as they fight over the beautiful Snow. Yes, Koo has brought Snow along with him (and his faithful aide Chin). Just by lying there looking coy and superior, and by being luscious, Snow seems to cause trouble – Tin is besotted.

The duels between Koo and Tin are deftly portrayed – using one of the staples of historical, Hong Kong movies, a tall, wooden tower, just the thing for aerial combat. So once again it's night, it's smoke, it's fire, it's weightless action on wires and flailing swords.

And the action keeps coming: in the military camp scenes Snow has her moment of glory when she teases and bests the Japanese commander, Thunder, who's revealed to be a tiny imp.

The military camp sequence is a kind of free-for-all, narratively, so that anyone who has an idea for something that Snow, or Tin, or Koo could do gets their idea put in the film. Like, one of the make-up girls suggests: what if Snow arrogantly teases General Tin, like she did with Shogun Thunder? Or, one of the sparks comes up with this nugget: how about General Koo waking from delirium to discover General Tin banging a gong (!) up on the look-out tower, while Snow lolls about on his lap?

The introduction of so many narrative sidetrackings and artificial conflicts weakens *The Swordsman 3: The East Is Red* considerably in its last half-hour. Whereas *The Swordsman 2* had a tightly-controlled narrative that managed to keep the primary plot in focus as well as giving the large ensemble cast interesting (and spectacular) things to do – all the way to the Grand Finish – *The Swordsman 3* stumbles and staggers. It veers off into swordplay btn Generals Koo and Tin, into Snow horsing around with Tin (just to spite Koo, perhaps – but also because Snow remains the masochistic devotee of Asia the Unobtainable to the very end. Indeed, the filmmakers have retained Snow as a character to embody what Asia has lost – love, humanity, etc. Snow becomes the precious beauty in life which Asia has cast aside in his/ her bid for power. But they also don't quite know what to do with Snow, apart from having Joey Wong lie there and look beautiful. Which of course Wong can accomplish with ease. Thus, in the Big Battle at the end of the third *Swordsman* flick, Snow has little to do except to look pained that Asia seems to be ignoring her (and she's injured, too). Snow's strategy seems to be to sulk and pout her way back into Asia's heart).

Anyway, after emphasizing too many minor and strange elements, *The Swordsman 3: The East Is Red* hurtles around the corner of the Hong Kong Movie Race Circuit, heading for the Final Stretch – with the Finish Line in sight (10 minutes away). And just what is a Hong Kong swordplay/ fantasy/ action flick going to do? Only have scenes of Big, Wild Action! For the finale, everybody else seems to have gone home (including all of the extras), and only three charas remain: Asia the Insane, Snow the Wistful Masochist, and General Koo the Paranoid Intermediary (who just wants everybody *to stop fighting, already!* And to *just get along!*).

No. No – because Asia the Unpleasable is a divinity as a spoilt child who, if it/ he/ she can't get what it/ he/ she wants, is going to *destroy* it! Yes – the signs were displayed in the scene in act one of this third *Swordsman* celluloid outing where Asia attacked Snow viciously. For being an impostor, yes, but also perhaps for simply being someone who really got to him/ her, who got under her/ his skin, and whom s/he really loved. Asia is the supreme egotist (vain but vicious), who demands total servitude from his/ her lovers. *Love me or die!* might be his/ her mantra. So Snow must die – and it can only be Asia who kills her.

The moral teaching in the finale of *The Swordsman 3* is: recognize and love what you have, not what you desire. Very Taoist/ Buddhist: be *here* (not *there*). Or as North American schmaltz like *The Wizard of Oz* or a Disney cartoon might put it, *there's no place like home*. Ain't that right, Toto? Oh yes, ma'am, it is – especially when 'home' is a colossal nation like the People's Republic of China! (Which has a head-start on North America of several thousand years for weaving myths and legends about heroes and gods).

For the finale of *The Swordperson 3*, the filmmakers have brought back the national navies – so the smackdown takes place on wooden ships at sea. Unfortunately, we have already seen this in the incredible nighttime sequence where Asia the Naughty laid siege to Snow and the Sun Moon Sect's vessel (the finale, filmed in full daylight, simply doesn't have the same impact and atmosphere).[53] But Ancient, Chinese magic does allow for scenes not often used in the Western pirate/ maritime movie – flying ships! (Asia's magic raises ships out of the water: as well as flying boats, we have boats landing on top of each other, boats running aground, and of course, boats exploding). And other non-Western scenes occur – the heroes soaring on sails ripped from ships thru the sky, pounding each other with bolts of energy shot from the palms.

The finale of *The Swordsman 3* is filled with endless bits of business in the cat-and-mouse tussle between General Koo and Asia the Inflammable – such as Koo wielding a cannon to fire at Asia, Asia responding by using her/ his flying needles to pin Koo to the cannon, and then Koo to the bulwark. One moment we're up in the air on the masts, the next we're in the hold. A memorable beat has Asia and Koo using sails (still attached to the square yard-arms) as weapons, striking each other with them, while hurtling thru the air.

The 'anything goes' approach to filmmaking is one of the appeals of Hong Kong action (and comedy) cinema – here it includes Asia the Indomitable's military costume, as if he or she's the commander of an empire of one soul, her/ himself.

But this final segment of the climax of *The Swordsman/woman 3* lacks many dramatic and cinematic elements to make it convince. The staging doesn't make sense at times, as if much of the footage was achieved with stand-ins, and there wasn't enough coverage to smooth over the cracks (which happens occasionally with Hong Kong movies). A giveaway is the decision to have Asia the Intractable and General Koo placed always far apart – so in the reverse angles (and in the wide shots, of course), Koo or Asia can be a double.[54] But if the production team were also making one or more films at the same time, all of this is understandable.

Yes, like many Hong Kong pictures, the ending of *The Swordsman 3: The East Is Red* has everything falling apart, emotions running wild and unchecked, and a high body count. General Koo, for ex, seems to expire in a boiling mass of fire as a ship explodes, and Asia the Inexplicable spirits the dead Snow away on a flying sail into the sunset (there's a lovely, weepy close-up of the two stars, Joey Wong and Brigitte Lin). Asia

---

53 The flat, cloudy skies don't help.
54 That diminishes Asia, though: such as how s/he demands that Koo hand over Snow, from a distance, when s/he is clearly much more powerful than Koo, and can stride in and take Snow at any time.

the Unstoppable, we note, survives.

It's not always a convincing dramatic/ aesthetic solution, it's not always a satisfying ending in terms of narrative or thematic structure, but the Chaos plus Death[55] plus Shouting plus Explosions ending of many a Hong Kong movie is certainly crowd-pleasing (in the noise and mad visuals, the filmmakers hope the audience will forget about the flaws in the script). So, yes, lots of stuff blows up, fires rage, and characters die... Roll the credits!

---

[55] 'It could be argued that *everything* in *The East Is Read* leads to death, for it may be the bloodiest film with the highest death count in Tsui Hark's filmography' (Lisa Morton, 100).

The Swordsman 2 (1992).

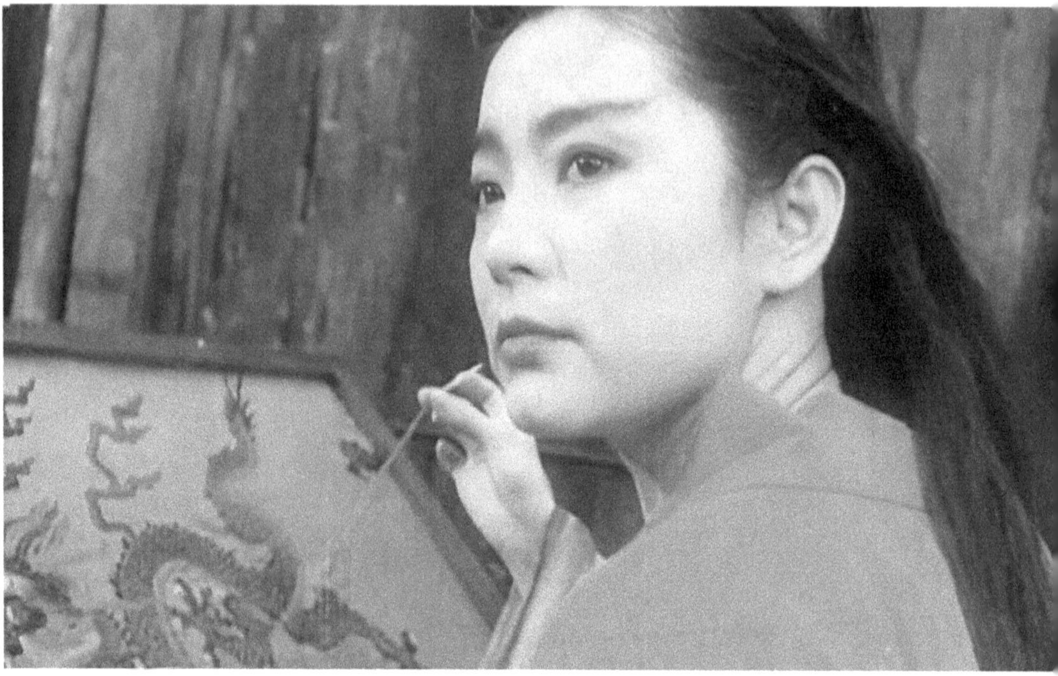

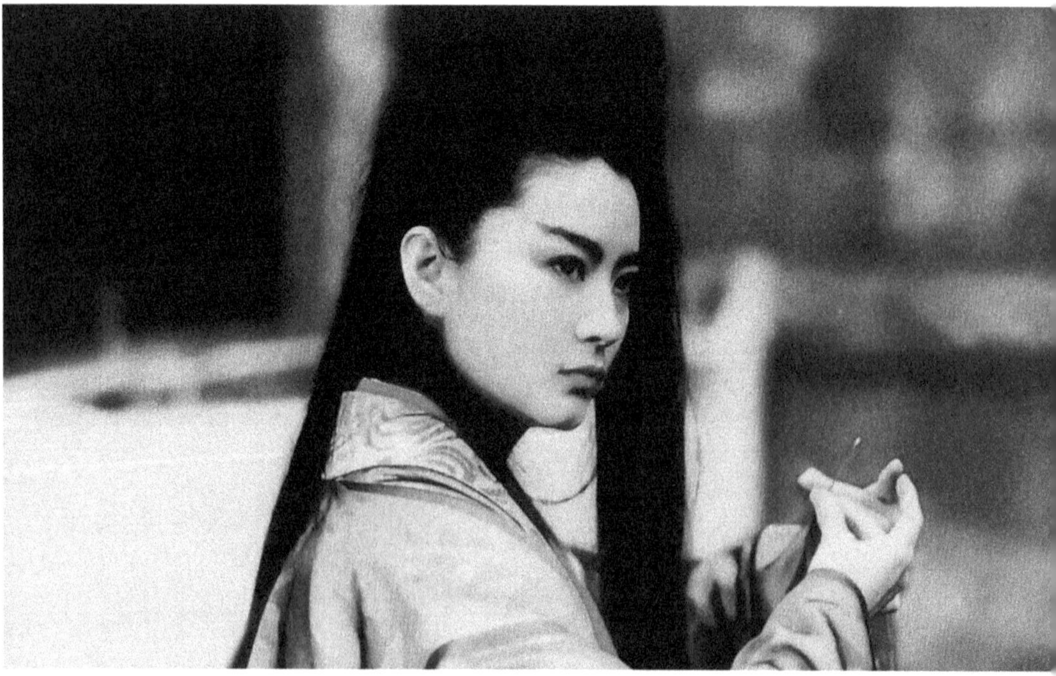

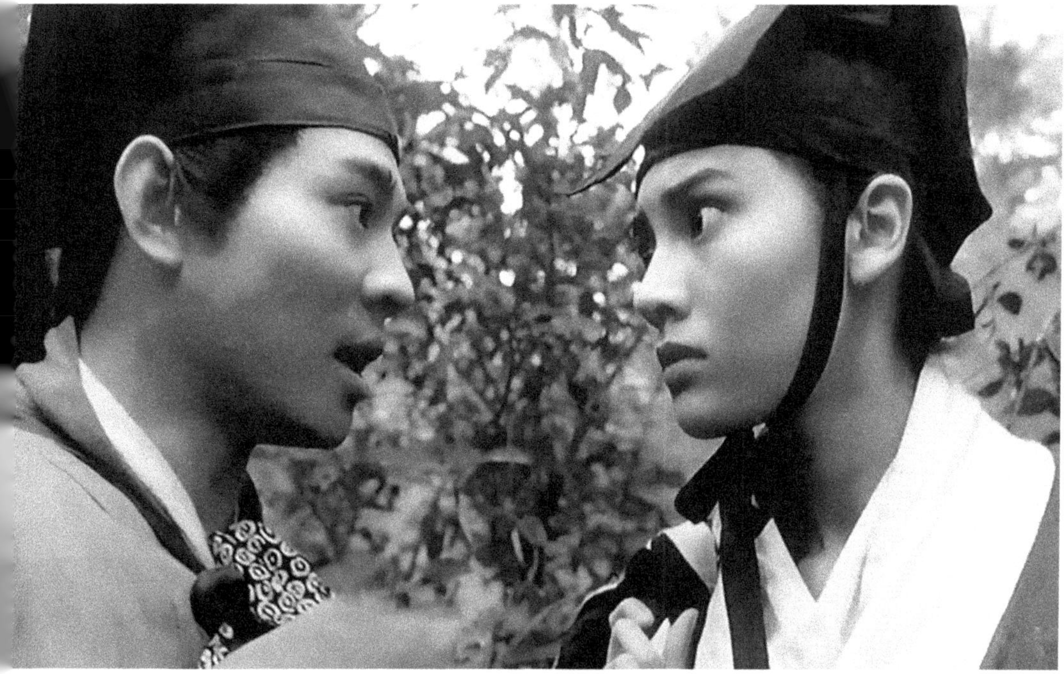

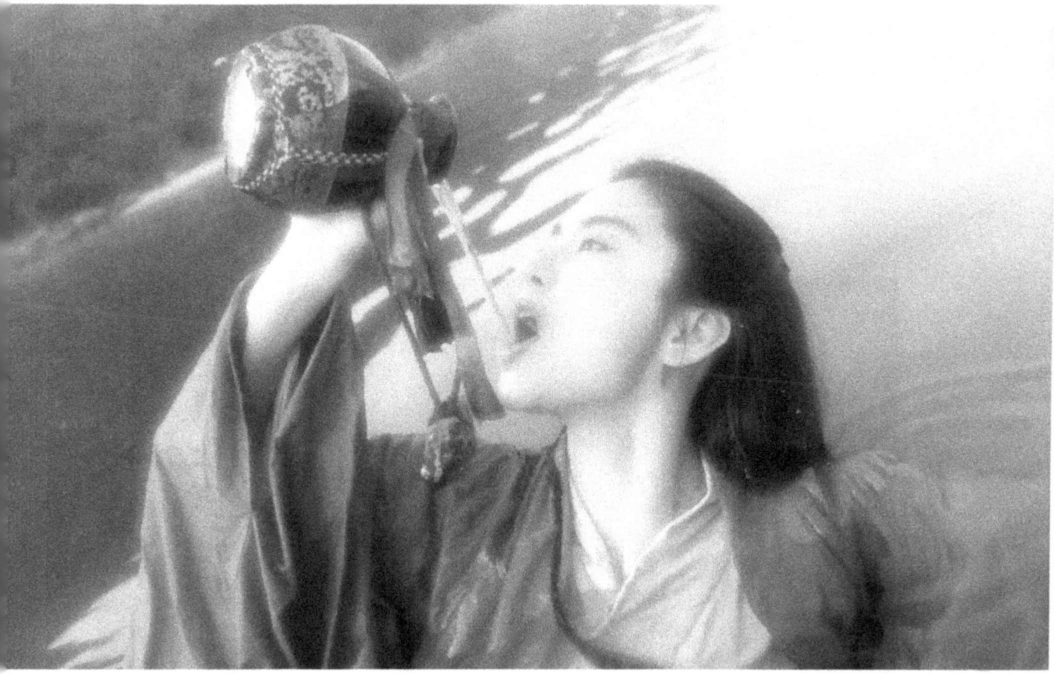

The Swordsman 3 (1993), this page and over.

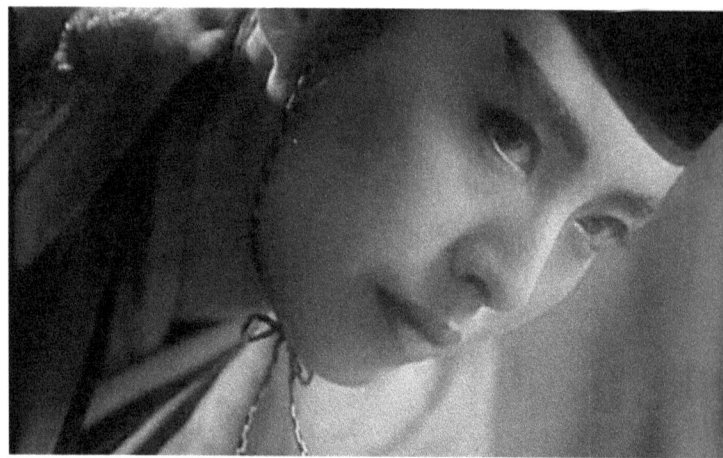

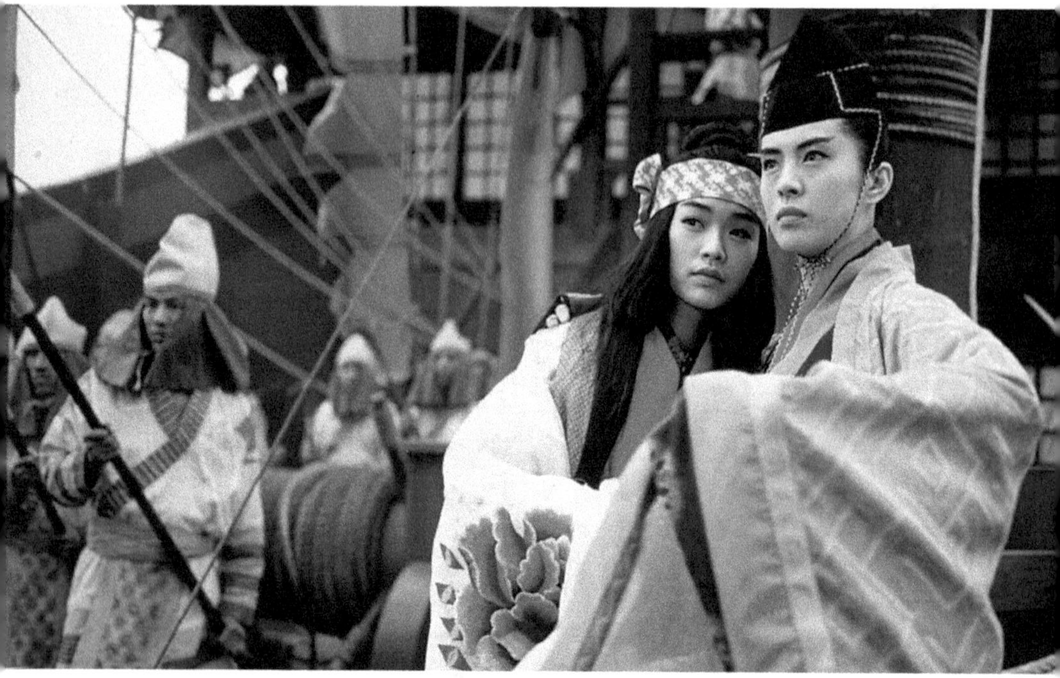

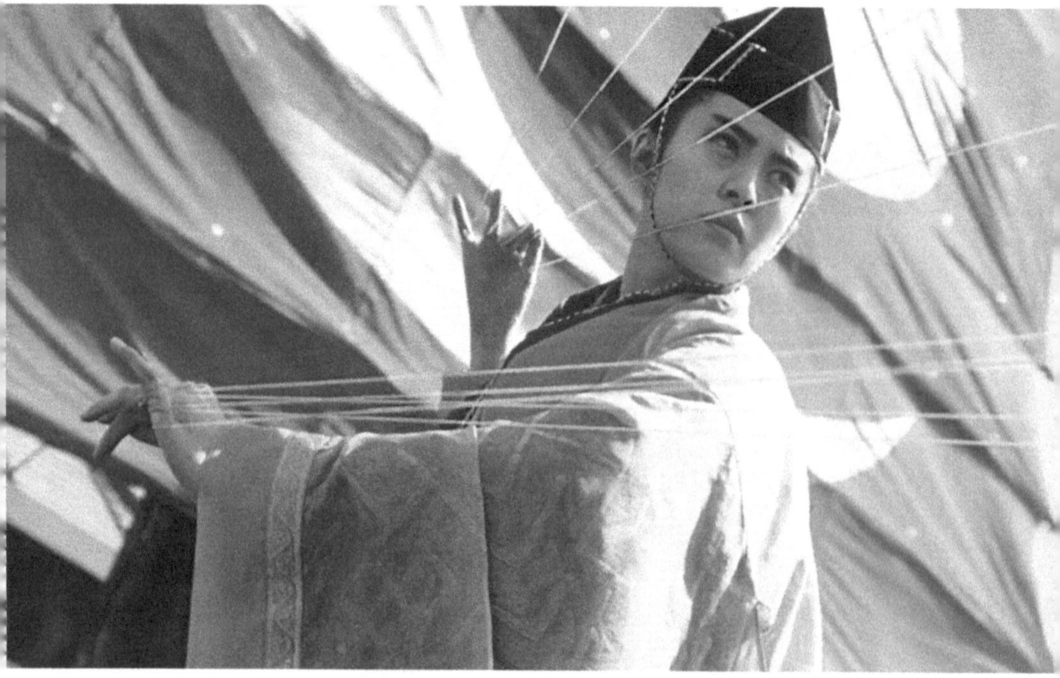

APPENDIX

ROYAL TRAMP

Lu Ding Ji

Any big success in the Hong Kong film industry immediately receives cash-in movies and also spoofs. One of the finest of the send-ups of the *Swordsman* series was the Wong Jing and Stephen Chow comedy *Royal Tramp* (*Lu Ding Ji*, 1992).

Royal Tramp (with a sequel that followed rapidly – only a few months later) was a hugely enjoyable romp in the form of a broad, often crude pantomime spoofing the recent spate of swordplay movies in Hong Kong, and the *Swordsman* films (1990-1993) in particular. *Royal Tramp* was a massive hit in Canton (with over HK $40 million at the box office), and a sequel was swiftly produced – it was released less than two months later (and imitations appeared, as usual).

Royal Tramp was very much a Wong Jing production – Wong produced, directed and wrote the film (though Gordon Chan was an uncredited co-director; some sources credit Tony Ching with co-direction. Certainly some of the action scenes are staged in Ching's style. As we know, Wong was happy to hand over the direction of the action scenes in his movies completely to Ching). This was common in Hong Kong.

Louis Cha (Jin Yong, d. 2018) provided the story, from his book *The Deer and the Cauldron* (a.k.a. *The Duke of Mount Deer*). Prod. by Jimmy Heung and Stephen Shui for Win's Movie Productions, and distributor Golden Harvest, David Chung and Joe Chan were DPs, Jason Mok was art dir., Kenneth Yee Chung-man and Shirley Chan were costume designers, Chuen Chi edited, William Wu composed the score, and the action dirs. were Tony Ching, Yuen Bun, Dion Lam, Ma Yeuk-sing and Yeung Ching-ching. Released July 30, 1992. 106 mins.

The cast is an all-star line-up that included Sharla Cheung-man, Deric Wan Siu-lun, Chingmy Yau Suk-ching, Ng Man-tat, Elvis Tsui Kam-kong, Damian Lau Chung-yan, Sandra Ng Kwun-yu, Vivian Chen Te-yung, Fennie Yuen Kit-ying, Nat Chan Pak-cheung, and Brigitte Lin Ching-hsia.[1]

---

[1] Lin appears at the end, advertizing the sequel, when the Empress Dowager escapes.

(Several appeared in the *Swordsman* series).

Headlining the movie is of course Chow Sing-chi, a.k.a. Stephen Chow. *Royal Tramp* is a star vehicle, with Chow dominating the movie and appearing in most scenes. Chow plays the familiar cowardly goof in the midst of mayhem, a seemingly ordinary guy thrust into extraordinary circumstances, the kind of role that Bob Hope played, or Woody Allen in his early comedies (the funny ones). It works – because the character is easy to identify with – he might be anybody – and he plays off every group of characters (and scores laughs off them, too, of course).

The *Royal Tramp* movies were based on *The Deer and the Cauldron* by Louis Cha (Jin Yong) which had already been adapted, and were adapted again in movies and television series (in fact, one occurred the year after *Royal Tramp*, starring Tony Leung). Films appeared in 1983, 1993 and 2011, and TV shows in 1978, two in 1984, 1998, 2001, 2008, and 2014.

❋

The premise of *Royal Tramp* is an appealing hook: Stephen Chow plays an undercover agent (called Wilson Bond a.k.a. Wai Siu-bo) in Ming Dynasty China (1368-1644), as rival organizations and governments vie for power (the fallen Ming Dynasty versus the invading Ching Dynasty). Bond ends up working as a double agent – for Chan Kan-nam from the Heaven and Earth Society and for the Kang Xi Emperor. There's a special book in the mix, too – the Buddhist text *The Sutra of Forty-two Chapters.* The background and the story is in part, as usual in Hong Kong comedy cinema, a pretext or coat hanger for a series of skits and set-pieces. However, the story is also worked out and makes sense: one of the foundations for a successful comedy movie is that the audience buys into the characters, the story and the premise. (For Western audiences the primary plot may seem a little too complicated).

Royal Tramp was full of Wong Jingsms – nonsensical humour, crude jokes, pretty girls, overblown action scenes, and parodies of contemporary Hong Kong movies (Wong's movies send up local products far more often than Western or Hollywood films). *Royal Tramp* is Wong's familiar let's-please-everybody cookery approach: give the audience a bit of everything. It's a movie like a big pile of Chinese food placed on hot plates in front of a crowd in a restaurant, with the chef and his assistant eager to please. If you don't like chicken, there's beef; if you don't like noodles, there's rice. It's a movie with one over-riding goal: to entertain.

This is a movie that's easy to like, and easy to watch. Oh, and it's very funny. There's no question that the combination of Wong Jing and Stephen Chow is cinematic gold dust. *Royal Tramp* is a very confident film comedy: it knows how to deliver this material. And it also seems that the actors and the crew are enjoying themselves (even if they actually weren't, because this was a period in Hong Kong film history when everybody was extremely over-worked. The sequel, for example, came out less than two months after this movie, with much of the same crew and cast).

There are some very enjoyable turns from the cast – Chingmy Yau

Suk-ching is at her kittenish best as the Emperor's sister, Princess Kin-ning; Stephen Chow's regular straight man Ng Man-tat is terrific as the effete eunuch Hoi Da-fu, as is another stalwart comic of this era, Nat Chan Pak-cheung as Duran; Sharla Cheung is delightfully imperious and nasty as the fake Empress Dowager, Lung'er; Elvis Tsui chews the scenery as the arch villain O'Brian (a.k.a. Oboi); and Fennie Yuen and Vivian Chen Te-yung are an adolescent sexual fantasy as the twin Seung-yee bodyguards for the hero.

Meanwhile, some roles are played straight, to make the plot work in *Royal Tramp* (and because not everybody can be goofing off) – such as Damian Lau Chung-yan, dependable and righteous as Swordsman Chan Kan-nam; and Deric Wan Siu-lin as the earnest, young Emperor Kang Xi.

❁

The humour is pure Wong Jing at his schoolboy naughtiest – not one joke about penises, but many; eunuchs and castration are running gags, too. For example, Wilson Bond examines a bunch of animal members in glass jars on a shelf, including the penis of the eunuch Hoi (he uses a magnifying glass to see it, looking right into the camera). In *Goldfinger* (1964) James Bond was strapped to a table with a giant circular saw – in *Royal Tramp*, Wilson Bond is tied down with a bunch of guys about to castrate him.

Wong Jing staples such as brothels and prostitutes, group sex, and eunuchs also appear in *Royal Tramp.* It's not all frantic action or frantic comedy, however – parts of *Royal Tramp* are extended farcical scenarios, like Wilson Bond being given lovely twins to act as his bodyguards (Nam Seung-yee and her sister). As expected from Wong Jing, the twins feel what the other one is feeling, so there are gags featuring erotic play (massages, etc), and a lengthy scene where Princess Kin-ning visits Bond and he hides the girls behind him in his bed, but they act as his arms as he pretends to be alone.

Stephen Chow and Ng Man-tat milk the sleazy aspects of being a eunuch repeatedly in scenes featuring the two of them at Hoi Da-fu's digs. This is giggly, teenage humour, unapologetically crude (characters grab each other's crotches, for example, to check on their castrated status).

❁

The action in *Royal Tramp* is in the over-the-top, Peking Opera style, which suits the broad, vaudeville approach of the movie – moves are swishy, exaggerated. *Royal Tramp* opens with a massive scene filmed in the familiar quarry in the New Territories, announcing the vibrant pageant of the movie (with colourful red and yellow costumes), the time period, and the warring groups. The scene introduces the super-villain of the piece, O'Brian (played by Hong Kong regular Elvis Tsui) and his ability to take on hordes of assailants with just his thumbnail (there are some gross gags, too – cutting a guy's head open, mass decapitations, and victims torn to pieces). Shots where five or six performers are flying on wires are pure Tony Ching in this scene, as are the images of multiple explosions in the ground detonated one after another, the ground collapsing, and soldiers being bayonetted on bamboo spikes. (Notice the dramatic structure of the movie – once this intense violence has been delivered, the movie steps away from it, and doesn't return to it for some time. In other words, the grotesque action in the opening scene is a function of the plot, to demonstrate the political threat and what's at stake, and to provide a narrative engine to make the story work. But the movie isn't actually interested it – we are waiting for Stephen Chow to make his entrance, which he does soon after the main titles, entertaining an audience at a brothel with his tall tales).

In *Royal Tramp*, Tony Ching and fellow choreographers such as Yuen Bun and Dion Lam send up the work they were performing for directors at the time such as Tsui Hark, John Woo, Derek Yee and Ringo Lam. Thus, the action has a loose, anarchic feel (even though the stuntwork and wirework can be even more difficult to achieve for comedy than for straight drama).

Several action scenes climax *Royal Tramp*, including a classic Tony Ching sequence: it's night, smoke wafts about, there are multiple performers in the air, swords flash, unusual weaponry is deployed (here, brass, Tibetan cymbals), and there are gross-out gags. To thicken the mix of the action – which is essentially the heroes taking on O'Brian and his mob (paying off the prologue) – the production added some warriors from Tibet. In true, Chingian style, the Tibetans (clad in red and yellow costumes) are soon flying about all over the place, and performing familiar, Chingian stunt gags, such as standing atop each other like circus acrobats, riding on the cymbals which they throw, and using the cymbals to chop up their victims (animation adds some pizzazz to the movement of the cymbals).

In addition, the duel between Swordsman Chan and O'Brian reprises gags that Tony Ching has been using throughout his career (going back to his first film as director, *Duel To the Death*), such as a swordsman descending from on high upside-down, sword extended. 27 years after *Royal Tramp*, in 2019, the same gags appeared in *Jade Dynasty*, directed by Ching.

ROYAL TRAMP 2

Lu Ding Ji 2 Zhi Shen Long Jiao

INTRO.

Royal Tramp 2 (*Lu Ding Ji 2 Zhi Shen Long Jiao,* 1992) was prod. by Win's Movie Productions and Golden Harvest. Prod. by Stephen Shiu and Jimmy Hueng, wr. and dir. by Wong Jing (some sources have Tony Ching co-directing both *Royal Tramp* movies, and some credit Gordan Chan with co-direction), from a story (*The Deer and the Cauldron*) by Louis Cha (Jin Yong). DP: David Chung. Music: Williams Hu. Art dir: Jason Mok Siu-Kei. Costumes: Kenneth Yee Chung-Man and Shirley Chan Koo-Fong. Sound editor: Benny Chu Chi-Ha. Editor: Chuen Chi. Action director: Tony Ching Siu-tung (plus five assistants).[2] Released Sept 24, 1992. 93 mins.

Colourful, fast-paced, and very silly, *Royal Tramp 2* boasts a superb cast which includes Stephen Chow Sing-chi, Damian Lau Chung-yan, Deric Wan, Paul Chun Kong, Law Lan Kent Tong, and an amazing number of leading ladies in Hong Kong cinema: Brigitte Lin Ching-hsia, Sharla Cheung-man, Natalis Chan, Chingmy Yau Suk-ching, Sandra Ng, Fennie Yuen, Vivian Chan, and Michelle Reiss.

Royal Tramp 2 was the follow-up to *Royal Tramp,* released earlier in the year, on July 30, '92. Both *Royal Tramp* movies were huge hits locally.

Royal Tramp 2 is a Stephen Chow comedy – which tells you all you need to know about the movie; thus, the star is in almost every scene, and is allowed to dominate the proceedings (Chow also carries most of the humour, as superstars usually do in comic star vehicles). Chow is once again playing Wilson Bond (Duke Wai Siu-bo in Chinese), an undercover agent (the role gives his character legitimate reasons for being in the middle of rival factions and different groups).

Whether or not Wong Jing actually directed all of the two *Royal Tramp* movies, or did some of it, or used assistants, they are very enjoyable and highly accomplished productions. Wong surely deserves some of the credit for these two great movies.

The demands of the screenwriting are considerable: first, the cast is huge, and requires a *lot* of planning and thought to keep track of all of them, and to give them all something significant to do (and don't under-

[2] Yuen Bun, Ma Yuk-Sing, Yeung Ching-Ching, Dion Lam Dik-On and Cheung Yiu-Sing.

estimate the egos of some of the actors involved!). Second, the superstar (Stephen Chow Sing-chi) has to be kept centre stage throughout. Third, the film has to deliver a lavish historical costume piece. Fourth, action and spectacle have to be integrated at regular intervals. Fifth, and above all, it has to be *funny*, it has to spoof *wuxia pian* like the *Swordsman* movies.

Royal Tramp 2 is partly a send-up of the *Swordsman* movies, as with 1993's *Holy Weapon* (also a collaboration between Tony Ching and Wong Jing, among others). So there is plenty of mistaken identity comedy, and cross-dressing, and brothel and hooker jokes, and lusts scuppered by circumstances, and authority figures brought down to size, and people not being what you thought they were.

The political background of *Royal Tramp 2* is the very familiar one of a more liberal, easy-going community being threatened by stern, unforgiving Manchu/ Imperial authorities. If you wish, it can be related in the simplistic terms of: Hong Kong versus the People's Republic of China.

Tony Ching Siu-tung was one of the action directors for *Royal Tramp 2* and displays his remarkable talents throughout the picture. The *Royal Tramp* movies, for action, are the equal of many other Hong Kong movies. As *Royal Tramp 2* has a historical setting (in the Qing Dynasty), the style of the action is in the usual swordplay genre, and in the usual Chingian manner of flamboyant wire-work, rapid sword slashes, fluttering robes, explosions, props that smash, and iconic poses.

As to Tony Ching Siu-tung's input in *Royal Tramp 2*, it's found in the many action sequences, and also in the action within otherwise dramatic scenes. *Royal Tramp 2* is another of those Hong Kong historical pictures where physical acting is emphasized: it's one of the delights of Hong Kong cinema: actors don't just stand there and mouth dialogue, they are in movement. (If you want to watch actors simply standing there and speaking, look at any Western television show. Hong Kong cinema is *more* than that).

Of the stand-out action scenes in *Royal Tramp 2*, there's an amazing ambush of the Imperial caravan in the countryside (filmed in the New Territories, again). It's a chaotic sequence of flying swordsmen and slashing blades.

THE FIRST ACT.

Royal Tramp 2 is a movie where, in the opening exposition scene, Sharla Cheung-man turns into Brigitte Lin Ching-hisa! Lin's Lung'er is the leader of the St Dragon Sect, hoping to gain power again (she has martial arts powers which will be lost to the man who takes her virginity).

The political background of Emperors and governments and dynasties and warring factions in *Royal Tramp 2* is just that – a background for a Stephen Chow comedy. And yet, *Royal Tramp 2* is also an impressively mounted production, with some marvellous costumes and settings. Or is it that Chinese cinema, and Hong Kong cinema, has been churning out historical films for so long, and at such a high rate, that everybody in the production can do this sort of movie in their sleep? Even the tea boy or the script girl could probably step into the director's shoes at a moment's notice and direct a costume picture (we know that many people behind the camera can – and have – replaced the director. In Hong Kong's non-unionized cinema, members of the crew take up other jobs as necessary).

THE MIDDLE ACT.

So in the middle act of *Royal Tramp 2* of course Stephen Chow Sing-chi gets a love scene with Brigitte Lin Ching-hsia (Lin who was formerly Sharla Cheung-man – a transformation from one Hong Kong super-babe into another). Lung'er, you see, has been poisoned, and can only be healed by lerrrve (it's another Wong Jingian potions/ poisons plot).[3] And Lin, after lovemaking, becomes the coy, simpering girl we always knew she was underneath the haughty exterior she usually projects (every movie featuring Lin pursues this uncovering of her 'true' persona).

Even the build-up to the love scene is couched within action cinema terms: Lung'er unfurls long, white banners in all directions, becoming a spider-woman for a moment (a favourite motif in Hong Kong fantasy cinema): it's woman as witch, predator, untameable nature.

As a visual motif, the sight of pieces of white cloth zooming thru the night air is something peculiar to Hong Kong movies (if there's a chance to include some billowing cloth blown by fans or the breeze, it will always be taken. Tony Ching Siu-tung is especially fond of fluttering material).

In an inspired beat, the white banners merge to form a cocoon in which the lovers do what lovers do. (Next morning, the structure, composed now of leaves, looks like an Andy Goldsworthy sculpture).

THE FINAL ACT.

The finale of *Royal Tramp 2* is of course a series of big set-pieces, where the main characters get to fight each other. Yen Shi-kwan as Fung Sek-fan is introduced halfway thru *Royal Tramp 2* to provide a villain for the hero to go up against (Yen often plays heavies – he's familiar from his customary villainous cackle).

So Fung Sek-fan encounters Wilson Bond in a rural setting for their second smackdown in *Royal Tramp 2* (they have already fought once, with Fung retreating for the time being. That action scene is also remarkable – the one in the countryside replays it, but bigger and wilder. There's a classic piece of Tony Ching's use of props – the henchmen wield large gold hoops, like a circus juggling act).

In a send-up of *The Swordsman 2*, Wilson Bond is dressed as Brigitte Lin Ching-hsia in perhaps her most famous role, as Invincible Asia. Thus, the tussle with Fung Sek-tan and his scarlet-clad henchmen is played for laughs at first. And now that Bond possesses 80% of Lung'er's powers, there's no way he can lose (well, he's also Stephen Chow, and he's the hero of this movie, so it's impossible for him to be defeated in any way).

So Tony Ching Siu-tung gets to spoof his own movie *The Swordsman*

---

[3] Wong Jing is very fond of gimmicks such as aphrodisiacs: they're always given or taken by the wrong person, or aimed at the wrong person. Also magical potions and poisons. It's typical in a Wong picture that the victim has to make love by a certain time, as here in *Royal Tramp 2*.

2 with some silly bits of business in amongst the flying, the wire-work, and the flashing, slashing swordplay (such as Wilson Bond twisting the nipples of the hapless henchmen). Props, swords and stuntmen are soaring about all over the place, as usual in a Ching set-piece, and this sequence would be enough for many action movies, but *Royal Tramp 2* goes further, adding one more Big Set and one more Big Fight.

So, falling thru a hole in the ground (made by Fung Sek-fan being hurled by the high energy of Wilson Bond), the action shifts into a studio set. It's that favourite of historical action movies – an underground palace/ chamber/ lair. So we have the flickering torches, elaborate statuary, a mound of gold, and pools on each side of a walkway.

The action escalates from astonishing, acrobatic swordplay (where the combatants are in constant motion, moving across the screen, and performing tumbles and spins at the same time), to wizardly bolts of energy being hurled at each other.

In one highpoint, there's a Ching Siu-tung speciality – fountains of water exploding upwards from the pools (water placed inside oil barrels filled with explosives). Ching's team had deployed this gag with amazing effect in the *Chinese Ghost Story* movies as well as the *Swordsman* series.

In the end, Fung Sek-fan is impaled fatally upon a statue. Cleverly, Wilson Bond and his chums use the body of Fung to stand in for his master, Chan Kan-nam, at an execution.

In the customary *dénouement* scene (set in the customary location – on horseback in the countryside), everyone congratulates themselves for being so wonderful (or something like that). Wilson Bond is accompanied by several wives (i's tough being the hero), for the Ride Off Into the Sunset.

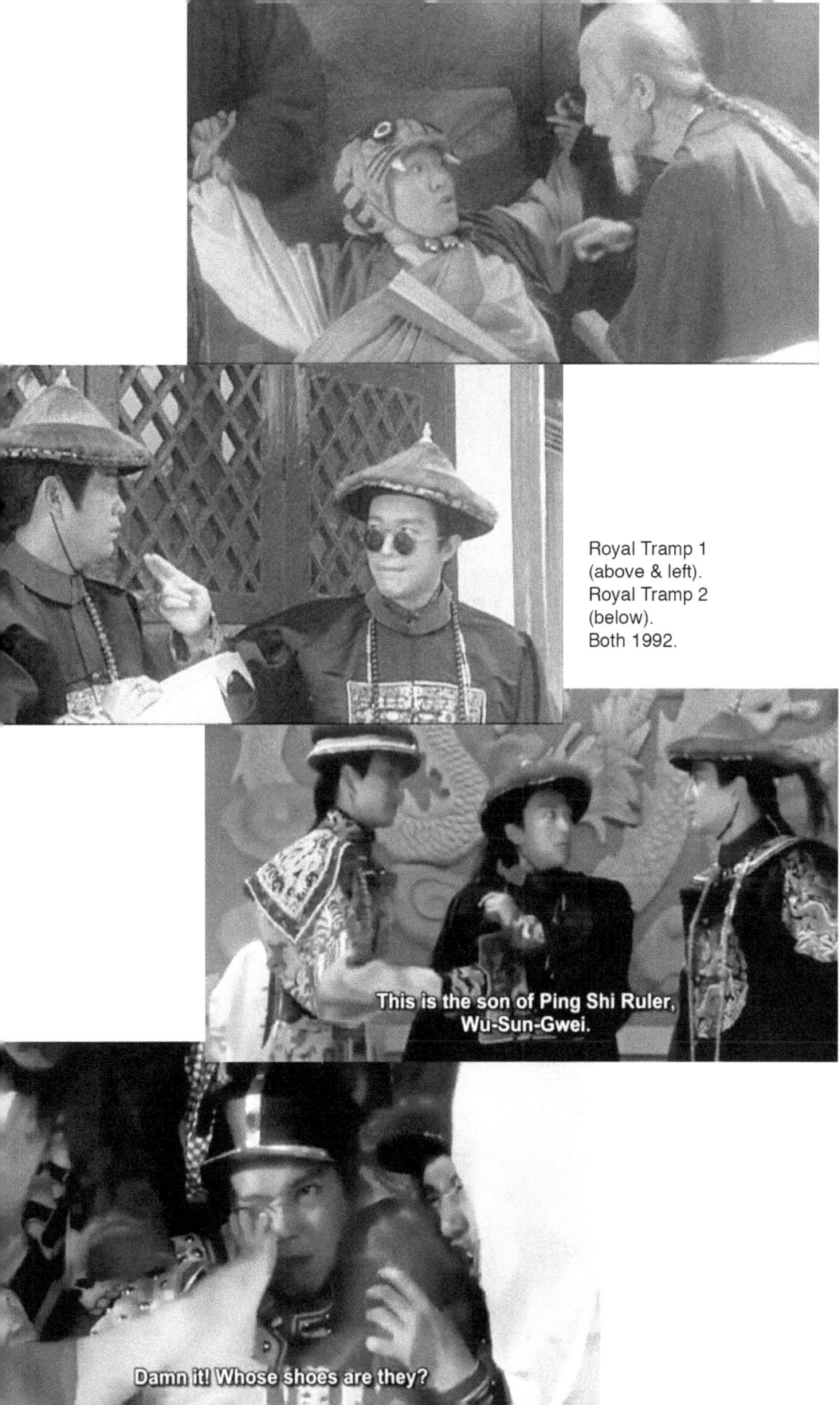

Royal Tramp 1 (above & left).
Royal Tramp 2 (below).
Both 1992.

FILMOGRAPHY

TONY CHING SIU-TUNG

MOVIES AS DIRECTOR

Duel To the Death (1983)
The Witch From Nepal (1986)
A Chinese Ghost Story (1987)
The Terracotta Warrior (1989)
The Swordsman (1990 – co-directed)
A Chinese Ghost Story 2 (1990)
The Raid (1991 – co-directed)
A Chinese Ghost Story 3 (1991)
Swordsman 2 (1992)
Swordsman 3 (1993 – co-directed)
The Heroic Trio (1993, co-directed)
The Executioners (1993, co-directed)
Wonder Seven (1994)
Dr. Wai In "The Scripture With No Words" (1996)
The Longest Day (1997)
Conman In Tokyo (2000)
Naked Weapon (2002)
Belly of the Beast (2003)
An Empress and the Warriors (2008)
The Sorcerer and the White Snake (2011)
Jade Dynasty (2019)

MOVIES AS ACTION DIRECTOR

The Fourteen Amazons (1972)
The Rats (1972)
Love and Vengeance (1973)
Shaolin Boxer (1974)
The Tea House (1974)
Kidnap (1974)
Lady of the Law (1975)
Negotiation (1977)
He Who Never Dies (1979)
Monkey Kung Fu (1979)
The Bastard Swordsman (1979)
The Sentimental Swordsman (1979)
Dangerous Encounter - 1st Kind (1980)
The Spooky Bunch (1980)
The Sword (1980)
The Master Strikes (1980)
Gambler's Delight (1981)
Return of the Deadly Blade (1981)
Sword of Justice (1981)
The Story of Woo Viet (1981)
Rolls, Rolls, I Love You (1982)
Once Upon a Rainbow (1982)
Swordsman Adventure (1983)
Twinkle Twinkle Little Star (1983)
Cherie (1984)
Happy Ghost 3 (1986)
Peking Opera Blues (1986)
A Better Tomorrow 2 (1987)
The Eighth Happiness (1988)
I Love Maria (1988)
The Killer (1989)
All About Ah-Long (1989)
The Fun, the Luck and the Tycoon (1990)
Casino Raiders 2 (1991)
Son On the Run (1991)
New Dragon Gate Inn (1992 – co-directed)
Moon Warriors (1992)
Twin Dragons (1992)
Royal Tramp (1992)
Royal Tramp 2 (1992)
Gambling Soul (1992)
Justice, My Foot! (1992)
Lucky Encounter (1992)
Flying Dagger (1993)
Future Cops (1993)

Holy Weapon (1993)
The Mad Monk (1993)
Butterfly and Sword (1993)
City Hunter (1993)
Love On Delivery (1994)
A Chinese Odyssey I: Pandora's Box (1995)
A Chinese Odyssey 2: Cinderella (1995)
The Stuntwoman (1996)
Warriors of Virtue (1997)
Hong Niang (1998)
The Blacksheep Affair (1998)
The Assassin Swordsman (2000)
The Duel (2000)
My School Mate, the Barbarian (2001)
Invincible (2001)
Shaolin Soccer (2001)
Hero (2002)
Spider-Man (2002 – uncredited)
House of Flying Daggers (2004)
The Curse of the Golden Flower (2006)
Krrish (2006)
In the Name of the King: A Dungeon Siege Tale (2007)
The Warlords (2007)
Dororo (2007)
Legend of Shaolin Kungfu I: Heroes in Troubled Times (2007)
Butterfly Lovers (2008)
Kung Fu Dunk (2008)
The Treasure Hunter (2009)
Future X-Cops (2010)
Just Call Me Nobody (2010)
Legend of Shaolin Kungfu 3: Heroes of the Great Desert (2011)
Krrish 3 (2013)

TV SERIES

The Spirit of the Sword (1978)
It Takes a Thief (1979)
The Roving Swordsman (1979)
Reincarnated (1979)
Reincarnated 2 (1979)
Dynasty (1980)
Dynasty 2 (1980)
Legend of the Condor Heroes (1983)
The Return of the Condor Heroes (1983)
The New Adventures of Chor Lau Heung (1984)
The Duke of Mount Deer (1984)
The Return of Luk Siu Fung (1986)
The New Heaven Sword and Dragon Sabre (1986)
The Storm Riders (a.k.a. *Wind and Cloud*, 2002)
The Storm Riders 2 (a.k.a. *Wind and Cloud 2*, 2004)
The Royal Swordsmen (2005)

FILMOGRAPHY

TONY CHING SIU-TUNG

FILMS AS DIRECTOR

DUEL TO THE DEATH, 1983

(A.k.a. *Sang Sei Kyu/ Sheng Si Jue*). Production: Paragon Films. Distributor: Golden Harvest. Producers: Raymond Chow Man-Wai and Catherine Chang Si-kan. Script: David Lai, Manfred Wong and Ching Siu-tung. Released: Jan 13, 1983. 86 mins.

THE WITCH FROM NEPAL, 1986

(*Qi Yuan* in Mandarin, a.k.a. *The Nepal Affair/ Affair From Nepal/ A Touch of Love*). Production: Golden Harvest/ Paragon Films. Producer: Anthony Chow. Script: Chui Jing-Hong. Released: Feb 27, 1986. 89 mins.

A CHINESE GHOST STORY, 1987

(Mandarin: *Qiannu Youhun = Sien: Female Ghost*, a.k.a. *Fair Maiden, Tender Spirit*). Production: Film Workshop/ Cinema City. Producers: Tsui Hark, Claudie Chung Jan and Qianqing Liu. Exec. producer: Zhong Zheng. Script: Yuen Kai-Chi. Released: July 18, 1987. 98 mins.

THE TERRACOTTA WARRIOR, 1989

(*Chin Yung/ Gu Gam Daai Zin/ Yon Qing* in Cantonese, a.k.a. *Fight and Love With a Terracotta Warrior*). Production: Art & Talent Group Inc. Exec. producer: Kam Kwok-Leung. Producers: Tsui Hark, Zhu Mu and Hon Pau-chu. Script: Pik Wah Lee. Released: Apl 12, 1990. 106 mins. (145 mins).

THE SWORDSMAN, 1990

(Cantonese = *Siu Ngo Gong Woo,* Mandarin = *Xiao Aoi Jianzhu* = *Laughing and Proud Warrior*). Production: Film Workshop/ Golden Harvest. Producers: Tsui Hark, Tommy Law Wai-Tak and Chu Feng Kang. Script: Kwan Man-Leung, Daai Foo Ho, Huang Ying, Tai-Mok Lau, Yiu-ming Leung, and Jason Lam Kee To. Co-directed with Raymond Lee, King Hu, Tsui Hark, Andrew Kam Yeung-Wa and Ann Hui. Released: Apl 5, 1990. 115 mins.

A CHINESE GHOST STORY 2, 1990

(Mandarin: *Qiannü Youhun Zhi Renjian Dao* = *Sien Female Ghost II: Human Realm Tao*). Production: Film Workshop/ Golden Princess. Producer: Tsui Hark. Script: Lau Tai-mok, Lam Kei-to and Leung Yiu-ming. Story: Tsui Hark and Yuen Kai-Chi. Released: July 13, 1990. 98/ 104 mins.

THE RAID, 1991

(*Choi Suk Ji Wang Siu Chin Gwan*). Production: Film Workshop and Cinema City. Producer: Tsui Hark. Script: Tsui Hark and Yuen Kai-chi. Story: Michael Hui Koon-Man. Co-directed with Tsui Hark. Released: Mch 28, 1991. 100 mins.

A CHINESE GHOST STORY 3, 1991

(*Qiannü Youhun III Dao Dao Dao*). Production: Golden Princess/ Film Workshop. Exec. producers: Chui Bo-Chu and Roger Lee Yan-Lam. Producer: Tsui Hark. Co-producer: Cho King-Man. Script: Roy Szeto Cheuk-hon and Tsui Hark. Released: July 18, 1991. 99 mins.

THE SWORDSMAN 2, 1992

(Cantonese: *Siu Ngo Kong Woo II Dong Fong Bat Baai;* Mandarin: *Xiao-ao Jianghu II Dongfang Bubai* = *Laughing and Proud Warrior: Invincible Asia*). Production: Film Workshop/ Long Shong Pictures/ Golden Princess. Producer: Tsui Hark. Assoc. producers: Chi-Wai Cheung and Wai Sum Shia. Script: Hanson Chan Tin-suen, Elsa Tang Pik-yin and Tsui Hark. Released: June 26, 1992. 108 mins.

THE SWORDSMAN 3, 1993

(A.k.a. *The East Is Red.* Mandarin: *Dongfang Bùbài – Fengyún Zàiqi* = *Invisible Asia 3: Turbulence Again Rises*). Production: Film Workshop/ Long Shong Pictures/ Golden Princess. Producers: Tsui Hark and Lau Jou. Script: Tsui Hark, Charcoal Tan Cheung and Roy Szeto Chak-Hon. Co-directed with Raymond Lee Wai-man. Released: Jan 21, 1993. 93 minutes.

THE HEROIC TRIO, 1993

(*Dung Fong Saam Hap*). Production: China Entertainment Films and Paka Hill Productions. Producer: Tony Ching. Script: Sandy Shaw Lai-King. Co-directed with Johnny To Ke-fung. Released: Feb 12, 1993. 83 mins.

THE EXECUTIONERS, 1993

(*Xian Dai Hao Xia Zhuan*, a.k.a. *The Heroic Trio 2*). Production: China Entertainment Films and Paka Hill Film. Producers: Johnnie To Ke-fung, Tony Ching and Yeung Kwok-fai. Script: Susanne Chan and Sandy Shaw Lai-King. Co-directed with Johnnie To Ke-fung. Released: Sept 30, 1993. 97 mins.

WONDER SEVEN, 1994

(*7 Jin Gong*). Production: China Entertainment Films. Producer: Catherine Hun. Script: Charcoal Tan Cheung, Elsa Tang Bikyin and Tony Ching. Story: Manfred Wong Man-Chun. Released: Apl 1, 1994. 88 mins.

DR WAI IN "THE SCRIPTURE WITH NO WORDS", 1996

(*Yale: Mo Him Wong,* a.k.a. *Mao Xian Wang*). Production: Win's Entertainment and Eastern Production. Producers: Tsai Mu-ho, Wong Sing-ping, Charles Heung Wah-keung and Tiffany Chen Ming-Ying. Script: Lam Wai-Lun, Roy Szeto Cheuk-hon and Sandy Shaw Lai-King. Released: Mch 14, 1996. 87/ 91 mins.

CONMAN IN TOKYO, 2000

(*Zung Waa Dou Hap*). Production: Star East and Best of the Best and Partners. Producer: Wong Jing. Script: Law Yiu-fai. Released: Aug 31, 2000. 103 mins.

NAKED WEAPON, 2002

(*Chek Law Dak Gung*). Production: Media Asia/ Jing Productions. Producers: Wong Jing and John Chong. Script: Wong Jing. Released: Nov 15, 2002. 92 mins.

BELLY OF THE BEAST, 2003

Production: G.F.T. Entertainment/ Salon Films/ Studio Eight Productions/ Emmett/ Furla Films. Producers: George Furla, Gary Howsam, Jamie Brown, Randall Emmett, Steven Seagal and Charles Wang. Script: Thomas Fenton and James Townsend. Released: Dec 30,

2003. 91 mins.

AN EMPRESS AND THE WARRIORS, 2008

(*Jiang Shan Mei Ren = The Kingdom and a Beauty*). Production: Beijing Polyabana Publishing Co./ United Filmmakers Organization/ China Film Co-Production Corp./ Big Pictures, Ltd. Execuive producers: Eric Tsang and Kuo Hsing Li. Producers: Claudie Chung Jan, Gin Lau Sin-hing, Peter Chan and Dong Yu. Script: James Yuen, Tan Cheung and Tin Nam Chun. Released: Mch 19, 2008. 99 mins.

THE SORCERER AND THE WHITE SNAKE, 2011

(*Baak Se Cyun Syut Zi Faat Hoi,* a.k.a. *The Emperor and the White Snake*, a.k.a. *Madame White Snake*, a.k.a. *It's Love*). Production: China Juli Entertainment Media/ Distribution Workshop/ Different Digital Design Ltd. Exec. producer: Pang Yau-Fong. Producers: Chui Po Chu, Chi Wan Tse and Yang Zi. Script: Charcoal Tan Cheung, Tsang Kan Cheung and Roy Szeto Cheuk-hon. Released: Sept 28, 2011. 100 mins.

JADE DYNASTY, 2019

(*Zhu Xian*). Production: Huxia Film Distribution/ New Classics Pictures/ Shanghai Taopiaopiao Film Culture/ Youku Pictures/ I.Q.I.Y.I. Pictures. Producer: Ning Li. Line producers: Huang Qunfei, Jia Xu and Tony Ching. Script: Shen Jie and Song Chaoyun. Released: Sept 13, 2019. 101 mins.

TONY CHING SIU-TUNG FILMS AS ACTION DIRECTOR

THE SWORD, 1980

(*Jian* a.k.a. *Ming Jian*). Production: Golden Harvest. Producer: Raymond Chow Man-Wai. Script: Lau Shing-Hon, Clifford Choi Gai-Gwong, Wong Ying, Patrick Tam Kar-Ming, Lo Chi-Keung and Lau Tin-Chi. Direction: Patrick Tam Kar-ming. Released: Aug 14, 1980. 84 mins.

DANGEROUS ENCOUNTER – 1ST KIND, 1980

(*Diyi Leixing Weixian = First Kind of Danger,* a.k.a. *Dangerous Encounter of the First Kind, Don't Play With Fire* and *Playing With Fire*). Production: Fotocine Film Production Ltd. Producer: Thomas Wing-Fat Fung. Script: Tsui Hark and Roy Szeto Cheuk-hon. Direction: Tsui Hark. Released: Dec 4, 1980. 92 mins.

TWINKLE TWINKLE LITTLE STAR, 1983

(*Xing Ji Dun Tai*). Production: Shaw Brothers. Producer: by Mona Fong Yat-wah. Script: Alex Cheung Kwok-ming, Manfred Wong Man-jun, John Au Wa-hon, Sandy Shaw Lai-king, Lawrence Cheng Tan-shui and Yuen Gai-chi. Direction: Alex Cheung Kwok-ming. Released: Feb 12, 1983. 93 mins.

PEKING OPERA BLUES, 1986

(*Dao Ma Dan = Knife Horse Actresses*). Production: Cinema City/ Film Workshop. Producers: Claudie Chung-jan and Tsui Hark. Script: Raymond To Kwok-wai. Direction: Tsui Hark. Released: Sept 6, 1986. 104 mins.

A BETTER TOMORROW 2, 1987

(*Jing Hung Bun Sik II* in Cantonese, *Ying Xiong Ben Se II* in Mandarin = *Heroic Character II*). Production: Cinema City. Producer: Tsui Hark. Script: Tsui Hark and John Woo. Direction: John Woo (Ng Yu-sam). Released: Dec 17, 1987. 104 mins.

I LOVE MARIA, 1988

(*Roboforce*). Producers: Tsui Hark and John Sham. Script: Yuen Kai-chi. Direction: David Chung Chi-man. Released: Mch 10, 1988. 96 mins.

THE KILLER, 1989

(*Dip Huet Seung Hung* in Cantonese, *Die Xue Shuang Xiong* in Mandarin = *Bloodshed Brothers*, 1989). Production: Film Workshop/ Golden Princess/ Magnum. Script: John Woo. Producer: Tsui Hark. Direction: John Woo. Released: July 6, 1989. 105 mins.

JUST HEROES, 1989

(A.k.a. *Tragic Heroes*, *Yi Dan Qun Ying* in Cantonese). Production by Magnum Films. Producers: Alan Ng, David Chiang, Danny Lee, and Tsui Hark. Exec. prod. by Chang Cheh. Script: Ni Kuang, Tommy Hau and Yiu Yau Hung. Direction: John Woo and Wu Ma. Released: Sept 14, 1989. 97 mins.

THE BANQUET, 1991

(*Hao Men Ye Yan*). Producers: Ng See-yuen and John Sham. Script: Choi Ting-ting. Direction: Clifton Ko-chi, Alfred Sum, Joe Tin, Kin Cheung and Tung Cheung Cho. Released: Nov 30, 1991. 97 mins.

NEW DRAGON GATE INN, 1992

(*Xin Long Menm Ke Zhan* in Mandarin). Production: Film Workshop and Seasonal Films. Producers: Tsui Hark and Ng See-yuen. Script: Tsui Hark, Charcoal Tan Cheung and Hiu Wing. Direction: Raymond Lee Wai-man and Tsui Hark. Released: by Aug 27, 1992. 103 mins.

CITY HUNTER, 1993

(*Sing Si Lip Ya*). Production: Golden Harvest/ Golden Way Films/ Paragon Films. Producer: Chua Lam. Script and direction: Wong Jing. Released: Jan 14, 1993. 105 mins.

THE MAD MONK, 1993

(*Ji Gong*). Production: Cosmopolitan Film Productions. Producer: Mona Fong Yat-wah. Script: Sandy Shaw Lai-king. Direction: Johnnie To Ke-fung. Released: July 29, 1993. 85 mins.

FUTURE COPS, 1993

(*Chiu Kap Hok Hau Ba Wong*). Production: Wong Jing's Workshop and Fantasy Productions Inc.. Producers: John Higgins and Sherman Wong Shui-Hin. Script and direction: Wong Jing. Released: July 15, 1993. 95 mins.

LOVE ON DELIVERY, 1994

(*Po Huai Zhi Wang*, a.k.a. *King Of Destruction*). Production: Cosmopolitan Films. Script: Vincent Kok Tak-chiu. Direction: Stephen Chow Sing-chi and Lee Lik-Chi. Some credits have Tony Ching as co-director with Lee. Released: Feb 3, 1994. 100 mins.

A CHINESE ODYSSEY, 1995

(*Daiwah Saiyau* and *Sai Yau Gei: Daai Git Guk Ji-Sin Leui Kei Yun*). Production: Xi'an Film Studio and Choi Sing Film Company. Producer: Yeung Kwok-fai. Script: Wu Cheng-en. Direction: Jeffrey Lau. Released: Jan 21, 1995 and Feb 4, 1995. 87 and 95 mins.

WARRIOR OF VIRTUE, 1997

(*Wu Xing Zhan Shi*). Production: Joseph, Ronald, Dennis K., Jeremy and Christopher Law, Yoram Barzilai, Lyle Howry and Patricia Ruben. Distribution: Metro Goldwyn Mayer. Script: Michael Vickerman and Hugh Kelley. Direction: Ronny Yu. Released: May 2, 1997. 101 mins.

BLACKSHEEP AFFAIR, 1998

(*Meltdown 2, Another Meltdown* and *Bi Xie Lan Tian*). Production: Win's Entertaiment/ Eastern Film Production. Producer: Alex Law Kai-yui. Presenters: Charles Heung Wah-keung and Chui Po-chu. Script: Roy Szeto Cheuk-hon and Alex Law. Direction: Lam Wai-lun. Released: Feb 14, 1998. 90 mins.

THE DUEL, 2000

(*Jue Zhan Zi Jin Zhi Dian*). Production: Win's Entertainment. Producers: Wong Jing and Manfred Wong. Script: Manfred Wong. Direction: Andy Lau Wai-keung. Released: Feb 3, 2000. 106 mins.

SHAOLIN SOCCER, 2001

(*Siu Lam* in Cantonese, *Shàolín Zúqiú* in Mandarin). Production: Universe Entertainment and Star Overseas. Producer: Yeung Kwok-Fai. Script: Tsang Kan-cheung and Stephen Chow Sing-chi. Direction: Lee Lik-chi and Stephen Chow. Released: July 12, 2001. 112 mins.

INVINCIBLE, 2001

Production: T.B.S. Producers: Steven Chasman, Janine Coughlin and Jim Lemley. Executive producers: Bruce Davey, Mel Gibson, Jet Li, and John Morayniss. Script: Carey Hayes, Chad Hayes, Michael Brandt, Derek Haas, and Jefrey Levy. Direction: Jefrey Levy. Released: Nov 18, 2001. 87 mins.

SPIDER-MAN, 2002

Production: Marvel/ Columbia/ Laura Ziskin Prods. Producers: Laura Ziskin and Ian Bryce. Script: David Koepp. Direction: Sam Raimi. Released: May 3, 2002. 121 mins.

HERO, 2002

(Mandarin: *Yingxiong;* Cantonese: *Jing Hung*). Production: China Film Co-Production Corporation/ Elite Group Enterprises/ Zhang Yimou Studio/ Metropole Organisation/ Miramax Films/ Beijing New Picture Film. Executive producers: Shoufang Dou and Weiping Zhang. Producers: Bill Kong, Sook Yhun and Zhang Yimou. Script: Feng Li, Zhang Yimou and Bin Wang. Direction: Zhang Yimou. Released: Oct 24, 2002. 99 mins.

HOUSE OF FLYING DAGGERS, 2004

(*Shí Miàn Mái Fú*). Production: China Film Co-Production Corporation/ E.D.K.O. Films/ Elite Group/ Zhang Yimou Studio/ Beijing New Pictures. Executive producer: Weiping Zhang. Producers: Bill Kong, Zhenyan Zhang and Zhang Yimou. Script: Bin Wang, Li Feng, Peter Wu and Zhang Yimou. Direction: Zhang Yimou. Released: July 15, 2004. 119 mins.

KRRISH, 2006

Production: Filmkraft Productions. Producer: Rakesh Roshan. Script: Sanjay Masoomi, Sachin Bhowmick, Rakesh Roshan, Akash Khurana, Honey Irani and Robin Bhatt. Direction: Rakesh Roshan. Released: June 23, 2006. 175 mins.

CURSE OF THE GOLDEN FLOWER, 2006

(*Manchéng Jìndài Huángjinjia*, a.k.a. *The City of Golden Armor,* a.k.a. *Autumn Remembrance*). Production: E.D.K.O. Film/ Bejing New Pictures Film/ Elite Group Enterprises. Producers: Zhang Weiping, Bill Kong and Zhang Yimou. Script: Zhihong Bian, Nan Wu, and Zhang Yimou. Direction: Zhang Yimou. Released: Dec 21, 2006. 114 mins.

THE WARLORDS, 2007

(*Tau Ming Song* a.k.a. *The Blood Brothers*). Production: Media Asia/ China Film Group/ Morgan & Chan. Producers: Andre Morgan and Peter Chan. Script: Xu Lan, Chun Tin-nam, Aubery Lam, Huang Jianxin, Jojo Hui, He Jiping, Guo Junli and James Yuen. Direction: Peter Chan. Released: Dec 12, 2007. 127 mins.

IN THE NAME OF THE KING, 2007

Production: Brightlight Pictures/ Boll K.G. Productions/ Herold Productions. Producers: Dan Clarke, Shawn Williamson, Uwe Boll and Wolfgang Herold. Script: Doug Taylor. Direction: Uwe Boll. Released: April 11, 2007. 127 mins.

DORORO, 2007

Production: Toho/ Tokyo Broadcasting System/ Twins Japan/ Yahoo Japan/ W.O.W.O.W./ Universal/ Dentsu/ Mainichi Broadcasting System/ Hokkaido Broadcasting Company/ Asahi Shimbun/ Stardust Pictures. Producers: Takashi Hirano and Atsuyuki Shimoda. Script: Osamu Tezuka, Masa Nakamura and Akihiko Shiota. Direction: Akihiko Shiota. Released: Mch 15, 2007. 139 mins.

THE BUTTERFLY LOVERS, 2008

(*Jian Die*). Production: Brilliant Idea Group/ China Film Co-Production Corp./ Xian Mei Ah Culture Communciation Ltd. Producer: Catherine Hun. Script: Chris Ng Ka-keung, Yeung Sin-ling, Wong Nga-man, Jingle Ma Choh-shing and Chan Po-chun. Direction: Jingle Ma Choh-shing. Released: Oct 9, 2008. 102 mins.

KUNG FU DUNK, 2008

(*Gonfu* or *Guanlan* in Cantonese). Production: Shanghai Film Group/ Emperor Motion Pictures/ MediaCorp Raintree. Executive producers: Albert Yeung, Zhonglun Ren and Wu Tun. Producers: Zhao Xiaoding, Pengle Xu, Albert Lee and Yiu Kay Wah. Script: Kevin Chu Yen Ping, You-Chen Wang and Lam Chiu Wing. Direction: Kevin Chu Yen-ping. Released:

Feb 7, 2008. 98 mins.

THE TREASURE HUNTER, 2009

(*Ci Lung*). Production: Chang Hong Channel Film & Video. Producers: Han Sanping, Han Xiaoli, Jiang Tai, Raymond Lee, Pei Gin-yam, Du Yang, Ding Li, Dong Zhengrong and Han Xiao. Script: Charcoal Cheung Tan, Yip Wan-chiu, Lam Chiu-wing, Lam Ching-yan and Shao Huiting. Direction: Kevin Chu Yen-ping. Released: Dec 9, 2009. 105 mins.

FUTURE X-COPS, 2010

(*Wei Lai Jing Cha*). Production: China Film Group Corp. Producers: Ken Nickel, Haicheng Zhao, Ming Li, Sanping Han, Jason Han and Venus Keung. Direction and script: Wong Jing. Released: Apl 15, 2010. 101 mins.

THE IRON FORT'S FURIOUS LION, 2010

(*Irumbukkottai Murattu Singam*). Production: A.G.S. Entertainment. Producers: Kalpathi S. Aghoram, Kalpathi S. Ganesh and Kalpathi S. Suresh. Script and direction: Chimbu Deven. Released: May 7, 2010. 140 mins.

JUST CALL ME NOBODY, 2010

(*Da Xiao Jiang Hu*). Production: Polybona Film Distribution Co.,Ltd. Producers: Kevin Chu Yen-ping, Don Yu-dong, Maxx Tsai, Jeffrey Chan and Zhao Benshan. Script: Ning Cai Shen. Direction Kevin Chu Yen-ping. Released: Dec 3, 2010. 94 mins.

KRRISH 3, 2013

Production: Filmkraft Productions. Executive producer: Shammi Saini. Producers: Sunaina Roshan and Rakesh Roshan. Script: Rakesh Roshan, Akash Khurana, Honey Irani, Sanjay Masoomi, Irfan Kamal, David Benullo, Rajshri Sudhakar and Robin Bhatt. Direction: Rakesh Roshan. Released: Nov 1, 2013. 152 mins.

RECOMMENDED BOOKS AND WEBSITES

One of the finest general introductions to the history of Hong Kong cinema, and a great place to start, is *Hong Kong Cinema* (1997) by Stephen Teo. David Bordwell and Kristin Thompson are consistently excellent commentators on film, in books such as *Film History: An Introduction* (2010) and Bordwell's account of Hong Kong cinema, *Planet Hong Kong: Popular Cinema and the Art of Entertainment* (2000).

Bey Logan's *Hong Kong Action Cinema* (1995) is an entertaining introduction to the action side of Hong Kong cinema (with many valuable illustrations). *Kung-fu Cult Masters: From Bruce Lee To 'Crouching Tiger'* (2003) takes a more theoretical approach to the same subject.

For surveys of films, Jeff Yang's *Once Upon a Time In China* (2003) is superb, as is *Hong Kong Babylon* (1997) by F. Dannen & B. Long (this book also features many interviews with the key players in the Hong Kong industry). Lisa Morton's *The Cinema of Tsui Hark* (2001) is an important early study.

Jackie Chan has attracted many studies and biographies, including *Jackie Chan* by C. Gentry (1997), *The Essential Jackie Chan Sourcebook* by J. Rovin & K. Tracy (1997), and *Dying For Action: The Life and Times of Jackie Chan* by R. Witterstaetter (1997). And Chan's own memoirs: *I Am Jackie Chan* (1998) and *Never Grow Up* (2018).

Among critical essays, I would recommend *At Full Speed: Hong Kong Cinema In a Borderless World* (1998, edited by E.C.M. Yau) and *The Cinema of Hong Kong* (2002), edited by P. Fu & D. Desser.

WEBSITES

Hong Kong Movie Database
Love Hong Kong Film
Hong Kong Cinemagic
Film Workshop
Jet Li   jetli.com

BIBLIOGRAPHY

ON TSUI HARK

B. Accomando. "Army of Darkness: Hong Kong Director Tsui Hark Takes On the West", *Giant Robot*, 8, 1997
G. Hendrix. "Tsui Hark: Great Directors", *Senses of Cinema*, July, 2013
Howard Hampton. "Once Upon a Time In Hong Kong", *Film Comment*, 33, 1997
Hal Hinson. "*Peking Opera Blues*," *Washington Post*, Oct 14, 1988
D. Houx. "The Underrated Insanity of Tsui Hark and Jean-Claude van Damme's *Knock Off*", *Badass Digest*, 2014
A. Hwang. "The Irresistible: Hong Kong Movie *Once Upon a Time In China* Series", *Asian Cinema*, 10, 1, 1998
Y. Lee. "Artist Provocateur – On Tsui Hark", Hong Kong International Film Festival, 23, 1999
P. Macias. "Animerica Interview: Tsui Hark", *Animerica*, 7, 10
The Making of A Chinese Ghost Story: The Tsui Hark Animation, Hong Kong, 1997
L. Morton. *The Cinema of Tsui Hark*, McFarland, Jefferson, North Carolina, 2001
C. Reid. "Interview With Tsui Hark", *Film Quarterly*, 48, 3, 1995
S. Short. "Tsui Hark", interview, *Time*, CNN, 2000
Chuck Stephens. "Tsui Hark's Planet Hong Kong", *Village Voice*, May 1, 2001
S. Tan. "Ban(g)! Ban(g)! *Dangerous Encounter – 1st Kind*", *Asian Cinema*, 8, 1, 1996
Stephen Teo. "Tsui Hark: Filmography", *Senses of Cinema* 17, Nov, 2001
Tsui Hark. Interview, in F. Dannen, 1997
Ben Umstead. "An Interview With Tsui Hark", *Twitch*/ N.Y.A.F.F., 2011, July 11, 2011

OTHERS

A. Abbas. *Hong Kong*, University of Minnoestoa Press, Minneapolis, 1997
J. Abert. *A Knight At the Movies: Medieval History On Film,* Routledge, London, 2003
G. Adair. *Vietnam on Film*, Proteus, New York, NY, 1981
—. *Hollywood's Vietnam*, Heinemann, London, 1989
R.C. Allen, ed. *Channels of Discourse: Television and Contemporary Criticism*, Methuen, London, 1987
R. Altman, ed. *Sound Theory, Sound Practice*, Routledge, London, 1992
—. *Film/ Genre*, British Film Institute, London, 1999
M. Anderegg, ed. *Inventing Vietnam*, Temple University Press, Philadelphia, PA, 1991
G. Andrew. *The Film Handbook*, Longman, London, 1989
—. *Stranger Than Paradise: Maverick Filmmakers In Recent American Cinema*, Prion, 1998
A. Assister & A. Carol, eds. *Bad Girls and Dirty Pictures: The Challenge To Reclaim Feminism*, Pluto Press, London, 1993
A. Auster. *How the War Was Remembered: Hollywood and Vietnam*, Praeger, New York, NY, 1988
R. Baker & T. Russell. *The Essential Guide To Hong Kong Movies*, Eastern Heroes, London, 1994
—. *The Essential Guide To the Best of Eastern Heroes*, Eastern Heroes, London, 1995
—. *The Essential Guide To Deadly China Dolls*, Eastern Heroes, London, 1996
M. Barker, ed. *The Video Nasties: Freedom and Censorship In the Media*, Pluto Press, London, 1984
—. & J. Petley, eds. *Ill Effects: The Media/ Violence Debate*, Routledge, London, 1997
L. Bawden, ed. *The Oxford Companion To Film*, Oxford University Press, Oxford, 1976
J. Baxter. *George Lucas*, HarperCollins, London, 1999
J. Beck, ed. *Animation Art*, Flame Tree Publishing, London, 2004

M. Beja. *Film and Literature: An Introduction*, Longman, London, 1979
R. Bergan & R. Karney. *Bloomsbury Foreign Film Guide*, Bloomsbury, London, 1988
I. Bergman. *Talking With Ingmar Bergman*, Dallas, TX, 1983
—. *Bergman on Bergman, Interviews with Ingmar Bergman*, eds. S. Björkman, *et al*, tr. P. B. Austin, Touchstone, New York, NY, 1986
—. *The Magic Lantern: An Autobiography*, London, 1988
C. Berry. *Perspectives On Chinese Cinema*, B.F.I., London, 1991
P. Biskind. *Easy Riders, Raging Bulls: How the Sex 'n' Drugs 'n' Rock 'n' Roll Generation Saved Hollywood*, Bloomsbury, London, 1998
—. *Down and Dirty Pictures: Miramax, Sundance and the Rise of Independent Film*, Bloomsbury, London, 2004
M. Bliss. *Between the Bullets: The Spiritual Cinema of John Woo*, Scarecrow Press, Lanham, MD, 2002
A. Block & L. Wilson, eds. *George Lucas's Blockbusting*, HarperCollins, New York, 2010
D. Bordwell & K. Thompson. *Film Art: An Introduction*, McGraw-Hill Publishing Company, New York, NY, 1979
—. *et al. The Classical Hollywood Cinema: Film Style and Mode of Production To 1960*, Routledge, London, 1985
—. *Narration In the Fiction Film*, Routledge, London, 1988
—. *Making Meaning*, Harvard University Press, Cambridge, MA, 1989
—. & N. Caroll, eds. *Post-Theory: Reconstructing Film Studies*, University of Wisconsin Press, Madison, WI, 1996
—. *Planet Hong Kong: Popular Cinema and the Art of Entertainment*, Harvard University Press, 2000
—. "Aesthetics in Action: *Kungfu*, Gunplay and Cinematic Expressivity", in E. Yau, 2001
—. *The Way Hollywood Tells It*, University of California Press, Berkeley, CA, 2006
J. Bower, ed. *The Cinema of Japan and Korea*, Wallflower Press, London, 2004
D. Breskin. *Inner Voices: Filmmakers In Conversation*, Da Capo, New York, 1997
A. Britton *et al. American Nightmare: Essays On the Horror Film*, Toronto, 1979
A. Brown. *Directing Hong Kong: The Political Cinema of John Woo and Wong Kar-Wai*, Routledge/ Curzon, 2001
R. Brown. *Overtones and Undertones: Reading Film Music*, University of California Press, Berkeley, CA, 1994
N. Browne *et al*, eds. *New Chinese Cinema*, Cambridge University Press, 1994
S. Bukatman. *Terminal Identity: The Virtual Subject In Postmodern Science Fiction*, Duke University Press, Durham, NC, 1993
G. Burt. *The Art of Film Music*, Northeastern University Press, 1994
B. Camp & J. Davis. *Anime Classics*, Stone Bridge Press, CA, 2007
J. Campbell. *The Power of Myth*, with B. Moyers, ed. B.S. Flowers, Doubleday, New York, NY, 1988
J. Chan. *I Am Jackie Chan*, with Jeff Yang, Pan Books, 1998
—. *Never Grow Up*, Simon & Schuster, London, 2018
J. Charles. *The Hong Kong Filmography: 1977-1997*, McFarland, 2000
R. Chu. "*Swordman II* and *The East Is Red*", *Bright Lights*, 13, 1994
C. Chun-shu & Shelley Hsueh-lun Chang. *Redefining History: Ghosts, Spirits, and Human Society in Pu Sung-ling's World, 1640–1715*, University of Michigan Press, Ann Arbor, 1998
D. Chute & Cheng-Sim Lim, eds. *Heroic Grace: The Chinese Martial Arts Film*, University of California, Los Angeles, Film and Television Archive, 2003
P. Clark. *Chinese Cinema: Culture and Politics Since 1949*, Cambridge University Press, 1987
J. Clements & H. McCarthy, eds. *The Anime Encyclopedia*, Stone Bridge Press, Berkeley, CA, 2001/ 2007/ 2015
S. Cohan & I.R. Hark, eds. *Screening the Male: Exploring Masculinities In Hollywood Cinema*, Routledge, London, 1993
J. Collins *et al*, eds. *Film Theory Goes To the Movies*, Routledge, New York, NY, 1993
D.A. Cook. *A History of Narrative Film*, W.W. Norton, New York, NY, 1981, 1990, 1996
P. Cook, ed. *The Cinema Book*, British Film Institute, London, 1985/ 1999
S. Cornelius & I. Smith. *New Chinese Cinema*, Wallflower Press, London, 2002
J. Crist, ed. *Take 22: Moviemakers On Moviemaking*, Continuum, New York, NY, 1991
F. Dannen & B. Long. *Hong Kong Babylon*, Faber, London, 1997
G. Deleuze & F. Guattari. *Cinema 1: The Movement Image*, Athlone Press, London, 1989
—. *Cinema 2: The Time Image*, Athlone Press, London, 1989
C. Desjardins. *Outlaw Masters of Japanese Film*, I.B. Tauris, London, 2005
D. Desser. *Eros Plus Massacre: An Introduction to the Japanese New Wave Cinema*, Indiana University Press, Bloomington, IN, 1988
L. Dittmar & G. Michael. *From Hanoi To Hollywood*, Rutgers University Press, NJ, 1991
J. Donald, ed. *Fantasy and the Cinema*, British Film Institute, London, 1989
K.J. Donnelly, ed. *Film Music*, Edinburgh University Press, Edinburgh, 2001
C. Ducker & Stuart Cutler. *The H.K.S. Guide To Jet Li*, Hong Kong Superstars, London, 2000
M. Eagleton, ed. *Feminist Literary Theory: A Reader*, Blackwell, Oxford, 1986

—. ed. *Feminist Literary Criticism*, Longman, London, 1991
A. Easthope, ed. *Contemporary Film Theory*, Longman, London, 1993
P. Ettedgui. *Production Design & Art Direction*, RotoVision, 1999
D. Fairservice. *Film Editing*, Manchester University Press, Manchester, 2001
K. Fang. *John Woo's A Better Tomorrow, The New Hong Kong Cinema*, Hong Kong University Press, Hong Kong, 2004
C. Finch. *Special Effects*, Abbeville, 1984
J. Finler. *The Movie Director's Story*, Octopus Books, London, 1985
—. *The Hollywood Story*, Wallflower Press, London, 2003
C. Fleming. *High Concept: Don Simpson and the Hollywood Culture of Excess*, Bloomsbury, London, 1998
J. Fletcher & A. Benjamin, eds. *Abjection, Melancholia and Love: The Work of Julia Kristeva*, Routledge, London, 1990
K. Fowkes. *Giving Up the Ghost: Spirits, Ghosts and Angels In Mainstream Comedy Films*, Wayne State University Press, Detroit, MI, 1998
A. Frank. *Horror Films*, Hamlyn, London, 1977
—. *The Horror Film Handbook*, Barnes & Noble, 1982
K. French, ed. *Screen Violence*, Bloomsbury, London, 1996
P. Fu & D. Desser, eds. *The Cinema of Hong Kong*, Cambridge University Press, Cambridge, 2002
Lisa Funnell. *Warrior Women: Gender, Race, and the Transnational Chinese Action Star*, State University of New York Press, 2014
M. Gallagher. "Masculinity In Translation: Jackie Chan", *Velvet Light Trap*, 39, 1997
—. *Tony Leung Chiu-wai*, British Film Instititute, 2018
L. Gamman & M. Marshment, eds. *The Female Gaze: Women as Viewers of Popular Culture*, Women's Press, London, 1988
J. Geiger & R. Rutsky, eds. *Film Analysis*, Norton & Company, New York, NY, 2005
K. Gelder & S. Thornton, eds. *The Subcultures Reader*, Routledge, London, 1997
—. ed. *The Horror Reader*, Routledge, London, 2000
J. Gelmis. *The Film Director as Superstar*, Penguin, London, 1974
C. Gentry. *Jackie Chan*, Taylor, Dallas, TX, 1997
Jean-Luc Godard. *Godard on Godard*, eds. J. Narobi & T. Milne, Da Capo, New York, NY, 1986
—. *Interviews*, ed. D. Sterritt, University of Mississippi Press, Jackson, 1998
L . Goldberg *et al*, eds. *Science Fiction Filmmaking In the 1980s*, McFarland, Jefferson, 1995
M. Goodwin & N. Wise. *On the Edge: The Life and Times of Francis Coppola*, William Morrow, New York, NY, 1989
B.K. Grant, ed. *Film Genre*, Scarecrow Press, Metuchen, NJ, 1977
—. ed. *Planks of Reason: Essays on the Horror Film*, Scarecrow Press, Metuchen, NJ, 1984
—. *Film Genre Reader II*, University of Texas Press, Austin, TX, 1995
—. ed. *The Dread of Difference: Gender and the Horror Film*, University of Texas Press, Austin, TX, 1996
E. Grosz. *Sexual Subversions*, Allen & Unwin, London, 1989
—. *Jacques Lacan: A Feminist Introduction*, Routledge, London, 1990
—. *Volatile Bodies,* Indiana University Press, Bloomington, IN, 1994
—. *Space, Time and Perversion*, Routledge, London, 1995
K. Hall. *John Woo: The Films*, McFarland & Co., Jefferson, N.C., 1999
L. Halliwell. *Halliwell's Filmgoer's Companion*, 7th edition, Granada, London, 1980
D. Hamamoto & S. Liu, eds. *Countervision: Asian-American Film Criticism*, Temple University Press, Philadelphia, PA, 2000
S. Hammond. *Hollywood East*, Contemporary Books, Lincoln, IL, 2000
P. Hardy, ed. *The Aurum Encyclopedia of Science Fiction*, Aurum, London, 1991
C. Heard. *Ten Thousand Bullets: The Cinematic Journey of John Woo*, Lone Eagle Publishing Co., L.A., 2000
S. & N. Hibbin. *The Official James Bond Movie Book*, Hamlyn, London, 1989
G. Hickenlooper. *Reel Conversations: Candid Interviews With Film's Foremost Directors and Critics*, Citadel, New York, NY, 1991
J. Hillier. *The New Hollywood*, Studio Vista, London, 1992
—. *American Independent Cinema: A Sight & Sound Reader*, British Film Institute, London, 2001
L.C. Hillstrom, ed. *International Dictionary of Films and Filmmakers: Directors*, St James Press, London, 1997
Sam Ho, ed. *The Swordsman and His Juang Hu: Tsui Hark and Hong Kong Film*, Hong Kong University Press, Hong Kong, 2002
Hong Kong Film Archive. *The Making of Martial Arts Films*, Hong Kong Provisional Urban Council, 1999
Hong Kong International Film Festival. *Hong Kong Panorama*, Leisure and Cultural Services Department
Hong Kong International Film Festival. *Hong Kong New Wave: Twenty Years After*, Provisional Urban Council of Hong Kong, 1999

Hong Kong International Film Festival. *Hong Kong Cinema '79-'89,* Leisure and Cultural Services Department, 2000
D. Hudson. *Draculas, Vampires, and Other Undead Forms*, Rowman & Littlefield, 2009
D. Hughes. *Comic Book Movies*, Virgin, London, 2003
L. Hughes. *The Rough Guide To Gangster Movies,* Penguin, 2005
L. Hunt. "Once Upon a Time In China: Kung Fu From Bruce Lee To Jet Li", *Framework*, 40, 1999
—. *Kung-fu Cult Masters: From Bruce Lee To 'Crouching Tiger',* Wallflower Press, London, 2003
J. Hunter. *Eros In Hell: Sex, Blood and Madness In Japanese Cinema*, Creation Books, London, 1998
J. Inverne. *Musicals*, Faber, London, 2009
L. Irigiaray. *The Irigaray Reader,* ed. M. Whitford, Blackwell, Oxford, 1991
S. Jackson & J. Jones, eds. *Contemporary Feminist Theories*, Edinburgh University Press, Edinburgh, 1998
S. Jaworzyn, ed. *Shock: The Essential Guide To Exploitation Cinema*, Titan Books, London, 1996
S. Jeffords. *Hard Bodies: Hollywood Masculinity In the Reagan Era*, Rutgers University Press, New Brunswick, NJ, 1994
E. Jeffreys & L. Edwards, eds. *Celebrity In China*, Hong Kong University Press, Hong Kong, 2010
K. Kalinak. *Settling the Score: Music and the Classical Hollywood Film*, University of Wisconsin Press, Madison, WI, 1992
B.F. Kawin. *Mindscreen: Bergman, Godard and First-Person Film*, Princeton University Press, Princeton, NJ, 1978
—. *How Movies Work*, Macmillan, New York, NY, 1987
P. Keough, ed. *Flesh and Blood: The National Society of Film Critics on Sex, Violence, and Censorship*, Mercury House, San Francisco, CA, 1995
M. Kinder. *Playing With Power In Movies*, University of California Press, Berkeley, CA, 1991
P. Kolker. *The Altering Eye: Contemporary International Cinema*, Oxford University Press, New York, NY, 1983
—. *A Cinema of Loneliness: Penn, Stone, Kubrick, Scorsese, Spielberg, Altman*, Oxford University Press, New York, NY, 2000
P. Kramer. *The Big Picture: Hollywood Cinema From Star Wars To Titanic*, British Film Institute, London, 2001
—. *The New Hollywood*, Wallflower Press, London, 2005
J. Kristeva. *About Chinese Women,* tr. A. Barrows, Marion Boyars, London, 1977
—. *Desire In Language: A Semiotic Approach To Literature and Art*, ed. L.S. Roudiez, tr. T. Gora *et al*, Blackwell 1982
—. *Powers of Horror: An Essay on Abjection,* tr. L.S. Roudiez, Columbia University Press, New York, NY, 1982
—. *Revolution In Poetic Language*, tr. M. Walker, Columbia University Press, New York, NY, 1984
—. *The Kristeva Reader*, ed. T. Moi, Blackwell, Oxford, 1986
—. *Tales of Love*, tr. L.S. Roudiez, Columbia University Press, New York, NY, 1987
—. *Black Sun: Depression and Melancholy*, tr. L.S. Roudiez, Columbia University Press, New York, NY, 1989
—. *Strangers To Ourselves*, tr. L.S. Roudiez, Harvester Wheatsheaf 1991
J. Kwok Wah Lau. "Imploding Genre, Gender and History: *Peking Opera Blues*", in J. Geiger, 2005
M. Lanning. *Vietnam At the Movies*, Fawcett Columbine, New York, NY, 1994
R. Lapsley & M. Westlake, eds. *Film Theory: An Introduction*, Manchester University Press, Manchester, 1988
Shing-hou Lau, ed. *A Study of the Hong Kong Martial Arts Film*, Hong Kong International Film Festival, 1980
—. *A Study of the Hong Kong Swordplay Film, 1945-80*, Hong Kong International Film Festival, 1981
Law Kar, ed. *Fifty Years of Elecric Shadows*, Hong Kong International Film Festival, 1997
M. Lee. "*Once Upon a Time In China*", Criterion, 2021
J. Lent. *The Asian Film Industry*, Austin, TX, 1990
T. Leung Siu-hung. "Mastering Action", Hong Kong Cinemagic, March, 2006
E. Levy. *Cinema of Outsiders: The Rise of American Independent Film*, New York University Press, New York, NY, 1999
J. Lewis. *The Road To Romance and Ruin: Teen Films and Youth Culture*, Routledge, London, 1992
—. *Whom God Wishes To Destroy: Francis Coppola and the New Hollywood*, Duke University Press, Durham, NC, 1995
—. ed. *New American Cinema*, Duke University Press, Durham, NC, 1998
—. *Hollywood v. Hard Core: How the Struggle Over Censorship Created the Modern Film Industry,* New York University Press, New York, NY, 2000

J. Leyda. ed. *Film Makers Speak: Voices of Film Experience*, Da Capo, New York, NY, 1977
V. LoBrutto. *Sound-On-Film*, Praeger, New York, NY, 1994
B. Logan. *Hong Kong Action Cinema*, Titan, London, 1995
S. Lu, ed. *Transnational Chinese Cinemas*, University of Hawaii Press, Honolulu, 1997
H. Ludi. *Movie Worlds: Production Design In Film*, Mengers, Stuttgart, 2000
B. McCabe. *The Rough Guide To Comedy Movies*, Rough Guides, London, 2005
R. Maltby. *Harmless Entertainment: Hollywood and the Ideology of Consensus*, Scarecrow Press, Metuchen, NJ, 1983
—. & I. Craven. *Hollywood Cinema: An Introduction*, Blackwell, Oxford, 1995
—. *Hollywood Cinema*, 2nd ed., Blackwell, Oxford, 2003
E. Marks & I. de Courtivron, eds. *New French Feminisms: an anthology*, Harvester Wheatsheaf, Hemel Hempstead, 1981
G. Mast *et al*, eds. *Film Theory and Criticism: Introductory Readings*, Oxford University Press, New York, NY, 1992a
—. & B Kawin. *A Short History of the Movies*, Macmillan, New York, NY, 1992b
C. Marx. *Jet Li*, Martial Arts Masters, Rosen Publishing Group, 2002
T.D. Matthews. *Censored*, Chatto & Windus, London, 1994
F. McConnell. *Storytelling and Mythmaking*, Oxford University Press, New York, NY, 1979
S.Y. McDougal. *Made Into Movies: From Literature To Film*, Holt, Rinehart and Winston, New York, NY, 1985
M. Medved. *Hollywood vs. America*, HarperCollins, London, 1992
R. Meyers. *Martial Arts Movies*, Citadel Press, NJ, 1985
—. *Great Martial Arts Movies*, Citadel Press, NJ, 2001
D. Millar. *Cinema Secrets: Special Effects*, Apple Press, 1990
T. Miller *et al*, eds. *Global Hollywood*, British Film Institute, London, 2001
T. Moi. *Sexual/ Textual Politics: Feminist Literary Theory*, Methuen, London, 1983
J. Monaco. *The New Wave: Truffaut, Godard, Chabrol, Rohmer, Rivette*, Oxford University Press, New York, NY, 1977
—. *American Film Now*, New American Library, London, 1979
—. *How To Read a Film*, Oxford University Press, Oxford, 1981
R. Murray. *Images In the Dark: An Encyclopedia of Gay and Lesbian Film and Video*, Titan Books, London, 1998
S. Neale. *Cinema and Technology*, Macmillan, London, 1985
—. & M. Smith, eds. *Contemporary Hollywood Cinema*, Routledge, London, 1998
—. *Genre and Contemporary Hollywood*, Routledge, London, 2002
J. Nelmes, ed. *An Introduction To Film Studies*, Routledge, London, 1996
D. Neumann, ed. *Film Architecture: From Metropolis To Blade Runner*, Prestel-Verlag, New York, NY, 1996
K. Newman. *Nightmare Movies*, Harmony, New York, NY, 1988
—. *Millennium Movies*, Titan Books, London, 1999
G. Nowell-Smith, ed. *The Oxford History of World Cinema*, Oxford University Press, Oxford, 1996
D. O'Brien. *Spooky Encounters: A Gwailo's Guide To Hong Kong Horror,* Headpress, 2004
T. Ohanian & M. Phillips. *Digital Filmmaking*, 2nd ed., Focal Press, Boston, MA, 2000
J. Orr. *Contemporary Cinema*, Edinburgh University Press, Edinburgh, 1998
B. Palmer *et al*. *The Encyclopedia of Martial Arts Movies*, Scarecrow Press, NJ, 1995
A. Paludan. *Chronicle of the Chinese Emperors*, Thames & Hudson, 1998
L. Pang. *Masculinities and Hong Kong Cinema,* Kent State University Press, 2005
D. Parkinson. *The Rough Guide To Film Musicals*, Penguin, London, 2007
J. Parish. *Jet Li: A Biography*, Thunder's Mouth Press, New York, 2002
F. Patten. *Watching Anime, Reading Manga*, Stone Bridge Press, CA, 2004
D. Peary & G. Peary, eds. *The American Animated Cartoon*, Dutton, New York, NY, 1980
—. *Cult Movies 2*, Vermilion, London, 1984
—. *Cult Movies 3,* Sigwick & Jackson, London, 1989
C. Penley, ed. *Feminism and Film Theory*, Routledge, London, 1988
D. Petrie. *Screening Europe: Image and Identity In Contemporary European Cinema*, British Film Institute, London, 1992
P. Phillips. *Understanding Film Texts*, British Film Institute, London, 2000
M. Pierson. *Special Effects*, Columbia University Press, New York, NY, 2002
L. Pietropaolo & A. Testaferri, eds. *Feminisms In the Cinema*, Indiana University Press, Bloomington, IN, 1995
D. Pollock. *Skywalking: The Life and Films of George Lucas*, Crown, New York, NY, 1983, 1990, 2000
M. Polly. *Bruce Lee*, Simon & Schuster, New York, 2018
S. Prince, ed. *Screening Violence*, Athlone Press, London, 2000
D. Prindle. *Risky Business: The Political Economy of Hollywood*, Westview, Boulder, CO, 1993
N. Proferes. *Film Directing Fundamentals*, Focal Press, Boston, MA, 2001
M. Pye & Lynda Myles. *The Movie Brats: How the Film Generation Took Over Hollywood*, Faber, London, 1979
T. Reeves. *The Worldwide Guide To Movie Locations*, Titan Books, London, 2003

P. Rice & P. Waugh, eds. *Modern Literary Theory: A Reader*, Arnold, London, 1992
D. Richie. *The Films of Akira Kurosawa*, University of California Press, Berkeley, CA, 1965
R. Rickitt. *Special Effects*, Aurum, London, 2006
B. Robb. *Screams and Nightmares*, Titan Books, London, 1998
J. Robertson. *The British Board of Film Censors*, Croom Helm, 1985
D. Robinson. *World Cinema*, Methuen, London, 1981
W.H. Rockett. *Devouring Whirlwind: Terror and Transcendence In the Cinema of Cruelty*, Greenwood Press, New York, NY, 1988
S. Rohdie. *The Passion of Pier Paolo Pasolini*, British Film Institute, London, 1995
J. Romney & A. Wootton, eds. *Celluloid Jukebox: Popular Music and the Movies Since the 50s*, British Film Institute, London, 1995
P. Rosen, ed. *Narrative, Apparatus, Ideology: A Film Theory Reader*, Columbia University Press, New York, NY, 1986
J. Rosenbaum. *Placing Movies*, University of California Press, Berkeley, CA, 1995
R. Rosenblum & R. Karen. *When the Shooting Stops... The Cutting Begins: A Film Editor's Story*, Da Capo Press, New York, NY, 1979
J. Ross. *The Incredibly Strange Film Book: An Alternative History of Cinema*, Simon and Schuster, 1993
The Rough Guide To China, Penguin, 2017
R. Roud. *Jean-Luc Godard*, Thames & Hudson, London, 1970
J. Rovin & K. Tracy. *The Essential Jackie Chan Sourcebook*, Pocket Books, New York, 1997
M. Rubin. *Thrillers*, Cambridge University Press, Cambridge, 1999
K. Russell. *A British Picture: An Autobiography*, Heinemann, London, 1989
V. Russo. *The Celluloid Closet: Homosexuality In the Movies*, Harper & Row, New York, NY, 1981
K. Sandler. *Reading the Rabbit: Explorations In Warner Bros. Animation*, Rutgers University Press, Brunswick, NJ, 1998
A. Sarris. *The American Cinema*, Dutton, New York, NY, 1968
T. Sato. *Currents In Japanese Cinema*, Kodansha, New York, 1982
D. Schaefer & L. Salvato, eds. *Masters of Light*, University of California Press, Berkeley, CA, 1984
T. Schatz. *Hollywood Genres*, Random House, New York, NY, 1981
—. *Old Hollywood/ New Hollywood*, UMI Research Press, Ann Arbor, MI, 1983
—. *The Genius of the System: Hollywood Filmmaking In the Studio Era*, Pantheon, New York, NY 1988
F. Schodt. *Inside the Robot Kingdom: Japan, Mechatronics and the Coming Robotopia*, Kodansha, Tokyo, 1988
—. *Manga! Manga! The World of Japanese Magazines*, Kodansha International, London, 1997
—. *Dreamland Japan: Writings On Modern Manga*, Stone Bridge Press, Berkeley, CA, 2002
P. Schrader. *Transcendental Style In Film: Ozu, Bresson, Dreyer*, Da Capo Press, 1972
A. Schroeder. *Tsui Hark's Zu: Warriors From the Magic Mountain*, Hong Kong University Press, Hong Kong, 2004
R. Schubart. *Super Bitches and Action Babes: The Female Hero In Popular Cinema, 1970-2006*, McFarland, 2007
M. Schumacher. *Francis Ford Coppola*, Bloomsbury, London, 2000
M. Scorsese. *Scorsese On Scorsese*, ed. D. Thompson & I. Christie, Faber, London, 1989, 1995
Screen Reader I: Cinema/ Ideology/ Politics, Society for Education in Film & TV, 1977
Screen Reader II: Cinema and Semiotics, British Film Institute, London, 1982
C. Sharrett, ed. *Crisis Cinema*, Maisonneuve Press, Washington, DC, 1993
—. *Mythologies of Violence In Postmodern Media*, Wayne State University Press, 1999
M. Shiel & T. Fitzmaurice, eds. *Screenng the City*, Verso, London, 2003
D. Shipman. *The Story of Cinema*, Hodder & Stoughton, London, 1984
T. Shone. *Blockbuster: How the Jaws and Jedi Generation Turned Hollywood Into a Boom-Town*, Scribner, London, 2005
E. Showalter, ed. *The New Feminist Criticism*, Virago, London, 1986
E. Siciliano. *Pasolini: A Biography*, Bloomsbury, London, 1987
L. Sider et al, eds. *Soundscapes: The School of Sound Lectures 1998-2001*, Wallflower Press, London, 2003
M. Singer. *A History of the American Avant-Garde Cinema*, American Federation of the Arts, New York, NY, 1976
P. Adams Sitney, ed. *The Film Culture Reader*, Praeger, New York, NY, 1970
—. ed. *The Avant-Garde Film: A Reader of Theory and Criticism*, New York University Press, New York, NY, 1978
—. *Visionary Film: The American Avant-Garde, 1943-1978*, 2nd ed., Oxford University Press, New York, NY, 1979
G. Smith. *Epic Films*, McFarland, Jefferson, NC, 1991
J. Smith. *Looking Away: Hollywood and Vietnam*, Scribner's, New York, NY, 1975
T.G. Smith. *Industrial Light and Magic: The Art of Special Effects*, Columbus Books, 1986

E. Smoodin. *Animating Culture: Hollywood Cartoons From the Sound Era*, Roundhouse, 1993
—. ed. *Disney Discourse: Producing the Magic Kingdom*, Routledge, London, 1994
V. Sobchack. *The Limits of Infinity: The American Science Fiction Film*, A.S. Barnes, New York, NY, 1980
—. *Screening Space: The American Science Fiction Film*, Ungar, New York, NY, 1987/ 1993
J. Squire, ed. *The Movie Business Book*, Fireside, New York, NY, 1992
J. Staiger. *Interpreting Films*, Princeton University Press, Princeton, NJ, 1992
—. *Perverse Spectators: The Practices of Film Reception*, New York University Press, New York, NY, 2000
N. Stair. *Michelle Yeoh*, Rosen Publishing Group, 2001
B. Steene. *Ingmar Bergman*, Twayne, Boston, MA, 1968
L. Stern. *The Scorsese Connection*, British Film Institute, London, 1995
D. Sterritt. *The Films of Jean-Luc Godard*, Cambridge University Press, Cambridge, 1999
G. Stewart. *Between Film and Screen: Modernism's Photo Synthesis*, University of Chicago Press, Chicago, IL, 1999
M. Stokes & R. Maltby, eds. *Identifying Hollywood Audiences*, British Film Institute, London, 1999
J. Storey, ed. *Cultural Theory and Popular Culture*, Harvester Wheatsheaf, Hemel Hempstead, 1994
J.M. Straczynski. *The Complete Book of Scriptwriting*, Titan Books, London, 1997
J. Stringer. "Problems With the Treatment of Hong Kong Cinema As Camp", *Asian Cinema*, 8, 2, 1996
—. ed. *Movie Blockbusters*, Routledge, London, 2003
C. Sylvester, ed. *The Penguin Book of Hollywood*, Penguin, London, 1999
K. Tam & W. Dissanayake. *New Chinese Cinema*, Oxford University Press, Hong Kong, 1998
A. Tarkovsky. *Sculpting In Time: Reflections On the Cinema*, tr. K. Hunter-Blair, Faber, London, 1989
C. Tashiro. *Pretty Pictures: Production Design and the History Film*, University of Texas Press, 1998
Y. Tasker. *Spectacular Bodies: Gender, Genre and the Action Cinema*, Routledge, London, 1993
R. Taylor et al, eds. *The B.F.I. Companion To Eastern European and Russian Cinema*, British Film Institute, London, 2000
S. Teo. *Hong Kong Cinema*, British Film Institute, London, 1997
—. "Tsui Hark", in C. Yau, 1998
B. Thomas. *Video Hound's Dragon: Asian Action and Cult Flicks*, Visible Ink Press, 2003
K. Thompson & D. Bordwell. *Film History: An Introduction*, McGraw-Hill, New York, NY, 1994/ 2010
—. *Storytelling In the New Hollywood*, Harvard University Press, Cambridge, MA, 1999
D. Thomson. *A Biographical Dictionary of Film*, Deutsch, London, 1995
S. Thrower, ed. *Eyeball: Compendium: Sex and Horror, Art and Exploitation*, F.A.B. Press, Godalming, Surrey, 2003
C. Tohill & P. Tombs. *Immoral Tales: Sex and Horror Cinema In Europe 1956-1984*, Titan Books, London, 1995
J. Trevelyan. *What the Censor Saw*, Michael Joseph, London, 1973
A.D. Vacche. *Cinema and Painting*, Athlone Press, London, 1996
K. Van Gunden. *Fantasy Films*, McFarland, Jefferson, NC 1989
—. *Postmodern Auteurs: Coppola, Lucas, De Palma, Spielberg and Scorsese*, McFarland, Jefferson, NC 1991
M.C. Vaz. *From Star Wars To Indiana Jones*, Chronicle, San Francisco, CA, 1994
—. & P.R. Duignan. *Industrial Light & Magic*, Virgin, London, 1996
G. Vincendeau, ed. *Encyclopedia of European Cinema*, British Film Institute, London, 1995
—. ed. *Film/ Literature/ Heritage: A Sight & Sound Reader*, British Film Institute, London, 2001
P. Virillio. *War and Cinema*, Verso, London, 1992
D. Vivier & T. Podvin. "Through the Lens of Arthur Wong", Hong Kong Cinemagic, Jan 2005
H. Vogel. *Entertainment Industry Economics*, Cambridge University Press, Cambridge, 1995
C. Vogler. *The Writer's Journey: Mythic Structure For Storytellers and Screenwriters*, Pan, London, 1998
J. Wasko. *Movies and Money*, Ablex, NJ, 1982
—. *Hollywood In the Information Age*, Polity Press, Cambridge, 1994
E. Weiss. & J. Belton, eds. *Film Sound: Theory and Practice*, Columbia University Press, New York, NY, 1989
T. Weisser. *Asian Cult Cinema*, Boulveard Books, New York, NY, 1997
O. Welles. *This is Orson Welles*, HarperCollins, London, 1992
P. Wells. *Understanding Animation*, Routledge, London, 1998
D. West. *Chasing Dragons: An Introduction To the Martial Arts Film*, I.B. Tauris, London, 2006
L. Williams, ed. *Viewing Positions: Ways of Seeing Film*, Rutgers University Press, New

Brunswick, NJ, 1995
T. Williams. "To Live and Die In Hong Kong", *Cineaction*, 36, 1995
—. "Kwan Tak-hing and the New Generation", *Asian Cinema*, 10, 1, 1998
—. "Space, Place and Spectacle: the Crisis Cinema of John Woo", in P. Fu, 2002
R. Witterstaetter. *Dying For Action: The Life and Times of Jackie Chan*, Warner Books, New York, 1997
M. Wolf. *The Entertainment Economy,* Penguin, London, 1999
P. Wollen: *Signs and Meaning In the Cinema*, Secker & Warburg, London, 1972
J. Woo. Interview, in J. Arroyo, 2000
—. *Interviews; Conversations With Filmmakers Series*, ed. R. Elder, University Press of Mississippi, 2005
M. Wood. *Cine East: Hong Kong Cinema Through the Looking Glass*, F.A.B. Press, 1998
R. Wood. *Hollywood From Vietnam To Reagan... and Beyond*, Columbia University Press, New York, NY, 2003
T. Woods. *Beginning Postmodernism,* Manchester University Press, Manchester, 1999
J. Wyatt. *High Concept: Movies and Marketing In Hollywood*, University of Texas Press, Austin, TX, 1994
J. Yang *et al. Eastern Standard Time: A Guide To Asian Influence On American Culture*, Houghton Mifflin, Boston, MA, 1997
—. *Once Upon a Time In China*, Atria Books, New York, NY, 2003
E.C.M. Yau, ed. *At Full Speed: Hong Kong Cinema In a Borderless World*, University of Minnesota Press, Minneapolis, MN, 1998
Z. Yimou. *Zhang Yimou: Interviews, Conversations With Filmmakers Series*, ed. F. Gateward, University Press of Mississippi, 2001
Judith T. Zeitlin. *Historian of the Strange: Pu Songling and the Chinese Classical Tale*, Stanford University Press, Stanford, CA, 1993
Y. Zhang & X. Zhiwei, eds. *Encyclopedia of Chinese Film*, Routledge, 1998
J. Zipes. *The Enchanted Screen: The Unknown History of Fairy-tale Films*, Routledge, New York, NY, 2011
S. Zizek. *Enjoy Your Symptom Jacques Lacan In Hollywood and Out*, Routledge, New York, NY, 1992
—. *The Fright of Real Tears: The Uses and Misuses of Lacan In Film Theory*, British Film Institute, London, 1999

JEREMY ROBINSON has published poetry, fiction, and studies of J.R.R. Tolkien, Samuel Beckett, Thomas Hardy, André Gide and D.H. Lawrence. Robinson has edited poetry books by Novalis, Ursula Le Guin, Friedrich Hölderlin, Francesco Petrarch, Dante Alighieri, Arseny Tarkovsky, and Rainer Maria Rilke.

Books on film and animation include: *The Akira Book* • *The Art of Katsuhiro Otomo* • *The Art of Masamune Shirow* • *The Ghost In the Shell Book* • *Fullmetal Alchemist* • *Cowboy Bebop: The Anime and Movie* • *The Cinema of Hayao Miyazaki* • *Hayao Miyazaki: Pocket Guide* • *Princess Mononoke: Pocket Movie Guide* • *Spirited Away: Pocket Movie Guide* • *Blade Runner and the Cinema of Philip K. Dick* • *Blade Runner: Pocket Movie Guide* • *The Cinema of Donald Cammell* • *Performance: Donald Cammell: Nic Roeg: Pocket Movie Guide* • *Pasolini: Il Cinema di Poesia/ The Cinema of Poetry* • *Salo: Pocket Movie Guide* • *The Trilogy of Life Movies: Pocket Movie Guide* • *The Gospel According To Matthew: Pocket Movie Guide* • *The Ecstatic Cinema of Tony Ching Siu-tung* • *Tsui Hark: The Dragon Master of Chinese Cinema* • *The Swordsman: Pocket Movie Guide* • *A Chinese Ghost Story: Pocket Movie Guide* • *Ken Russell: England's Great Visionary Film Director and Music Lover* • *Tommy: Ken Russell: The Who: Pocket Movie Guide* • *Women In Love: Ken Russell: D.H. Lawrence: Pocket Movie Guide* • *The Devils: Ken Russell: Pocket Movie Guide* • *Walerian Borowczyk: Cinema of Erotic Dreams* • *The Beast: Pocket Movie Guide* • *The Lord of the Rings Movies* • *The Fellowship of the Ring: Pocket Movie Guide* • *The Two Towers: Pocket Movie Guide* • *The Return of the King: Pocket Movie Guide* • *Jean-Luc Godard: The Passion of Cinema* • *The Sacred Cinema of Andrei Tarkovsky* • *Andrei Tarkovsky: Pocket Guide*.

'It's amazing for me to see my work treated with such passion and respect. There is nothing resembling it in the U.S. in relation to my work.'
(Andrea Dworkin)

'This model monograph – it is an exemplary job, and I'm very proud that he has accorded me a couple of mentions… The subject matter of his book is beautifully organised and dead on beam.'
(Lawrence Durrell, on *The Light Eternal: A Study of J.M.W. Turner*)

'Jeremy Robinson's poetry is certainly jammed with ideas, and I find it very interesting for that reason. It's certainly a strong imprint of his personality.'
(Colin Wilson)

'*Sex-Magic-Poetry-Cornwall* is a very rich essay... It is a very good piece… vastly stimulating and insightful.'
(Peter Redgrove)

CRESCENT MOON PUBLISHING

web: www.crmoon.com e-mail: cresmopub@yahoo.co.uk

ARTS, PAINTING, SCULPTURE

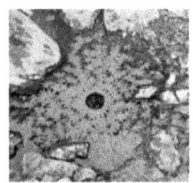

The Art of Andy Goldsworthy
Andy Goldsworthy: Touching Nature
Andy Goldsworthy in Close-Up
Andy Goldsworthy: Pocket Guide
Andy Goldsworthy In America
Land Art: A Complete Guide
The Art of Richard Long
Richard Long: Pocket Guide
Land Art In the UK
Land Art in Close-Up
Land Art In the U.S.A.
Land Art: Pocket Guide
Installation Art in Close-Up
Minimal Art and Artists In the 1960s and After
Colourfield Painting
Land Art DVD, TV documentary
Andy Goldsworthy DVD, TV documentary
The Erotic Object: Sexuality in Sculpture From Prehistory to the Present Day
Sex in Art: Pornography and Pleasure in Painting and Sculpture
Postwar Art
Sacred Gardens: The Garden in Myth, Religion and Art
Glorification: Religious Abstraction in Renaissance and 20th Century Art
Early Netherlandish Painting
Leonardo da Vinci
Piero della Francesca
Giovanni Bellini
Fra Angelico: Art and Religion in the Renaissance
Mark Rothko: The Art of Transcendence
Frank Stella: American Abstract Artist
Jasper Johns
Brice Marden
Alison Wilding: The Embrace of Sculpture
Vincent van Gogh: Visionary Landscapes
Eric Gill: Nuptials of God
Constantin Brancusi: Sculpting the Essence of Things
Max Beckmann
Caravaggio
Gustave Moreau
Egon Schiele: Sex and Death In Purple Stockings
Delizioso Fotografico Fervore: Works In Process 1
Sacro Cuore: Works In Process 2
The Light Eternal: J.M.W. Turner
The Madonna Glorified: Karen Arthurs

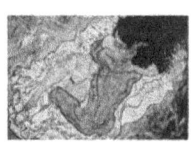

LITERATURE

J.R.R. Tolkien: The Books, The Films, The Whole Cultural Phenomenon
J.R.R. Tolkien: Pocket Guide
Tolkien's Heroic Quest
The *Earthsea* Books of Ursula Le Guin
Beauties, Beasts and Enchantment: Classic French Fairy Tales
German Popular Stories by the Brothers Grimm
Philip Pullman and *His Dark Materials*
Sexing Hardy: Thomas Hardy and Feminism
Thomas Hardy's *Tess of the d'Urbervilles*
Thomas Hardy's *Jude the Obscure*
Thomas Hardy: The Tragic Novels
Love and Tragedy: Thomas Hardy
The Poetry of Landscape in Hardy
Wessex Revisited: Thomas Hardy and John Cowper Powys
Wolfgang Iser: Essays and Interviews
Petrarch, Dante and the Troubadours
Maurice Sendak and the Art of Children's Book Illustration
Andrea Dworkin
Cixous, Irigaray, Kristeva: The *Jouissance* of French Feminism
Julia Kristeva: Art, Love, Melancholy, Philosophy, Semiotics and Psychoanalysis
Hélène Cixous I Love You: The *Jouissance* of Writing
Luce Irigaray: Lips, Kissing, and the Politics of Sexual Difference
Peter Redgrove: Here Comes the Flood
Peter Redgrove: Sex-Magic-Poetry-Cornwall
Lawrence Durrell: Between Love and Death, East and West
Love, Culture & Poetry: Lawrence Durrell
Cavafy: Anatomy of a Soul
German Romantic Poetry: Goethe, Novalis, Heine, Hölderlin
Feminism and Shakespeare
Shakespeare: Love, Poetry & Magic
The Passion of D.H. Lawrence
D.H. Lawrence: Symbolic Landscapes
D.H. Lawrence: Infinite Sensual Violence
Rimbaud: Arthur Rimbaud and the Magic of Poetry
The Ecstasies of John Cowper Powys
Sensualism and Mythology: The Wessex Novels of John Cowper Powys
Amorous Life: John Cowper Powys and the Manifestation of Affectivity (H.W. Fawkner)
Postmodern Powys: New Essays on John Cowper Powys (Joe Boulter)
Rethinking Powys: Critical Essays on John Cowper Powys
Paul Bowles & Bernardo Bertolucci
Rainer Maria Rilke
Joseph Conrad: *Heart of Darkness*
In the Dim Void: Samuel Beckett
Samuel Beckett Goes into the Silence
André Gide: Fiction and Fervour
Jackie Collins and the Blockbuster Novel
Blinded By Her Light: The Love-Poetry of Robert Graves
The Passion of Colours: Travels In Mediterranean Lands
Poetic Forms

POETRY

Ursula Le Guin: Walking In Cornwall
Peter Redgrove: Here Comes The Flood
Peter Redgrove: Sex-Magic-Poetry-Cornwall
Dante: Selections From the Vita Nuova
Petrarch, Dante and the Troubadours
William Shakespeare: Sonnets
William Shakespeare: Complete Poems
Blinded By Her Light: The Love-Poetry of Robert Graves
Emily Dickinson: Selected Poems
Emily Brontë: Poems
Thomas Hardy: Selected Poems
Percy Bysshe Shelley: Poems
John Keats: Selected Poems
Joh n Keats: Poems of 1820
D.H. Lawrence: Selected Poems
Edmund Spenser: Poems
Edmund Spenser: Amoretti
John Donne: Poems
Henry Vaughan: Poems
Sir Thomas Wyatt: Poems
Robert Herrick: Selected Poems
Rilke: Space, Essence and Angels in the Poetry of Rainer Maria Rilke
Rainer Maria Rilke: Selected Poems
Friedrich Hölderlin: Selected Poems
Arseny Tarkovsky: Selected Poems
Arthur Rimbaud: Selected Poems
Arthur Rimbaud: A Season in Hell
Arthur Rimbaud and the Magic of Poetry
Novalis: Hymns To the Night
German Romantic Poetry
Paul Verlaine: Selected Poems
Elizaethan Sonnet Cycles
D.J. Enright: By-Blows
Jeremy Reed: Brigitte's Blue Heart
Jeremy Reed: Claudia Schiffer's Red Shoes
Gorgeous Little Orpheus
Radiance: New Poems
Crescent Moon Book of Nature Poetry
Crescent Moon Book of Love Poetry
Crescent Moon Book of Mystical Poetry
Crescent Moon Book of Elizabethan Love Poetry
Crescent Moon Book of Metaphysical Poetry
Crescent Moon Book of Romantic Poetry
Pagan America: New American Poetry

MEDIA, CINEMA, FEMINISM and CULTURAL STUDIES

J.R.R. Tolkien: The Books, The Films, The Whole Cultural Phenomenon
J.R.R. Tolkien: Pocket Guide
The *Lord of the Rings* Movies: Pocket Guide
The Cinema of Hayao Miyazaki
Hayao Miyazaki: *Princess Mononoke*: Pocket Movie Guide
Hayao Miyazaki: *Spirited Away*: Pocket Movie Guide
Tim Burton : Hallowe'en For Hollywood
Ken Russell
Ken Russell: *Tommy*: Pocket Movie Guide
The Ghost Dance: The Origins of Religion
The Peyote Cult
Cixous, Irigaray, Kristeva: The *Jouissance* of French Feminism
Julia Kristeva: Art, Love, Melancholy, Philosophy, Semiotics and Psychoanalysis
Luce Irigaray: Lips, Kissing, and the Politics of Sexual Difference
Hélène Cixous I Love You: The *Jouissance* of Writing
Andrea Dworkin
'Cosmo Woman': The World of Women's Magazines
Women in Pop Music
HomeGround: The Kate Bush Anthology
Discovering the Goddess (Geoffrey Ashe)
The Poetry of Cinema
The Sacred Cinema of Andrei Tarkovsky
Andrei Tarkovsky: Pocket Guide
Andrei Tarkovsky: *Mirror*: Pocket Movie Guide
Andrei Tarkovsky: *The Sacrifice*: Pocket Movie Guide
Walerian Borowczyk: Cinema of Erotic Dreams
Jean-Luc Godard: The Passion of Cinema
Jean-Luc Godard: *Hail Mary*: Pocket Movie Guide
Jean-Luc Godard: *Contempt*: Pocket Movie Guide
Jean-Luc Godard: *Pierrot le Fou*: Pocket Movie Guide
John Hughes and Eighties Cinema
Ferris Bueller's Day Off: Pocket Movie Guide
Jean-Luc Godard: Pocket Guide
The Cinema of Richard Linklater
Liv Tyler: Star In Ascendance
Blade Runner and the Films of Philip K. Dick
Paul Bowles and Bernardo Bertolucci
Media Hell: Radio, TV and the Press
An Open Letter to the BBC
Detonation Britain: Nuclear War in the UK
Feminism and Shakespeare
Wild Zones: Pornography, Art and Feminism
Sex in Art: Pornography and Pleasure in Painting and Sculpture
Sexing Hardy: Thomas Hardy and Feminism

The Light Eternal is a model monograph, an exemplary job. The subject matter of the book is beautifully organised and dead on beam. (Lawrence Durrell)
It is amazing for me to see my work treated with such passion and respect. (Andrea Dworkin)

CRESCENT MOON PUBLISHING
P.O. Box 1312, Maidstone, Kent, ME14 5XU, Great Britain. www.crmoon.com

cresmopub@yahoo.co.uk   www.crescentmoon.org.uk

www.ingramcontent.com/pod-product-compliance
Lightning Source LLC
Chambersburg PA
CBHW060538100426
42743CB00009B/1570